≈ *Letter to a Stranger*

Letter to a Stranger

≈ ESSAYS TO THE ONES WHO HAUNT US

Edited by

COLLEEN KINDER

Foreword by

LESLIE JAMISON

ALGONQUIN BOOKS OF CHAPEL HILL 2022

Published by
Algonquin Books of Chapel Hill
Post Office Box 2225
Chapel Hill, North Carolina 27515-2225

a division of
Workman Publishing
225 Varick Street
New York, New York 10014

Library of Congress Cataloging-in-Publication Data

Names: Kinder, Colleen, editor. | Jamison, Leslie, author of foreword.
Title: Letter to a stranger : essays to the ones who haunt us / edited by
    Colleen Kinder ; foreword by Leslie Jamison.
Description: First Edition. | Chapel Hill, North Carolina : Algonquin Books
    of Chapel Hill, 2021. | Summary: "An anthology of short, intimate
    second-person essays by a diverse range of writers, each honoring a fleeting
    encounter with a stranger met while traveling that left a profound and
    lasting impact; with a foreword by bestselling author Leslie Jamison"—
    Provided by publisher.
Identifiers: LCCN 2021019229 | ISBN 9781643751245 (Trade Paperback) |
    ISBN 9781643752235 (ebook)
Subjects: LCSH: Voyages and travels. | Memory. | Self-actualization
    (Psychology)
Classification: LCC G465 .L475 2021 | DDC 910.4—dc23
LC record available at https://lccn.loc.gov/2021019229

10 9 8 7 6 5 4 3 2 1
First Edition

For my mother—the reason I love books.
For my father—the reason I wander, and dare.

CONTENTS

Foreword by Leslie Jamison xv
Introduction by Colleen Kinder 1

≈ SYMMETRY

≈ MYSTERY

≈ CHEMISTRY

≈ GRATITUDE

≈ WONDER

≈ REMORSE

≈ FAREWELL

≈ Foreword

by Leslie Jamison

We are born into a world of strangers. We spend our lives turning them into beloveds and ghosts: the ones we need, the ones we ache for, the ones we lose, the ones we brush up against and never really know, who stay with us anyway. These are letters written to those ones—the ones we glimpsed from buses and bathroom stalls, from the corners of our eyes; the ones we tripped, the ones who caught us, the ones we kissed without knowing their names, the ones who bewildered us, who made us feel alive.

The first time Colleen told me about the idea of asking people to write letters to strangers—*the ones we're haunted by*, she said, and I knew instantly what she meant—we were walking through a late-summer night in New Haven. The air was warm and damp. There was a hill beneath our feet. The dampness made the night feel weighted, as if its humidity held all those memories we're always carrying around inside of us as secret stowaways.

Colleen and I had been strangers once, but she was the opposite of a stranger by then. We'd cried with each other more times than I could count. We'd invented a dialect that only we spoke. *We're on geologic time*, I sometimes told her, meaning that the arc of our friendship would stretch for the rest of our lives. So she wasn't a stranger to me, but something about her relationship to strangers moved me deeply—the ways they lit small fires inside of her.

And these letters she was imagining, they would be written toward strange intimacies that didn't live in geologic time, that dwelled instead in the sudden supernovas of fleeting encounters.

Immediately, I knew the stranger I would write about: a one-legged traveling magician I'd crossed paths with several times when I lived in Nicaragua. He'd been drunk every time I'd seen him. I'd been drunk every time I'd seen him. I suspected maybe the letter would be about that, but honestly I didn't really know *what* it would be about. I just knew it would be a letter to him. And when I wrote it, several weeks later, it came out dark and gleaming and alive, as if it had already existed inside of me, fully formed. A secret stowaway. It just needed a home. The invitation of a letter had given it a home. This invitation said: *Write to this man, even if you don't know why you want to.* It said: *Write into that mystery.*

My letter to the traveling magician wasn't the account of an entire life; it was an account of brushing up—just briefly—against the infinitude of another person, and feeling him brush up against my own. It opened up a seam in my memory and asked me to peer through it. It was a fissure. This is a book of fissures. They live in all of us.

Who are the other strangers I could have written letters to? The mother in a Seattle bookstore who told me about her son's struggle to kick his heroin addiction while I thought about my own baby sleeping across town—how both of us loved our children with all of ourselves, and couldn't protect them from everything. Or the man on a Brooklyn street corner who helpfully informed me that my daughter's lip was bleeding as I held her, crying, in my arms. What did he know about the ways I was trying to figure out how to be a single mother? Or maybe the man who maybe date-raped me one night in Granada, years earlier, the one whose name I can never remember, the one who insulted the book of Frank O'Hara poems on my nightstand before he took off my clothes. Or else—from that same summer—the boy who slept some nights on the street outside my rented room, the one whose dreams I'd never know.

As I write these words, I'm riding a train headed north along the Hudson River, surrounded by strangers: The teenage boy with acne, furiously messaging someone on his phone. The elderly sisters on their way to Rochester. The businessman I first pegged as brash and inconsiderate, who seems to be—when he speaks—stuttering and fumbling and kind.

We spend so much of our lives in the company of people whose names we'll never know, people we'll never meet again. How rarely we honor them. How rarely we admit to ourselves the strange, unannounced ways they can lodge inside of us.

These essays invite our stowaways to climb up from beneath the deck. These essays don't say, *I knew you*. They say, *I never really knew you*. They confess their own partial gazes. They open up territories we didn't know we had inside of us. They offer themselves as vessels for our least official ghosts. They confess the magic lanterns of meaning and speculation that we project onto strangers' lives. They confess the ways we make them characters in our stories. They try to liberate them from these roles. They say, *You were more*. They say, *You were unknown to me*. They say, *Here is some of my unknowing*.

Art is often trying to strike up a conversation with strangers. The flâneur prowls the city, gazing at strangers. The street photographer prowls the city, gazing at strangers. In his poem, "To a Stranger," Walt Whitman calls out through the fissure: "Passing stranger! You do not know how longingly I look upon you, / You must be he I was seeking, or she I was seeking . . . / You give me the pleasure of your eyes, face, flesh, as we pass—you take of my beard, breast, hands in return."

He writes: "I am to think of you when I sit alone, or wake at night alone."

He writes: "I am to see to it that I do not lose you."

In *Don't Let Me Be Lonely*, Claudia Rankine describes a conversation with a New York City cab driver as they drive uptown on the West Side Highway. "[F]rom that space of loneliness," she writes, "I can feel the cab driver watching me in his rearview mirror." He is from Pakistan; she is a Black American. He asks her, "[H]ave you noticed these white people, they think they are better than everyone else?" She says, "Have I noticed? Are you joking? You're not joking." He says, "But the things they say to me. They don't know anything." When he asks her what she does for a living, she says, "I'm thinking as if trying to weep." But when they pull up to her building, he asks, "Why with such a nice smile are you trying to weep?"

In that cab, it's all there: the ways strangers hardly know us at all, and how toxic this unknowing can become—*The things they say to me. They don't know anything*—but also those sudden moments of penetration, not comprehension so much as contact. The ways they see our weeping, even if they do not know where it comes from. From the space of loneliness, we feel someone's gaze. From the space of loneliness, we gaze at them.

These letters are gifts. The invitation to write a letter is a gift. The invitation of the fissure is a gift. It's a way of encountering the world that stays attuned to the incompleteness of our vision: the infinitude of what we can see, and the infinitude of what we can't. These letters say: *I never had you. I never knew you. I am to see to it that I do not lose you.*

≈ *Letter to a Stranger*

≈ *Introduction*

Dear Stranger,

All writers have a peculiar devotion to strangers. The writer, after all, cloisters herself away in a quiet room, withdraws from the voices and faces she knows best, just to find and weave the words that might grace the consciousness of some distant, anonymous reader. The dream is to send unshakeable characters down the corridors of the reader's mind. To haunt you, that is, through painstakingly chosen words.

But the reverse is also true: you, stranger, haunt the storyteller. I learned this back in 2013, when I began asking writers about the strangers lurking in the back rooms of memory.

You might say I was living through a haunted time in my life, that the word *ghost* was over-operative in my days. I was biding the aftermath of a broken love, wishing the specter of my ex would quit flickering through every Brooklyn crowd. Even at my writing desk, the past weighed heavily. I'd lived abroad for years, pitching articles set everywhere from a Chinese megacity to the tiniest of Nicaraguan isles. Always, in delivering the basics that editors asked of me, I felt neglectful of the deeper, truer stories—the ones with crackle and emotion, high stakes and true vulnerability. I was writing endlessly about places but neglecting what animated them: the people I encountered there.

The Dominican cab driver who chased down the bus on which I'd mindlessly left my luggage. The little girl who lived upstairs from me in Havana, whose maturing voice marked the passage of time over the many years I returned to visit Castro's frozen-in-time Cuba. The South African woman who steered me away from a fool's errand of a hike up the Cape Town foothills and brought me to her flat instead, for a soulful chat about how to craft a life on your own terms.

I hardly knew these people, and yet they felt fire-branded into my memory. So when a hero of mine gave a talk about a stranger he couldn't forget, I paid rapt attention. Pico Iyer was speaking to my writing students at Yale, and I'd assigned them some favorite Iyer essays, including a gorgeous portrait of Iceland. I figured Iyer would hold forth on the craft of that story, perhaps enlighten us on his research process. Instead, our guest author went rogue, talking about a magnetic stranger he'd met while reporting in Reykjavík: a woman with piercing blue eyes with whom he wandered the streets for hours, swapping thoughts and life histories. It was so clear to me, listening to Iyer, that nothing about that 1987 assignment in Iceland had impacted him more than this stranger. She was the invisible heroine of the piece we'd pored over.

In the weeks after Iyer's talk, I couldn't shake the sense that something was off-kilter and needed righting. Shouldn't there be a publication for precisely such memories? If serendipity is such an essential ingredient in any journey, why wasn't there more room for it in the journey's recounting—on the page?

Necessity is one mother of invention; frustration is another one. I'd never dreamed of founding a magazine, but doing so began to feel urgent. Because when I asked fellow writers whether they ever came home from a reporting trip with better stories than those they'd gone seeking, the answer wasn't just "yes"; it was "always."

Off Assignment, a nonprofit magazine I cofounded with Vince Errico, became the container for those tales, and "Letter to a Stranger" was our flagship column. *Write a letter to a stranger you can't shake*, we challenged itinerant journalists and essayists. *Write to figure out why.*

I was awestruck by the very first "Letter to a Stranger" essays that blipped into my inbox: a missive from Leslie Jamison, addressed to a drunk magician in Nicaragua who wouldn't quit her memory. Another letter, from Lavinia Spalding, followed shortly after—a focused and searing account of a dalliance on a Thai beach. As for journalist Ted Conover, he sort of already *had* a "Letter to a Stranger" in progress, a side-story jotted down while on a *New Yorker* assignment in Rwanda almost twenty years earlier.

"It was as if these early contributors had not just written letters," observed Managing Editor Katy Osborn in *OA*'s manifesto, "but exhumed them; dug them out of some dusty room of memory." She summed up our seminal essays as "a stack of ghost stories so thick with personal meaning that one could imagine them having had actual weight within their authors."

The letter, it turned out, was the perfect vessel for that weight. a form brief and intimate, one keen on collapsing distance. What electrified *OA* early on was the sense that we'd found a literary shape that corresponded with a species of story already alive inside the writer. I remember so well, so viscerally, where I was sitting when I read a submission by fiction writer Carlynn Houghton—a missive addressed to a baby she'd miscarried on a road trip. Seated at my desk, I needed—immediately—to go outside and walk out the force of her story. That essay blew open our notions of what

"Letter to a Stranger" could be. Houghton had done it: sent her own ghost down the corridors of my mind, where it could—and does—exquisitely, lastingly haunt me.

This book stitches together the most extraordinary responses to the "Letter to a Stranger" challenge, essays by a formidable cast of writers from all corners of the literary world, as diverse themselves as the strangers they invoke. What energizes their every letter, though, is the quest to unpack a common underlying mystery: *Why can't I shake you, stranger?*

Why—of all the people Meron Hadero met on her family's return trip to Ethiopia—does her memory hover like a hawk around the man who sold her shoddy film? What *was it* about the effusive lady in the Provincetown bistro that shook loose memories of T Kira Madden's departed father? Why does novelist Julia Glass still find traces of a pushy Italian stranger in her fiction, decades after she rebuffed him in Florence? How can a person so ephemeral leave such eternal mark?

The eternal ephemeral. In this collection, I'm struck not just by the spectrum of geographies—stories set on the subway in Berlin and a rickshaw in Mandalay, the forest of Okinawa and the dim streets of Yonkers—but by the well-baked human wisdom embedded in them. They're replete with observations about how to live and what to seek, about how we can startle one another awake even in the most ordinary hours of our lives.

Elizabeth Kolbert writes to a loner she converged with while reporting in the Peruvian Andes, whose cryptic smile left her wondering. Emily Matchar brings hindsight to bear on a youthful journey, writing to an orphaned toddler who once tagged along with her in Mexico. Gregory Pardlo transports us to the French train station where a feisty drunk thrust him into lasting alliance with his mother-in-law. Jenessa Abrams narrates an encounter closer to home but no less charged—a dalliance with a gambler she met on jury duty, who ignited her desire. "I knew almost nothing about you, which is its own sort of nirvana," Abrams writes. "The small window when we can still be anyone to each other."

I've learned so much from the essays in your hands: namely, that any nagging ghost makes for a glorious muse; that memory goes to work on the rough drafts of our pasts like a ruthless editor, whittling them down until all we see clearly are the scenes that glint with significance; that while every society is stocked with teachers and mentors—the official and credentialed sort—there are invisible ranks of guides and quiet sages out there, edifying us in the most unexpected places. Yes, our families and institutions raise us, grow us up—but so does serendipity, the cast of characters who are randomly assembled in our path, dissolving quicker than we can spin around and ask, "What was your na—?"

A full six years have passed since Pico Iyer visited my classroom and unwittingly told a story that unleashed hundreds more. I write to you now from such a different phase of life, one no longer perfumed by aloneness or defined by my quest to move beyond loss. By the time I sat down to curate this anthology, I was no longer wandering the world as much; no longer sniffing around so hungrily for human wisdom or scanning the room for a soulmate. I'd found the latter, and—although my husband and I lived between four different countries—I felt, in so many ways, more settled. And then a magazine sent me on assignment.

It was a reporting trip—the first I'd taken in years, since becoming the face of *Off Assignment*, really—and I undertook it in a state entirely new to me: pregnant. I was reeling with wonder at the news when I departed to report on Eastern Canada, but it was far too early to tell anyone outside of my family and closest friends. How I yearned to proclaim the wild truth that my husband and I had set in motion a *life!* It took me a couple of days of wandering Quebec and wolfing down sesame bagels and pain au chocolat like only a pregnant woman can before I realized I could tell anyone on the road my fullest truth, precisely because I would never see them again.

How delicious this freedom was. Soon I was drawing forth prenatal tales from strangers all through Canada's Maritime provinces. I thrilled to know that Susan in New Brunswick craved Slurpees when she was pregnant, that Liz in Halifax couldn't tolerate a sniff of pork. After bonding with Peter over the appearance of a moose out our train's window, I could ask about his family and respond honestly about mine: it was *just* beginning. These intimacies, these surrogate friends: I needed them, craved them as hard as I craved carbs and crackers and all things containing cheese. Never was it clearer to me that strangers occupy such a distinct sphere in our lives, extending to us a particular magic, exclusive permissions. And as long as our lives keep changing—as they must—the workings of that magic and the fruits of that permission will keep evolving, too.

The tiny life secreted away in my body illuminated that truth, but so did the vast change about to sweep the world: a pandemic. Right when I turned this book over to my publisher, the world was reeling from a virus, one that hid the contours of smiles behind masks and recast human touch as mortal threat. Overnight, the cast of characters in our lives shrank from hundreds to three or five or one, as the "germ circle" became our only circle. A new sentiment toward strangers found me: nostalgia. I missed the days when I could shoot the breeze with someone at an airport terminal, or swap a laugh with a fellow shopper in the cereal aisle. Amidst coronavirus, this book feels like an artifact of a more innocent time. A bygone world in which any passerby could lean over the stroller I now push down my street, for a close glimpse of my newborn baby.

Reader: I hope these stories haunt you. I hope they spoil you with wisdom while enchanting you, line by line, continent by continent, stranger upon stranger. I hope they also make clear that intimacy and connection aren't just the province of the main players in our lives—the lovers and neighbors, siblings and parents, colleagues and coaches. There's magic and comfort in that, just as there is in knowing that—however strange it may seem to withdraw from loved ones to reach anonymous readers—communion between reader and writer isn't just possible; it's sacred. "Writing is, in the end," as Pico Iyer puts it, "that oddest of anomalies: an intimate letter to a stranger."

Surely, you have your own hallowed archive of brushes with strangers. Whoever those figures are, may this folio of stories carry you well beyond that personal canon, putting you in touch with the multitude of ways that we touch and heal and hurt and enliven one another, way out there on the edges of our lives.

—Colleen Kinder, Buffalo, NY

≈ SYMMETRY

≈ *To the Traveling Magician*

GRANADA, NICARAGUA

by Leslie Jamison

You came around the bar each night and so did I. Funny to say "the bar" as if there were only one, when Calle la Calzada was nothing but, their plastic chairs bearing slogans for Toña and Victoria, the national beers, flocked by children begging money for glue.

You were on crutches and missing part of one leg—I can't remember which, right or left—from the knee down, and I doubt you remember me getting drunk, but I remember you getting drunk, or rather—I remember you being drunk, as if you'd always been and would always be, as if you'd been born that way. It was nothing violent, more like a glaze across your being. You said you were a traveling magician and I guess you were. You taught me the words for what you did, *trucos de magia*, but I never saw you perform one.

This was in Granada, Nicaragua, during the summer of 2007. You don't remember my name, I'm sure, and I don't remember yours—because you didn't really need one, and I didn't really need one. You were the one-legged magician, like a figure from the tarot deck, and I was just another American girl who maybe glanced back for a couple seconds to look at your damage. The bar we haunted was the bar everyone haunted. We were interchangeable parts in a machine beyond our reckoning, both troubled travelers, and there were spares for both of us, extras, waiting in the wings; more where we came from.

Our bar was the bar where I went after I got my nose broken by a stranger in the street and it was the bar where I went every night my nose didn't get broken by a stranger in the street, because I liked getting drunk where other people would already be drunk before I even got started. I never liked beer, but I drank it a lot because it was basically just beer and rum on offer. I drank rum, too. Rum and cokes were called *Nica libres* instead of *Cuba libres*—the revolution in Nicaragua had been like a little sibling, formed in its elder's image.

Those were the early days of Ortega's second lease on the dream, and it went black for hours at a time each night. The government was figuring out how to make electricity a public industry. We'd buy tamales from the woman at the corner of the Parque Central and eat them somewhere with candles, or without candles—just feeling with our hands—and some nights, we piled into unmarked black taxis and rode down by the lake to Oscar's, where people danced and snorted lines of coke, where little black flies lifted in a fluttering scrim over the water at dawn. I worked at a school, and so that's where I spent my hangovers; I remember gulping orange soda in the gully behind the classrooms, picking corn chips from a crinkling bag, and teaching kids how to tuck their fingers down so they could learn subtraction.

You went away, or I went away, but drinking never did.

You were missing part of yourself and drinking anyway— fucking up magic tricks or failing to produce them, and drinking anyway—and I would think of you, years later, when I had a broken foot and drank anyway; when I had both hands gripping crutches and drank anyway; when I tripped and fell going down the steps of the double-wide trailer that was the bar, bandaged foot held aloft, crutches clattering to asphalt; when I made it home, went to bed, woke up the next morning, crutched through the next day—and drank again, inevitably, anyway.

Back then, I wanted to beg you to take better care of yourself— to tell you to treat your broken body as something worth attending to. And whatever in me had wanted to beg you, I knew—when I was tripping down those trailer stairs, or balancing a bottle against my crutches—I knew I needed to bring it back, to beg that of myself.

≈ To the Woman Who Found Me Crying Outside the Senate

WASHINGTON, DC

by Rachel Swearingen

You've been a part of the story since the beginning. You're the woman who finds me bawling in the bathroom outside the Senate. It's the late eighties. I'm from rural Wisconsin, in DC for a summer seminar. I'm president of the Young Republicans, a tiny part of a long-range plan to turn Wisconsin red. My family is working class and my father has just been laid off, and I want to make something of myself. I want to go to college. The party insider who recruited me tells me there has never been a better time to be a woman. I'm seventeen, not old enough to vote, but I campaign for men who drink highballs, who call me "little lady" and pat me on the head, saying, "You better watch out for this one. She's after your job."

You must have seen my ill-fitting, scuffed white pumps under the stall. "You alright in there?" you say. Your gruff, scotch-worn voice reminds me of women from back home. I emerge in a baby-blue Nancy Reagan suit, mascara snot on my face, my permed hair melting in the humidity. I'm carrying a briefcase my dad bought for me at a garage sale. You hand me a wad of toilet paper to blow my nose as I tell you about mock Congress, how my bill was just annihilated on live television. Tall private-school boys had jumped in front of me to get on TV. Months of work for nothing. They knew nothing about the research, gave stupid answers, hammed it up for the camera.

You light a cigarette—the reason you're in the bathroom. "Sweetheart," you say. "You've got to learn how to eat your own heart if you want to get into politics." Then you tell me to be a kid, to go out and find some trouble while I still can. This is the part I recount at parties because it was just the permission I needed to break curfew that night. The end of my budding political career. "My first and last political sex scandal," I'd joke.

You couldn't have been much older than I am now. The women I tell wonder what you were doing there. "Do you think she was a senator?" one will ask, and the others will laugh. "Are you kidding? Back then? How many were there?"

Turns out there were just two.

I told you I was tougher than I looked, despite the fact that I had just run crying from a fake meeting of Congress, and even the irreverent British boy who I had a crush on had laughed. I didn't mention the boy to you.

All that week, while I behaved, the other participants snuck out and had adventures. The special sit-down the local party member had arranged with my Republican senator was just a quick photo op. I had toured the House and Senate to find men delivering speeches to empty chambers. I had walked the halls, listened in on deal-making with lobbyists, and understood this was as far as I would go, or even wanted to go. There were back-slapping men everywhere, the scent of aftershave and lunchtime booze. If anyone noticed me, it was to leer. They hid nothing of their conversations because I was of no consequence.

When you coaxed me out of that stall, I didn't want to be what I was. A Midwesterner. A good girl. Most likely a Democrat who would never be able to eat her own heart. That same day, I had snuck away from my group to walk around DC and had seen disparity and segregation. I had visited my Democratic congressman's unglamorous office and sat down for a long meeting. He had one aging secretary and wore a knit-brown leisure suit. No cameras. He looked me in the eyes and talked about the importance of public service.

For years, I told the story, and you were the wizened crone shooing me out into the world, giving me the Don't Let the Assholes Bring You Down talk. But most fiction writers know that a minor character can never be solely at the service of the protagonist. Everyone has their own agenda. You looked so alone and stressed. Your dark hair was turning brittle with silver. You were cigarette-and-work-all-night skinny. I was too young to imagine the sort of life you inhabited.

That night, I stuffed my bed and asked my roommate from the Bronx to cover for me while I snuck off campus with the British boy. I wore a red-white-and-blue short set with zero irony. In a nearby golf course, we watched fireflies, talked, and kissed. It was two or three in morning when we saw the headlights of a golf cart coming at us, driven by one of the law students who was responsible for us. He had a megaphone and was shouting. My star-spangled outfit glowed as the boy and I ran across sandpits. We were alive and laughing. We were breaking the rules. We kept running until they caught us.

The law student delivered us to the director of the program. He was taking his bar exam that morning. I had to write an apology.

The director told me she was filing a copy with admissions, that she would see to it I never returned to Georgetown or became a page. When I told the boy how sorry I was that I had gotten him in trouble, he said not to worry. He was having tea with the ambassador in the morning. The next day, without showering or sleeping, I walked into the cafeteria of hushed teenagers to wait for a taxi. My roommate told me the RAs had come by the night before to give me a leadership award and discovered I was gone. Also, she said, "People are saying they found you naked on a golf course with a foreigner."

On the airplane home, I wrote in my journal about my ruined life. I barely mentioned you. That summer, I went to the library to ask how to call London and used the money I made working at a hardware store to send the boy roses. I thought I was in love with him. I didn't yet realize that what I wanted was to be him.

When I tell the story now, I see you in your skirt and blouse, pacing the Senate halls, stealing into the rare women's bathroom. I like to think of you taking your own advice, finding trouble that night, too. Maybe I became the centerpiece of your own funny story. The small-town girl sobbing behind a bathroom stall because she found out she was a Democrat. Or were there too many of us back then? All of us trying to climb the Hill in our borrowed shoes, reminding you of you?

≈ To the Father Paused Under the Tree

GRAND CANYON, ARIZONA

by Anjali Sachdeva

I met you because we were both seeking refuge. We were coming up the Bright Angel Trail, climbing from the bottom to the top of the Grand Canyon, more than 4,000 feet in elevation gain. Bright Angel is the superhighway of trails: broad, crowded, bare to the sun. But you had found the shadow of a tree, and sat down on a rock to catch your breath, and I joined you.

You looked forty-five or fifty, fit and tan, with an anonymously pleasant face. The kind of person I would pass without bothering to look at twice. You spoke first, asked me where I was from, and I answered warily. If my trip had taught me anything up to that point, it was that men assumed a young woman hiking alone was looking for either a lover or a father figure. I had been given advice about "taking it slow" and not "wearing myself out." In the air-conditioned dining hall in the canyon bottom, I had been propositioned by a married man who had not bothered to remove his wedding ring. By the time I met you I was not interested in being offered anything else.

But when I said I was from Pittsburgh you mentioned a distant relative there, and that led us to talking about your wife. I asked if you had children and you said two girls. You looked back down the path, and I realized they were with you, the three of them, hiking more slowly the steps you had already taken. We let that settle for a moment: their imminent presence, the limited time for talking.

You asked me if I wanted to have kids, a question I was asked often in those days, and one that I found irritating and invasive. But somehow, in that place, it seemed an honest inquiry that deserved an honest answer. I said I didn't know. That I thought about it a lot but I didn't think so. I was twenty-seven, well into adulthood, but such choices seemed far off still. You told me to think about it carefully because it was the only decision in life you could never take back. Like jumping off a cliff, you said. It got my attention. I was never good at decisions, always afraid of making the wrong choice, even about small things.

You looked down the trail again, said you loved your girls with all your heart, but that kids take over your life and it is never what it was before. I nodded; this was what I had always suspected about kids. I said I liked to take care of people, and you told me that was even more dangerous, that it made it easy to forget about the things that matter to you until it was too late.

I don't recall any bitterness in your voice as you spoke. All I remember is relief—from the sun, the antlike stream of people moving up and down the trail, the loneliness that always accompanied my stubborn desire to travel alone. But now I wonder what made you walk on ahead of your family. Was it simple impatience, the physical need to move at your own pace? Or was it a deeper desire, a longing to walk right away from them and into some other life, a feeling akin to the one that sent me in and out of canyons and forests and backcountry trails for fifteen years with no one accompanying me, a yearning for something wild and solitary?

It has been a decade since that hike, but I remember you more often than I do the parched air, the burn in my muscles, the excitement of reaching the top, the towering red sandstone walls of the canyon itself. I have two daughters of my own now. Having children has indeed been like jumping off a cliff, in that your old life recedes so quickly there is no time to think about it. You sometimes feel like you are flying, and sometimes like you are about to crash into the ground. Unlike other choices in my life, I've found great pleasure in the finality of this commitment, but I can't say that I have ever found whatever I was searching for in all those miles of hiking. I still have my craving for solitude, my longing for the wild. I think of you sometimes and wonder if it ever left you either.

When we stopped talking, we smiled at each other, and a moment later there was your wife and your children, coming around the bend in the trail. I felt the things we had said float between us like the heat, things too honest for people we loved. Then you said goodbye and walked back to meet them, to join your steps with theirs.

≈ To My Lost Trishaw Driver

MANDALAY, MYANMAR

by Pico Iyer

Travel is, deep down, an exercise in trust, and sometimes I think it was you who became my life's most enduring teacher. I had every reason to be wary when, in 1985, I clambered out of the overnight train and stepped out into the October sunshine of Mandalay, blinking amidst the dust and bustle of the "City of Kings." I wasn't reassured as you sprang out of the rickety bicycle trishaw in which you'd been sleeping, as you did every night, and I don't think the signs along the sides of your vehicle—B.SC. (MATHS) and MY LIFE—put my mind very much to rest.

To me it seemed like a bold leap of faith—a shot in the dark—to allow a rough-bearded man in a cap to peddle me away from the broad main boulevards and into the broken backstreets, and then to lead me into the little hut where you shared a tiny room with a tired compatriot. Yes, you gave me a piece of jade as we rode and disarmed me with the essays you'd written and now handed me on how to enjoy your town. But I'd grown up on stories of what happens when you're in a foreign place and recklessly neglect a mother's advice to never accept gifts from strangers.

Yet it required trust on your part, too, I realize now, to take in a shabby foreigner in a threadbare jacket, hauling a worn case off the third-class carriage and looking as if he hadn't washed in days (for the very good reason that he hadn't). In New York City—where I lived—it was not taxi drivers who were agents of violence, but their customers.

So we both took a chance, in the hope that we could turn an unscripted meeting into something durable. You won me over in your bare room when you started opening up all the albums in which you'd meticulously transcribed the names of every foreigner you'd taken a snapshot of and showed me the handwritten essays in which you shared your dreams (of earning a further certificate in mathematics; of inviting your parents to your graduation; of one day, perhaps, possessing your own trishaw).

When you pulled out from under your sagging cot a sociology textbook from Australia—*Life in Modern America*—the way someone else might have pulled out a poster of Jennifer Beals, the world I thought I knew began to feel remade. We might not have been friends yet, but you certainly felt like something closer than a stranger.

Days later, inevitably, I had to be on my way, to Thailand and Nepal; a few weeks later, we were on opposite sides of the world again. Within months, however, I was recognizing your handwriting as soon as I pulled out frayed envelopes from within our mailbox in California, quite often sent—for security's sake—from Bangkok, thanks to some helpful foreigner. You came to recognize my handwriting in return, I'm sure, in registered and untaped envelopes so that your less-than-trusting government would understand that I wasn't dealing in state secrets.

Mine were addressed to a "trishaw stand" outside a big city's central train station; yours to a house high up in the hills of Santa Barbara, home to glamorous blondes and millionaires' villas in the soap opera transmitted daily across your continent.

Then there was silence, and I started to read about the people's uprising in your country, and the government's vicious response. I lived with the evergreen question of how the most blue-skied and unfallen souls I'd met—Norman Lewis writes that taxi drivers in Rangoon used to tip their passengers—could produce and survive such brutal leaders. Was it the trust that had so moved me that left you and your friends so undefended?

I'd never know. But it was no longer safe for you to write, even via Bangkok. So when I described our encounter in my book, I deployed every ruse I knew to shield your identity, even as I was trying to do justice to the very real kindness and integrity of who you seemed to be. I changed your name, but I wanted to honor the details of your life, to highlight Kipling's famous claim that "[T]here is neither East nor West, border, nor breed, nor birth" when two souls meet, "though they come from the ends of the earth!"

One year later, your government changed the entire country's name, and the capital's, as well. The party that seemed to promise democracy won an election and was denied victory. Finally, fully fifteen years after our meeting, a letter from another stranger arrived, passing on some news. A traveler had followed the hints in my book, and tracked you down somehow in Mandalay. A different stranger's letter followed, with a photo. I was reassured that you were still alive; I was also chilled, because if strangers could locate you through my book, so too, perhaps, could the tireless surveillance agents of your government.

We began to correspond again, through a series of passing intermediaries, and then a letter arrived, directly from you, telling me how the extension of trust had played out in your life. A kindly couple from Texas—as moved by your story and sweetness as I had been—gave you the two hundred dollars you needed to realize your dream of possessing your own trishaw. A visitor from Italy, a little later, encouraged you to believe you could make good on an even greater dream—to take command of your very own camera.

You had always been a friend of hope, which is how you'd begun to make me one. So you sent the stranger all your savings, and then waited at a street corner at the time he'd mentioned. And waited and waited. Finally, you wrote, you recognized you'd been cheated of everything you owned. You'd been obliged to go back to your village and work for years to support your wife and children. Now, much older, less full of hope, you were back in your trishaw once more, sleeping in the big-city streets yet again, ready to extend trust to fresh strangers tumbling out of the overnight train in the early light.

I never know when the next letter from a stranger will arrive. You, too, I suspect. We don't even know, not having met for thirty-five years, how much to call one another friends. But you opened yourself up to the point where I feel I know you better than I do many of my lifelong companions. I live in the hope that, for all of my writing about us, I remain a friend, and not the stranger you should never have trusted.

I still write letters to old pals, often, and even in our sixties, we favor the jokes and personae we enjoyed when we were kids. But the letters I write to you—even the ones I don't write down—never stop evolving, because the decades keep speeding by and circumstances keep changing. Even as, in memory, we're still just kids in our twenties, on that bright late-autumn day in 1985, walking toward one another through the dusty sunshine, unsure of how much to trust, and whether it might not be better to remain forever strangers.

≈ To the Child on the Plane

THE CASCADES, OREGON

by Lia Purpura

I stood in the aisle stretching as pretense, but really it was to get a better look at you in action. I loved you instantly. It was your gestures—how you rubbed your freckly nose with the back of a hand, then pushed the long hair out of your face, no thought to smoothing or neatening. With legs tucked under, you loosened the seatbelt as far as possible—the way I still play with the letter of the law on planes.

You were a little loud but not whiney. Direct but not demanding. Athletic but not in a trained-up way—it looked like you knew how to think with your body. You yielded none of your seat space to your sister. You were older, eleven or twelve, and indulgent with the bag of toys, except when your mother had to referee time with the joke book.

When I was twelve, I would have loved a friend like you. I spent my girlhood cajoling reluctants to hike through woods, ride straight down hills, and stay in the ocean past bluing. You'd have met me anywhere. We'd have worn our jeans-and-T-shirt uniform; at that age, I hand-lettered a tee myself (simple black marker on a cast-off from my father that read, "The more I know of man, the more I love my dog," which worried my mother. People were often mean, though, and I did so love my dog).

Your mother's voice broke the spell. You and your sister were fighting over a snack and your mother called out a boy's name. *David!* What an unexpectedly steep disappointment. You were a *boy* child. And so it followed: of *course*, the ease of movement and claiming of territory; of *course*, the confident voice and reluctance to prettify. All I'd recognized as free, bold, and *girl* dissolved and slipped out of reach. Oh, *girl* the sensation was still present, but became again singular, mine to protect, not mirrored in another. *Girl* went inward and private, a way-of-being known best to animals and trees.

Still, you sent me right back to age twelve. I'd just gotten my period and when I went back out to ride my bike—new pad in place—I realized, with a shock so sharp it was physical, I'd have to carry a *bag* now. I could be ambushed by the need for supplies at any time, and I'd have to plan for proximity to bathrooms. In a panic, I thought I could just stuff one in my pocket like a tissue or dollar and go. But no. Too bulky. More to the point, we girls were meant to keep them out of sight. Hidden from whom? And how was discretion communicated? With the usual whispers, pantomimes, and codes. The gift of little zippered bags (in pink, the most useless form of camouflage). Such early training in accepting-but-not-naming boys as the central subject of my actions, soon to be the central subject of our collective fear, and yet in need of protection from the reality of our bodies.

A backpack took care of my concerns. Hands free, I could ride easily and hike. I still carry one to this day.

I got a look at your sister, too, before I went back to my aisle and seat. She seemed cool enough, but the usual sort of girl who made dolls talk and wore sparkly barrettes and bracelets—nice, though not someone I'd have had as a pal. You're the one I wondered about, long after that flight. Maybe you were a girl en route to being a boy. Or a boy who liked and would grow his girl-self. Or a long-haired kid refusing to take sides. Such are the possibilities available now, as they were not then. I am grateful for them. All I know is: you caught my eye, winged me back to a lightness, a power I held once so easily at the center of my body, a way of being I recognized immediately, a freedom that still presents as notable.

≈ *To My Arctic Vardøger*

PYRAMIDEN, NORWAY

by Alexander Lumans

Only six people live in Pyramiden, Norway. Abandoned in 1998, it was once a thousand-person Russian mining town. Now, my tour-group ship docks here, hundreds of miles north of the Arctic Circle. Through my cabin's porthole, I can barely make out a junkyard and a strange mountain, a factory and a tall signpost for the city. I want to reach through the glass and touch them. It's so fecundly cold here that the Soviet-era edifices will stay preserved for five hundred years. With a thirst to drink up every ounce of Arctic detail outside my window, I cannot fight that patent feeling of déjà vu: I have been here before. But this is the farthest I've ever been from anyone and anywhere.

Before my tour group disembarks the ship, you come aboard. You are one of the six people.

Standing perfectly straight in the ship's brassy saloon, you look unpreparedly cold in your road-cone-colored jumpsuit. You sport gray eyes and a sharp nose. Your clean goatee encircles some greater quietude, which I take as evidence that you do not speak English. You are either exactly my age of thirty-one, or twice that. You carry a rifle.

You step forward and speak in a strong, bell-clear Russian

accent: "My name is Sasha. Welcome to our ghost town. It is good to see people again." You pause. "Sometimes, we forget." And you do not say what or why.

Your name is mine. Or rather, yours is the Russian equivalent of mine: Alexander. I imagine becoming a version of you if I were to move here. (The ship's crew has already told me: out of everyone on board, I am the one they can most see moving to Pyramiden.) In this place, I envision you and I each leaving behind our old life problems, seeking the same Ice Age solutions—only you would have done so years before I ever arrived in the Norwegian Arctic.

At this point in time, I don't know the word for this sensation. But later I'll learn about the *vardøger*. A vardøger is known in Norse mythology as a spiritual predecessor. Unlike déjà vu or the Germanic *doppelgänger*, it is a guardian ghost with your voice, scent, or appearance that arrives in a place before you do, performing your actions in advance. In other words, when a vardøger appears, witnesses believe they've seen or heard the actual person show up before that person physically does. They say it is a phantom double.

You meet my tour group in the town square. I have the urge to draw you in my notebook, the one in which I've sketched the faces of glaciers I fear I will never see again. You wear a traditional Cossack coat under one of those iconic fur hats I always forget the name of. Your fingerless gloves tell me you have seen climates much worse than freezing. And your rifle peeks over your shoulder like a featherless wing. "For the bears," you say, which is another way of saying, "For your safety."

First you lead us to the cantina, where I run my hands over the crumbling mosaic tiles of a rogue polar bear squaring off against a Norse king; then to the pool house, where, in the drained swimming

pool, I pick up one of the old lane markers before it falls in half;
and then finally to the Culture House, where, in the dark theater, I
play a single note on the world's northernmost grand piano. I first
thought that someone went to the Arctic—this faraway territory
devoid of life—to feel alone. That is not the case. Through its calv-
ing glaciers and thin-aired silence, the Arctic has slowly revealed
itself to be a place where I sense the wavering fragility of living
things as well as the significance of profound self-reflection.

Here, all my solidified regrets feel more like abandoned What
Ifs; here, I most understand how each of us is their own great agent
of change. But in what direction should I hazard this change? I'm
south of nowhere, and still the compass needle of my potentials
keeps circling around the dial.

To our surprise, Pyramiden still has a working vodka bar. All
us tourists buy bottles. We drink them right there in gulps and
grimaces. I hate vodka; this is the best vodka I have ever tasted. In
the middle of the bar, I step into some imaginative tunnel where I
can see myself toasting and hugging. I fall into an ulterior nostalgia;
a kind of vardøger of the mind. I don't want to forget how all this
cold stone and arrested wood feels; I want to preserve the living
moment for five hundred years. Then you walk through the door,
put down your rifle, and pull me from my anticipatory reverie.

You look thrilled to share space with new voices and you look
terrified to talk without a script. We toast you. We desperately want
to know your story; *Why are you here?* is a way of asking, *Why am
I here?*

As a young man living in St. Petersburg, you fell in love with a
Russian woman. You married her with untamed abandon. She was
it. As you tell us about her, I can hear your quietude give way to a

voice long spent on the coin of old joy. I recognize it because it is how I often sound; I want to hold on to the skins of treasured memories the way Russians collect fox pelts for promised prosperity.

But your joy fast decays into a flat, frozen expression. Is she here?—I already know the answer.

She left you. Like that. For another man. You told us you did not know what to do with yourself. You were too young and too in love. So you left, too. You moved here. You tell us between sips of vodka, "Pyramiden was the only place I could confront—fully understand—my grief." I don't know if I have heard a more honest and more frightening sentence. It is difficult to tell, however, if you have succeeded.

Leaving the bar, I am a little drunk, like everyone, on spirits and memory. Knowing the ship will soon be leaving this place, I feel the definitive urge to have some private conversation with you. One in which you confirm that yes, I should abandon my current life—my long-distance relationship on unstable ground, my three adjunct jobs of no prospective futures, my big Western city with nowhere to fit in, my deepening depression that will slowly kill me—leave it all behind and move to Pyramiden. "Become me," I want you to command, which is to say, *Become yourself.*

No individual conversation occurs. Instead, we all say thank you. You say the same back, but why?

As you walk solo toward the town square, your rifle clings tightly to your back. (I have always wished I had asked to hold that gun and become you for the briefest moment.) You could simply continue walking: past the old mine's entrance and out into the snowy wilds. The temptation must strike you every day. To go out, confront your grief, and never let go. I admire that you are still here, holding on to this life you've created, acting as some mirrored reflection of another me yet to come.

Ahead of you, from around the corner of the cantina, appears a small blur. An Arctic fox in its dark summer coat. You walk up to the fox running in circles. It looks up at you like it wants to tell you a vital secret about the future. I hear you say something in Russian; the fox listens. You reach down and pet the wild animal like the two of you once shared a great trauma, or you soon will. Do you look at the fox and spot something familiar in its pointed face and gray fur? Did you look at me and see more of the same? You turn around to face the tour group and you give a final wave.

I still cannot get over your fingerless gloves in this spectral outpost of the Arctic. But I understand: you wear them so you do not forget what you have already touched—what you will touch again.

≈ *To the Girl in the Tattoo Parlor*

DALLAS, TEXAS

by Michelle Tea

Alaska. I met you in Dallas. You were leaning on the counter of a tattoo parlor, flipping through a book of flash. Your eyelids were painted like butterfly wings and you wore one of those plasticy track jackets from the eighties, purple and green and gold, that made a whooshing sound when your arms moved. Your shorts were so short I could see the tattoos coming up the back of your legs—a woman's eyes captured in a rearview mirror hung with a pair of dice. Chain link, shattered glass. I felt a throb of jealousy and feared that my own tattoos were basic. *Your tattoos are so cool,* I told you, and you responded with a smile. I knew you were an Aquarius, because I am, too, and I could feel all at once something spacey and brilliant and detached and engaged about you.

You said, "It's like you're the future me and I'm the past you," and there is no bigger compliment to get, as a forty-eight-year-old, than hearing that the coolest girl in Dallas would happily age into where I stood that day. I was wearing a rose-colored camisole and a pair of coral lady slacks, and the mural of maybe-basic tattoos scattered over my own body—hearts on my fingers; the word *Amethyst*, my birthstone, ornate on my neck; hands holding roses across my collarbone—saved me from looking like a slightly quirky business lady.

Alaska, I told you that I was not as cool as you when I was your age, and I wasn't being modest. When I was your age, in New England, I had a lousy boyfriend and I was blowing all my hard-earned money on a single semester in college. I was not cheerfully lounging around a tattoo parlor, taking in the framed flash that lined the walls—Japanese samurai and World War II motifs, the glowering devil masks and jumbled piles of dice, all of it lit with the hot glow of the neon on the back wall: TATTOO. The whole room was like an altar of sorts, and the two of us, Past and Future, were ready to offer our skin as a sacrifice.

Alaska, you can't tell me you like it here in Dallas. What is this place? I'm staying in an Airbnb, an apartment in a neighborhood of condos. It stinks like cheap cleaning products, like the murder of a previous guest had just been scoured away. I mean, I guess it's clean. I sat on the back stairs smoking last night, watching lightning crawl across the sky. I did like that, a Texan lightning storm. I thought I was staying in low-income housing, but in the morning, I walked through the neighborhood strewn with those scooters, tipped onto lawns like they'd been driven home drunk, and I wondered—students? I called a car on my phone and for blocks and blocks and blocks this went on, these condos, and I felt like I could have been in any sad spot in America.

This neighborhood, Deep Ellum, is the good one, though, right? I feel its growing wildness as afternoon ends, with more chaos to come as Sunday day drinkers transition into night. I'm getting a tattoo because I'm traveling and I'm bored and I'm in love, and it's a strange combination of sensations inside my body. It's less boring to travel now that my partner and I have opened up our relationship, when every day of work winks into a nighttime of possible dates with local strangers. But—I can't tell if you're queer or what, Alaska, but I just want to share that my current experiment of hooking up with a bunch of cisgendered straight guys has been kind of a bust. Like, with the exception of a single hot Scorpio with a tattooed neck in Portland, Oregon, it's been a real snooze fest. The one last night, before the lightning storm, was the worst yet. He didn't seem to get my joke about the low-income dorm I was staying in, and when I got to his place I saw it was the same kind of joint, only, like, funky, with a chandelier in the foyer. I thought because he'd lived in Oakland and was in the theater and practiced Non-Violent Communication child-rearing techniques with his kid that he'd be more interesting, but I have found that the stultifying effects of cisgendered white heterosexual maleness can trump anything. Turned out, that lightning was the best part of my night.

Alaska, I have to tell you, I do not like my tattoo. We were both getting baby-themed pieces—funny, right, another thing between us—but you got the only girl artist in the shop and I got that guy who looked like my depressed stepfather. My tattoo of a snake twining around a baby bottle, its fangs poised to strike the nipple, is too big and bright, too cartoony. I'd imagined it more classic and elegant, occult. My artist looked sad, like he knew I was disappointed, but I guess he'd looked that way from the start. Out front, we stood on opposite ends of the shop's long plate-glass window and smoked cigarettes, and sometimes I caught him looking at me regretfully. Meanwhile, the neighborhood had erupted into full wildness. A woman in a wheelchair bummed a cigarette off me, and the music was so loud it seemed to come from the darkening sky, from god's own boom box.

I wanted a tattoo because the love inside my heart had nowhere to go and made me feel wild and reckless and craving of sensation, and now I had it, throbbing on my arm, the skin around it bruising. In a sense, it doesn't matter if that tattoo is good or bad. I knocked on the window before I left, Alaska, and you looked up from your own tattoo of an evil baby, and the smile you gave me was so legit. I know you're not going to stay in Dallas, no matter how good the ramen is at Oni or the stock at Deep Vellum bookstore, your tattoo connection or your obvious thrift scores. I'll find you in another city, draped over the counter in a different tattoo parlor, the vixen on the back of your thigh forever peering into the cracked rearview at the highway she left behind.

≈ To the Face in the Subway Glass

BERLIN, GERMANY

by Annie Schweikert

To the girl on the Berlin U-Bahn who looked like me: I thought you were a mirror when I saw you. You had the same hard expression I knew had settled over my face, the same thin brown hair tucked behind your ear, the same aquiline nose that on men is called virile and on women is called "fucking huge." I hope that people made fun of your nose when you were young, and that when you brush your hair on a dry morning, you feel like a Medusa whose snakes have worn themselves thin and limp. I hope that hard expression makes you feel invincible. I hope it's also cost you a few dates.

To the girl on the Berlin U-Bahn who looked like me: I hope these things because I want to believe I am not alone. I saw you riding on a fluorescent-lit subway car in the country of my great-great-grandparents, where I could not quite speak the language and did not quite have a friend. I had descended into the bright, clean station from a street fair hawking fresh strawberries, homemade wurst, large-grained mustards, and rhubarb juice. Before that, I had idled the afternoon away at a karaoke competition in the place where the Berlin Wall once stood. It did not feel foreign, but of course it was, and that was exhausting. I didn't stand out but I didn't fit in, and by the time I stepped onto the train, my mouth had been set in a line for hours.

To the girl on the Berlin U-Bahn who looked like me: You're who I wanted to be at that moment. I'm sorry for staring.

≈ MYSTERY

≈ To the Loner at High Altitude

TRES CRUCES, PERU

by Elizabeth Kolbert

To say I did not know who you were would be an understatement. No one seemed to know who you were, or how you got there, or where you were going.

I met you in the Peruvian Andes, at almost 13,000 feet, an elevation at which the mere act of breathing becomes an adventure. With a group of scientists, I had driven almost six hours from Cusco, most of the way along an unpaved road. Finally, toward evening, we arrived at our destination: an abandoned building at a spot known as Tres Cruces. We'd just unloaded several days' worth of supplies when you appeared. You were disheveled, but cheerful. You had no bags or, it seemed, possessions of any kind. You asked, in Spanish, if you could stay with us. The scientists looked at one another uncomfortably. They conferred for a few minutes, in English.

The view from Tres Cruces probably ranks as one of the most spectacular in the world. It takes in thousands of square miles and extends down to the Alto Madre de Dios River, which flows into the Beni River, which flows into the Madeira, which eventually meets the Amazon. The building had been constructed as a hostel, but not enough tourists had been willing to make the kidney-rattling journey, and the place was now deserted. Normally, it was locked up; somehow, one of the scientists had obtained a key. How you knew we were there, I have no idea. Did you spot the lights of the van in the distance? Hear the chug of the motor? I wondered what you would have done had we not shown up. I don't think there was another structure for several miles in any direction.

The scientists decided to let you stay. Really, they didn't have much choice. The temperature at sunset was just above freezing; once it got dark, it would continue to drop. If you stayed, you'd have to be fed. Dinner that night—and for the several nights that followed—was simple: some rice, some cheese, an orange. There was no heat in the building, not to mention no electricity, so everyone walked around with headlamps, except, of course, you, who didn't have one. You were ravenous, and went through your portion so quickly that someone offered you more. It was, once again, the decent thing to do. But the mood of the group, which had been festive, turned tense. There was now a question hanging in the chilly air: What do we owe to a stranger?

For your part, you remained upbeat, almost eerily so. That's what struck me most about you, besides your improbable appearance— your smile. That night, you slept on the floor, as did everyone else. We'd all brought sleeping bags, which turned out to be just barely adequate. Did anyone offer you a blanket? Were there any blankets to offer? I can't recall. All I remember is that the next morning, you vanished just as mysteriously as you had materialized. One minute you were there, smiling to yourself, as if enjoying a private joke, and the next, you were gone. Some of the scientists had asked you about your life—I don't speak Spanish, so I couldn't understand the conversation—but, they told me, they hadn't learned much. You had claimed to be walking from your own village to another village, where you had relatives. But your story didn't add up, as the villages were too far apart to make the trip with no provisions. They had no idea how you got by. Nor were they sure you were quite sane.

Not long after you vanished, we started down the mountain, into the cloud forest. The trail we were following was a difficult one—so overgrown that sometimes it became a tunnel and we literally had to crawl along. Many times along the way, I felt sorry for myself. The tent I had brought along turned out to have been designed for a much drier climate; every night, when it rained, a pool of water collected by my feet. But, in part because of you, I was embarrassed by my self-pity. I still am. And although several years have passed, every now and then I think of you and your story, which I will never learn. The world is full of strangers. Mostly we turn away from them. But sometimes when we look, we find that they are smiling, though not necessarily at us.

≈ To the First Responder After the Storm

NEW ORLEANS, LOUISIANA

by David Parker Jr.

We met at the Parkview Tavern, when it was a way station for the weird. All around us lay the darkened wreckage of a city. After Hurricane Katrina, the bar was a tiny oasis of electricity and camaraderie in the very heart of New Orleans. Entergy had managed to restore power down several blocks of Carrollton Avenue, a main thoroughfare that stretched like a finger into Mid-City, all the way to Bayou St. John. Streetlights glowed eerily above the empty neutral grounds, casting shadows against abandoned storefronts and down rows of pitch-dark houses.

The neighborhood had a distinct smell, even after the Army Corps of Engineers managed to drain the city. The mud had baked into something that looked like the surface of another planet. The receding water left behind souvenirs, like the vivid orange stain of the waterline on every house and building, or like the motorboats wrecked at odd angles in the streets, miles from the lakefront.

Somehow, the owners of the Parkview had managed to dodge the debris, scrape the mud off their concrete floors, clean out, restock, and reopen. The bar was never anything fancy, but now it felt luxurious: electric lights, ceiling fans, refrigerated beer, flushing toilets, and a misfit jukebox that echoed into the dark streets.

You were sitting at one of the long picnic tables outside on the sidewalk patio. From the looks of it, you and your colleagues had been there for a while already: an impressive stack of emptied plastic beer cups stood before you. My friends were just now gathering—a motley assortment of writers, bartenders, and grad students who had ventured back into the city to inhabit what was left. We shared the long table with you, and you leaned in with a friendly style to join our chat. You seemed eager for some conversation, and that's when I learned you were here for the hurricane—for its aftermath.

A specialist in search and rescue, you'd come from another state. You had prowled the city streets for days and days in a shallow-bottomed boat, navigating around sunken cars to pluck survivors from rooftops, helping families flee to safety or saving patients marooned in sweltering hospitals that had turned into tragic islands with over-flowing morgues.

You looked the part. Dark blue EMS T-shirt stretched over well-muscled chest and arms. Dark, intelligent eyes. Olive-toned skin. A confident smile.

"What are you doing now?" I asked. It had taken over a month for city and military officials to allow residents back into New Orleans. The search and rescue missions should have been over by now.

"The mission has . . . evolved," you replied, in the cadence of an officer delivering orders. "Now I do search and recovery."

"Recovery?"

"The bodies," you replied.

"The bodies," I repeated, letting that sink in for a moment. "I didn't know they were still out there."

"Where did you think they were going to go?" you asked.

I felt a little embarrassed. "I just thought they were . . . collected already."

"We found all the easy ones," you said, peering into the last half of a beer in your hand. "Now we've got to find the ones buried under the mud and lost in the canals and crushed under houses."

"And this is what you do every day?"

"Every day."

I didn't press you for any more details, and you didn't volunteer them.

Instead, my friends and I bought you several rounds of beers as small tokens of appreciation. *Thank you for being here.* You were glad to get drunk, and we were glad to help. This was the time when everyone was glad to get drunk. Not party-drunk, mind you. Not Mardi Gras–drunk or Jazz Fest–drunk or Saints-game-drunk. Not French Quarter–brunch-drunk or second-line-dancing-drunk or drive-thru-daiquiris-in-the-park-drunk. This kind of drunk was more than a recreational activity; it was a strategic line of defense against the immense darkness that lay across the city.

But it didn't always work.

You got up to enjoy a piss in a bathroom with overhead lights and a working urinal. I remained at the picnic table and gazed out in the direction of City Park and beyond, where the ruined golf courses stretched along the bayou, almost all the way to Lake Pontchartrain. The affected area from Hurricane Katrina, when all combined, was supposedly the size of Great Britain.

The nights were so vast now that you could actually see thick blankets of stars over the metropolis, their brightness so enduring that hawks and coyotes moved back into the area for the first time in a century to hunt rabbits, cats, rats, nutria, and pigeons. The hawks hunted by day, and you could see them circling between the buildings and perched on torn roofs. Coyotes loped through the city at night, emerging from the lagoons of City Park to pad quietly through the streets.

"It's the fucking smell that gets to you," you said after you settled back onto your seat. You had bought yourself another whiskey and beer.

"The bathroom?" I asked. I thought it was pretty clean actually. By Parkview standards, anyway.

"No," you replied. "When you start to uncover the bodies. That smell. It's like getting punched. I can't get it out of my head sometimes."

"God," I said. "I can't imagine."

"No, you can't," you said, and that was the moment the night seemed to tilt toward an uncomfortable place. As you lost yourself in the whiskey and beer, you became more intense, more than friendly. Your eyes began to look bottomless, like they had spun out somehow. When conversation among the writers and students began drifting toward more esoteric topics like Proust's treatment of memory or the way Tim O'Brien crystalized tragedy, you became aggressive. "What? Do you think I'm fucking stupid?"

No one thought you were stupid, but everyone felt the air thicken. Conversation became an exercise in walking on eggshells. You tried to laugh, but it came out too loud. You tried to regain that easy camaraderie, but your anger was too close to the surface now. You challenged our opinions on everything from military patrols in the streets to what would happen to the New Orleans Saints now. "You got a problem with that?" you said to our friend Rick, who was sitting just to my right. When your eyes locked onto him, I realized that some part of you didn't want to have a conversation any longer. It wanted a fight. Something you could punch back.

We didn't want a fight, especially not with you. Something of a conversational clown show ensued. When you shot a challenge at someone, someone else deflected. If a verbal punch landed at my end of the table, chatter would swell at the other. Curfew was coming; maybe that would save us. We'd all be leaving soon. No one, in those days, wanted to get caught out after curfew.

But you must have gotten bored with us first. You got up to go inside and piss again, and you didn't come back to our table.

Eventually, you emerged from the smoky tavern with your colleagues and, together, began walking away from the bar, down the broken sidewalk, beneath the shadows of the live oaks. I watched you go with relief and guilt and gratitude. You walked unsteadily to the end of the block where the streetlight ended, and then kept going. There was no goodbye between us, so in my memory, you linger in that unfinished conversation over that unfinished beer, torn between those two rival impulses: camaraderie and violence.

≈ To the Boy Who Climbed onto My Hammock

MAZUNTE, MEXICO

by Emily Matchar

"I'm going to kill your baby," you said. *Voy a matar a tu nene.* You said this every time you saw me.

"I don't have a baby," I'd remind you, and then I'd pull you into my hammock and we'd swing back and forth and I'd tickle your belly until you giggled.

You were a nene yourself, Josué—three years old, the grandson of the woman who owned the beachfront palapa restaurant where I was renting a sleeping hammock. You spent your days underfoot in the restaurant kitchen, or napping in the shed, or wandering among the foreigners drinking Sol on the beach, looking for someone who might admire your toy truck.

You were angry, your grandmother said, because your mother had left you. She went north. There was a new boyfriend, a new baby. She didn't call anymore. Now you wouldn't stop talking about killing babies.

"You must remind him of his mother," your grandmother said to me, shrugging, sweeping sand off the kitchen's concrete threshold. "She had hair like you."

I was a senior in college, backpacking solo through southern Mexico for the summer, as happy as I'd been in my life. Everything was as new and electric as first love—juddering through the mountains on old Blue Bird school buses painted with the Virgin Mary, eating tamales sold warm from an enamel pot on the street corner, late-night hostel sing-alongs with cute British boys doing something called a "gap year." I used up half a roll of film in my first Oaxacan market—stalls piled high with cartoonish yellow chicken feet; an ochre-and-sienna rainbow of mole pastes; bull penises. "I'm sleeping in a hammock!" I wrote to my mother in North Carolina. "It's only $2 a night!"

I was a twenty-year-old American from the suburbs; *of course* I didn't have a nene, I thought. I wasn't even going to get married until I was at least thirty and had traveled the whole world. Who knew if I'd even have kids? I didn't usually like them.

But I liked you, Josué, with your grave brown eyes and your small, dusty feet and your strange threats. You may have wanted to kill my baby, but you also wanted as much of my attention as you could get. You hung off my neck while I brushed my teeth at the outdoor sink. You played with my flip-flops and zipped and unzipped all the zippers on my backpack. You sat in my lap in the morning while I drank Nescafé and consulted my guidebook.

I spent a week there in Mazunte. I bodyboarded in the gray Pacific and ate garlicky grilled fish and made out with an Australian cricketer. Every morning when I woke up in the palapa, there you were, kneeling in the sand with your toy truck. *Voy a matar a tu nene.* I'd laugh at your funny little gravelly voice, the words so incongruous on your rosebud lips. We'd play for a while and then I'd go off for the day with my sunhat and camera. When the week was over, I headed to Chiapas, then on to the rest of my life.

Seventeen years have passed, Josué, so you're as old as I was on that Oaxacan beach. And I do have a nene now; two in fact. The older one is as old as you were then.

My nene loves toy trucks, too. He has dozens, so many the shelf looks like a toy store. My nene has a bed with truck sheets, though he still pads into my bed in the night, sighing as he wriggles between me and his father, fully convinced this is his rightful spot. I've only been away from him once, for two nights, when he stayed with his grandparents and went to the zoo and two playgrounds and got ice cream for dinner.

The idea of leaving him and his brother—of their being left by me—makes me nauseated. Back then I'd imagined your mother as young and careless, speeding off with a handsome new boyfriend who didn't want the baggage of a toddler. But it must have been complicated. I know that now, at thirty-seven, the calamities of life having come to visit me and mine: the divorces, the breakdowns, the things that make you do things you never thought you'd do.

I was so oblivious then. Playing with you like a puppy, your existence a backdrop to my Amazing Adventure. But I'm not angry at my younger self. In a fair universe we would all start adulthood with that kind of obliviousness, the kind that comes from being sheltered and well-loved and wholly unacquainted with trauma and loss. The kind of obliviousness that allows you to think it's cute when a three-year-old threatens to kill your baby, rather than so deeply sad.

You'll never have that, of course. So I wish for you whatever else it is that you want now as a young man. A real truck. A college degree. A girlfriend. A nene of your own, one day. The ability to raise that nene to believe that bad things only happen far away, outside the shelter of your hammock.

≈ *To the Man I Believe Was Good*

PALERMO, ITALY

by Lauren Groff

You were what, seventy? Eighty? To a teenager, you were simply old, and somehow, in aging, you had lost your threat. This was the only day I spent in Sicily, having ridden there on a train that seemed only finger-bolted together, then a ferry that made sounds like a great and dying beast. I hadn't showered in days; I was hungry; I'd been alone for a week; I had almost run out of money; I wore a backpack the size of a toddler; and still, when I came out of the Palermo station, a prepubescent boy pinched my ass so hard in passing it later hurt to sit. I cursed him out, and when he laughed, I wept. This was not a shining moment in my life.

Palermo was hot and seemed populated mainly by pigeons, and the youth hostel had no available beds. I was resolute in my misery. I have a blurred impression of sun on ruins, tan buildings, dusty trees. This may or may not be Palermo in real life, but it is the Palermo of my imagination, and there it will stay. I have no desire to revisit this place.

After the pinch and the announcement of homelessness for the night, I sat at an outdoor table at a café to gather myself. There you came, Enrico Ferrante. You walked with a cane; your pants were creased. The skin of your face was flaking around the nose in dry spots. But you spoke beautiful English, and I remember we talked about Bach because you were very cultured and I'd had a musical theory class in the spring and so I said a few things about fugues. You bought my coffee, then you bought me some kind of drink that was so bitter I couldn't drink it, and only decades later tasted again as a Negroni. I loved it in this new incarnation of myself.

And then, as the sun started to go down over the little square where we sat, you suggested that I come home with you. You had leaned forward and were smiling gently. I noticed how clean your fingernails were and studied them, thinking.

Now I see that girl I was, dirty and blonde and skinny from hunger, and I want to shout at her, but I was raised in a warm, small place where people were mostly kind, and so that dusk, no alarm bells went off in me. Your apartment must have been like this: flecks of gold dust in the light of the window, a yellow cat, a piano and a great heavy chair passed down from your mother. I see it all so clearly, though in the end I never went with you, because, between the bitterness of coffee and the bitterness of Campari in my mouth, I understood that Palermo was no place for me, would never be my place, that there was something malign there. Places are like people, and sometimes inexplicable antipathies arise out of nowhere. Another train, another ferry that evening would come and take me away.

I left you with my address and you wrote me a gorgeous letter, but you included a photograph of yourself in a blue Polo shirt. "In front of my car," you'd written on the back, and the car was a cherry-red Lamborghini, but it was clearly also in motion, driving away from you. I was naïve but not entirely so, and it made me sad to think that you believed I'd believe this. And so I never answered, and I never discovered whether your gentleness that afternoon was truly kindness for a bedraggled stranger, or whether you were the predator two decades have taught me you might have been.

But this is the power of memory: the person who owns it can morph it to her desire. I'd like to judge you for the intense courtliness with which you treated me, the conversation, the sunlight in which we sat. I won't ever know the truth, but I choose to believe you were good and that your arrival took me away from worse. So thank you, Enrico Ferrante, for what didn't happen, for what you didn't do, for what I didn't find in that menacing dreamland of Palermo, for the way your gentle intervention sent me away.

≈ To the Man Who Saw Cobras Dance

AUROVILLE, INDIA

by Meera Subramanian

I was never any good at remembering names. You must have told me yours that evening in 2001, when you sat down next to me at the long outdoor table in the south of India. There were ten of us, brought randomly together at the guesthouse, emerging from our thatched-roofed cottages to dine together for the evening. But I only remember you, sitting to my left. That you were German but raised in India, and had lived an eclectic life, even dabbling in Bollywood movies. Not enough information to ever track you down. Dinner started in the last of the day's light, but we sat until long after darkness had fallen and candles were lit.

To my right was the man I was traveling with, my partner of eight years. I wonder if we seemed like a contented couple, an Asian American woman and the blue-eyed boyfriend she'd brought to her father's land. We were content, but in those end years, our ease only lasted as long as we were moving—and our travels were coming to an end. We'd been circling our way around South India, trying to remake our relationship, and had paused for that night in a place called Auroville when I met you at the long table.

Auroville is a living experiment, an attempt to remake civilization. Instead of nationality, there was intentionality; instead of competition, cooperation.

What had brought you to Auroville? I came because I still sought utopia, though I felt the possibility slipping away in tandem with my relationship. I was thirty-one, and my partner and I were taking a winter break from the community called Aprovecho that we lived in back in Oregon—a community that was not entirely unlike Auroville. It, too, was started by idealists who wanted to change the world. Auroville was founded in the late sixties; Aprovecho, in the early eighties. Like Aurovilians, we built experimental houses, cooked with solar power, preferred bikes over cars and cottage industries over desk jobs.

But we had no gurus or gods. We did not center our community around anything like the strange shining orb at the heart of Auroville, which looked like a spaceship and contained a giant crystal imported from Italy. We did not gather daily to meditate. No, we were escapees from mainstream America, thumbing our noses at the Joneses as we researched alternative energy, cultivated organic gardens and an old-growth forest, got drunk on wine made of grapes we'd grown and then stomped on with our bare feet.

But I write to you because I've never been able to shake the story you told me that night in the darkness. Do you remember? The one about the dancing snakes? You began with the caveat that it might not be true, but this is what you remember:

When you were just a boy, maybe five or six, your family was living in a remote town somewhere in India. You were outside by yourself one day, not far from the house, when you saw two cobras. They came together, you said, and rose up from the earth, winding the upper halves of their bodies together vertically, like water flowing uphill, intertwined. You watched them dance, you said, transfixed, a witness to something you sensed was forbidden.

I could barely see your face in the dim candlelight, but could tell you were speaking as if you were there again, a half century earlier, the curious, watchful little boy that the big man beside me had become. But only for a moment. Quickly, the spell broke. You leaned back in your chair, a middle-aged man again, but I'm sure I must have leaned forward as you told what happened next.

You said the maid came out. She saw you. She saw the snakes.

"That maid," you said, "she grabbed me and dragged me into the house!" You laughed. Repeatedly reprimanding you, she told you that one should never—never—watch cobras when they are together.

"They know," she said, "and they will come after you."

Your voice went down to a whisper. Precautions against the attack were made that night. Your parents raised your small bed high on blocks in your room. But the snakes came, you said. The cobras were after you. You were a sleepy boy, a young boy, and don't remember the details of the night, but you believe what you were told in the retelling, of the snakes that came for vengeance but missed their mark. The very next morning your mother and father bundled you up and fled for the train that would return you to the supposed safety of the city. You told me you never returned to the place of the dancing cobras again. It sounded like a loss you still carried.

I always assumed the cobras were mating. That what was illicit was watching the sinuous sexuality of the hooded snakes so revered in India. But years later, I have learned that they could just as easily have been two males, fighting. Things can be mistaken for one another: the violent and the erotic in the animal world, carefree travel and running away from something that can't be escaped.

Why was I so taken with you and your story, when my inner skeptic raised her eyebrow at the plausibility that the snakes returned? But I was. I saw them in your telling of the tale just as vividly as you must have seen them when your parents did the same. It made the impossible seem possible, just by speaking it into being. But you survived whatever happened to you that night. My relationship didn't survive our return to the Oregon woods. Words only take us so far.

We all make up stories. In the past, but also in the present. And even into the future, with or without great crystals set before us. What is the longing for utopia or the relationship that lasts forever if not a projection of our perfect storyline into the imperfect script of the world? Were the snakes lovers or mortal enemies? It matters as little as the truth of whether or not they returned that dark country night, remembrance and misremembrance intertwined in an ophidian embrace.

≈ To the Woman Who Wanted to Go Shoe Shopping

XI'AN, CHINA

by Vanessa Hua

It was 2008, just after Beijing's Olympic Games had daz-
zled the world—a coming-out party of sorts for modern China. My
husband and I headed to the very back row of the local bus, traveling east from downtown Xi'an. He'd joined me on a research trip
while I gathered stories and context for a novel set in China during
the Cultural Revolution. For a week or so, I'd been interviewing
Chinese peasants about their lives under Chairman Mao and visiting Communist Revolution sites. Now, we were on our way to the
foot of the Lishan Mountain to see the Terracotta Warriors, a buried
army designed to protect the country's first emperor in the afterlife.

Your eyes lit up when you spotted the two of us. My husband
is American, of Serbian and northern European descent. I'm also
American, but I don't have his sandy hair and green eyes. I'm the
daughter of Chinese immigrants. Every Chinese person we'd met
on our trip so far had assumed that only my husband was foreign,
was the American one. You must have leapt to the same conclusion
as we walked to the back of the bus where you sat with your young
son and your friend. Blunt in that familiar—that family—way, you
voiced your astonishment at the sound of my English banter.

"How does a Chinese person speak English so well?" you asked me.

I explained that I was born and raised in America, then, with a light smile added, "That's why my Chinese is so terrible."

A few days earlier, in a village outside of Beijing, I'd asked a granny with tiny feet a question in Mandarin. I had an interpreter with me to ensure I caught all the details of peoples' lives under Chairman Mao: what they grew, what animals they raised, what they ate for breakfast. But I wanted to establish a rapport with her by speaking Mandarin.

The ninety-year-old had stared blankly at me, as though she'd never heard the language I uttered. A moment later, though, when my husband uttered three words of Mandarin ("Wo bu dong," *I don't know*), the old lady proclaimed with delight, "Ta shuo zhong wen!" *He speaks Chinese!*

Our bus jounced along the rutted surface streets. You seemed to understand my Mandarin, so I kept talking, pausing every few beats to give the gist to my husband.

"I'm huaqiao. From America," I told you. A person of Chinese descent who lived abroad, among the 60 million in the diaspora, as numerous as all of Italy.

"I've heard of Chinese like that," your friend chimed in. "In Shanghai." It struck me that we may have been the first foreigners you'd ever met.

"ABC," I said. The acronym for "American-born Chinese," which made you all laugh, even if you didn't understand the meaning.

Your son looked at my husband. "Will he understand me?" your son asked. He might have been eight or nine years old. About the age of my twin boys now.

"He only speaks English," you explained to your son. "If you study hard, when you grow up, you can speak English. If you eat enough, you'll grow as tall as him."

I wished I didn't have to explain this to my husband. I wished Western standards of beauty hadn't swept through China, just as they had in the predominantly white suburbs east of San Francisco where I grew up. In middle school, I'd permed my straight black hair, trying to fit in, but still classmates teased me. I never wanted to be white, but I had Asian American friends who considered getting plastic surgery on their eyelids to make their eyes look bigger, less sleepy—more like a Barbie's. In every reflection—in windows, in mirrors—you measure yourself against portrayals of beauty, and find yourself lacking.

More passengers started getting on, crowding into the aisle, as the low-slung concrete blocks gave way to farmland. You asked me about our house, whether we planted food, and where the fat Americans lived.

"Middle of America," I said.

We laughed and you asked for my handle on QQ, an instant messaging service popular in China. That QQ hadn't caught on abroad startled you. The kind of startlement that Americans might experience when they discover something they love, something they assume is widespread—peanut butter, let's say—is not available elsewhere.

Before you got off the bus, you asked me if I wanted to go shoe shopping. I considered going. In China, I found my sizes more easily than back home, where I sometimes prowled the more fashionable quarters of the kid section. We didn't have time for detours, though—thoroughly American in that way. In a rush, on a schedule, even on vacation. Yet what you'd said to your son remained with me for years.

I still wonder why you cajoled him the way you did. Maybe he was a picky eater, perhaps small or short for his age. Maybe it was your own appearance that bothered you. Maybe when you stared in the mirror, you wished yourself taller or blonde, blue-eyed or fair-skinned. Was that it? That what you couldn't achieve for yourself, you wanted for your son?

He must be a teenager by now, in high school, at college, or now working. I suspect glimpsing a foreigner on the bus in western China isn't as remarkable now. Your son might dream of following one of your country's astronauts into space, or modeling himself after an action hero born from the booming Chinese film industry—stars you and your son can aspire to, who look more like you, who place the Middle Kingdom back at the center of the world.

≈ To the Chatty Man Who Pierced the Quiet

CANAAN, NEW HAMPSHIRE

by Peter Orner

It was after six in August. Canaan Street Lake, Canaan, New Hampshire. The sun yellow, a little bland, as if tired of shining all day. From where I sat, on a waterfront bench, the lake no longer glistened like new pavement. A lone duck, hoping against hope that I might have a sandwich to toss at it, paddled back and forth in the shallows, back and forth, not quacking, because even the duck had the decency to wait me out and not burst into my silence with a question.

You spoke without preface, just called out across the deserted beach: "You know how deep this lake gets?"

I'd come here to be alone, driven to Canaan from a few towns over, where I live. In New England this is interplanetary travel. I wanted to be alone across a border, not chatting with a stranger. Besides, I didn't have a clue how deep this lake gets. I said as much. But then, feeling I'd been too curt, I added, "Seems shallow though."

The lake is named after a street; how deep could it be? You said nothing. Maybe you could smell that I dreaded any response that might spur on conversation. You walked back to the parking lot.

You drove away. I hardly got a good look at you but I did catch a glimpse of Florida plates.

You know how deep this lake gets? Something about the way you asked. As if you weren't looking for an answer. Off-hand, just making conversation. But that question threw me out of my book, a book whose title I no longer recall. There's a degree of beauty in the question, isn't there? Let me state for the record that I will not spin this encounter into something profound. You just got me thinking. Two, three years later, I'm still thinking.

Not about the lake, but about those moments in our lives that have no significance. That are, and then were. A question shouted across an August beach. A useless attempt at an answer.

There's a Borges story, "Funes the Memorious," about a guy named Funes who remembers everything: every single solitary occurrence in his entire life. As in: *On such and such a day in 1922, at such and such time of day, at the corner of what and what, a dog barked.* It's almost like a carnival trick, and at first the narrator is floored, amazed, in awe. But soon enough, it's a horror story. Such memory leads, inevitably of course, to paralysis. Funes is confined to his bed, trapped in the ceaseless machinations of his own head. There's no forward, only the infinite, ever-growing heap: the past.

Think about it. I'm talking to you, idle lake-depth inquisitor. Now I'm interrupting you, wherever the hell you went (Tallahassee? Pensacola?), with a question out of the blue. Into the void you left. Me no longer on the beach but still on the beach, in that congealed light, that too-yellow margarine light.

And yet, as I remember this nonincident on the beach, I wonder, What if I've missed the point Borges was trying to make altogether? And no, I don't want to go back and read the story, I prefer to think on it, too, as a memory—the story as something I experienced as opposed to something I can fact-check. If I've got it wrong, I've got it wrong. What if the story is less a warning than a kind of odd call to arms against forgetting?

Myself, I tend to over-edit memories. I don't want to get bogged down. I collect only those moments charged with consequence, and too quickly disregard those moments that don't pass some sort of ill-defined memorability test. I've come to wonder whether I've got this wrong. What if our lives, ultimately, are made up of what we forget? That this limitless string of occurrences that were practically over the moment they happened—that's existence. And this whole time, I've been missing it.

So I call you back. Precisely because you seemed to mean nothing. *You know how deep this lake gets?* You were fiddling with your shoe. I'd forgotten this. That when you spoke, you were stooped over and trying to tighten your laces. Hold this. You're stooped but facing me across the beach. Bit of an awkward position but that's how it is.

I don't know actually, I say. Then, a beat. Another beat.

My duck swims back and forth.

Seems shallow though.

You didn't leave right away; hold that, too. The two of us, out there on the beach. You stopped adjusting your laces and stood. You stared out at the lake for a while. In the silence, so did I.

≈ To the Boo Radley of My Childhood

SYDNEY, AUSTRALIA

by Madelaine Lucas

Every childhood deserves a Boo Radley house and the Olympia Milk Bar was mine, although for years I didn't know your shop had a name. I was eight the year my father and step-mother moved in three doors down and we became your neighbors. Remember me then—twiggy limbs and home-cut bangs, blonde hair already tarnishing. The sign out the front of your shop was missing as many letters as I was teeth. It read: MILK AND SNACK, SMOKES, S_E_TS, like an unfinished game of hangman. To me, you looked impossibly old, emerging out of the dark, cool interior with your black eyes and gray pallor, your thinning white hair.

Nobody in the neighborhood remembered you as a young man—that was a different life, on another continent, an ocean away. Strange how I think of it that way—*the neighborhood*—as if I'd grown up in a small town instead of a largely anonymous urban corridor of car washes and discount dealerships, of apartments above struggling shop fronts on a long road that led away from the city, to the suburbs, to beaches. Soot blew in beneath our doorframe, blackening the soles of my feet. Every year, I had to have my blood tested for lead. I learned in that house to sleep against the sound of constant rushing traffic. *If you close your eyes,* my father said, *doesn't it sound like the ocean?*

I don't know what you made of us—me and my long-haired father, his fingers calloused from guitar strings and his day job soldering slivers of stained glass into kaleidoscopic patterns—but I doubt we haunted your imagination the way you haunted ours. We'd come into the Olympia together to buy milkshakes before going to the movies at the twin picture theater next door. It was my father's way of keeping you in business, I thought, though you were at best ambivalent toward your customers, serving them begrudgingly with as few words as possible. Your voice was low, thickly accented, and when you spoke at all it was something more akin to a groan. I never saw you smile.

We thought you were struggling. Why else would you leave the lights off during the day, so the shop was always full of shadows, and leave it lit at night only by a dim, bare yellow bulb? Why else were the boxes of Cherry Ripe and Milkybars and Twirl so dusty and mottled white where the chocolate had melted and reset, the cans of soft drink on the wooden shelves unrefrigerated and lukewarm, the signs for Cadbury and Nescafé and Streets ice cream dating back decades, aged to pale shades of blue and yellow by the sun?

I was still young enough to believe in magic then, in the stories I heard. I realize now you must have only been in your sixties, but I thought you were at least one hundred—if not older, beyond death, *undead.* I was a superstitious child, walking around knocking on wood, stepping carefully to avoid the cracks in the pavement, checking for my face in every mirror to make sure I was still part of the land of the living. You made it possible for me to see my childhood as something of a fable, and so to believe that it might hold the morals or rewards of a fairytale. In this world of step-mothers and haunted milk bars, there might be a coherence and a meaning to the things I couldn't yet understand, like my father's good but broken heart, my mother's absence.

So you were a vampire, a ghost, a zombie, depending on who was talking. All the locals had their versions of you. Did you know that they called you Vlad or Drac or Dr. Death because of the way you seemed to materialize out of the shadows, without a sound? There were whispers of a wife who once ran a beauty parlor in the space above, of a brother or a child who died in a mysterious accident, of the body of a bride still kept upstairs. The Milk Bar had to be a drug front, some said. What other reason could there be to keep such late hours when you had so few customers? My best friend and I had more childish theories—we were sure you slept in a crypt and flew around the neighborhood late at night, and we dared each other to peek through the gaps of the wooden fence at the back of your property to see what bones or relics might be hidden in your yard.

If this seems cruel, it's because I hadn't yet learned the lesson of Boo Radley—that these characters we craft from the figures of our childhood, strangers, reclusive *others* in our communities, are actually just people with lives and losses more human, more *mortal*, than we might care to imagine. Perhaps you would have told different stories about yourself if given the chance—but then again, perhaps you'd rather have been left alone in peace and privacy.

By the time I started high school and waited for the bus each morning at the stop in front of your shop, one of your windows was permanently broken, patched only occasionally with tape and brown paper. My father offered to repair it with leftover glass as a gesture of goodwill, but his offer was rebuked. You never needed anyone's sympathy, or pity.

It was only recently that I learned your name, when I read about how the local council had forced you to shut the shop because the ceiling was in danger of falling in. Once again, you waved away offers of support, fundraisers and donations offered by well-meaning fans to help with repairs and keep the Olympia open. Do you know that all these years later, adults who'd once visited your shop as kids speak on Facebook groups and Reddit forums of "the Haunted Milk Bar," "the Dark Place," and long to take their own children there, as my father had with me?

Your family name, Fotiou, is Greek, like Olympia, which stems from Olympus, the mythic home of the gods. You emigrated from the island of Lemnos in the fifties, but you didn't follow the familiar immigrant narratives, neither shedding your past to embrace Australian life nor staying closely knitted to the local Greek community. It's in your native tongue that one can find the root of the feeling I get when I think of the Olympia, all these years later. Far from the sugary, sentimental mood we associate with *nostalgia*, it originally described something more visceral, forged out of two words stitched together: *nostos* (return home) and *algia* (pain).

By the time I lived three doors down from you, I'd moved house every year since I was born—sometimes twice, if my mother and father both relocated, after they separated when I was four. It hurts, that kind of longing, the desire to go back to a place that feels like home. I knew what it was like to straddle two lives, never belonging truly in either one, because something would always be missing.

I'm older now. I've married, crossed oceans, become an immigrant myself. I've lived in many other places I've come to call home, but when I read about the Olympia's closure, it felt like the final curtain call of my childhood.

It's locked up now, your shop. I picture its interior just as it always was: frozen in time but not immune to its damages. The Formica tabletops peeling back at the edges, the greasy metal counter, the neon sign that was always burned out. What were you trying to preserve? Was the Milk Bar your monument to another time or place that felt more like home? Or do I just want to see it that way—twenty-one years later—still looking to stories to give meaning to what I've failed to understand?

You're no less of a ghost to me than you were then, when I was that sweet-breathed, gap-toothed girl holding tight to her father's hand. But I wonder more now about the realities of your life, the fabric of your own nostalgia. Those stories we told about you—they obscured who you were, but maybe they granted you the solitude you desired. Across generations, you bound a community together, even if you never really wanted to be part of it.

≈ To the Grandfather I Hardly Knew

SICILY, ITALY

by Peter Turchi

You were a difficult man, by all accounts. When my father was seventeen, he tried to enlist in the Navy, just like you had. Mistaking his stutter for an inability to discern letters on a chart, recruiters turned him away. Proud and hot-tempered, just like you, he went around the corner and read with no trouble for the Marines. You locked him out of the house.

There were other stories, worse: the one about you hanging him by his thumbs in the attic; the one about you throwing bottles at him after he repainted the family car to impress a girl—because, not knowing any better, he'd used house paint; and the one about you cutting open his thigh with a knife during a fight when he was home on leave, then telling him to claim the wound had happened during training.

How much of that is true?

All of it, my sister and I believed, because those were stories our mother told us, and the few times we saw you, you did nothing to contradict them. Your visits were hurricanes, predicted and monitored with growing alarm, then weathered, endured. On your drive down from New Jersey to Baltimore, if you had to pee, you peed into a jar; once arrived, you expected our parents to vacate their bedroom for you.

Stocky and strong, with hard, thick hands and a bulbous nose, you spoke louder than anyone I knew, your Sicilian accent so thick I could only guess what you meant. My sister and I would escape to her bedroom, or the backyard. Inevitably, at some point in every visit, an argument would erupt: you shouted, you accused, you made our father yell and our very quiet mother cry. When you left, the ill wind would linger for days.

After you died, your sons and their wives cleaned up what you left behind—a hoarder's house full of newspapers and trial-subscription magazines, cheap gadgets advertised on late-night TV, dirty plates, vacuum tubes, dog feces. Our father brought home some photos, books, ancient liquor bottles, and a stack of letters I discovered one night—typed missives you'd sent to other people but, for some reason, carbon-copied and kept.

I read the letters standing up, alone in our basement. In them: shocking revelations. Unspeakable even now. Also: harsh words about our mother, complaints that she and her parents looked down on you and your wife, always believed themselves superior. (Which was true.) And that she had raised us to dislike you, to be afraid of you. (Also true.) That when you wanted to talk to us, we were impatient to get away. (You thought we were arrogant; we were terrified.)

Not until you were gone did I begin to imagine there was more to the story. I learned about the exodus of Sicilians to the United States around the turn of the previous century; how you'd been treated like the Jews, like the Japanese, like the Irish in other eras, like Mexicans and Guatemalans today.

I learned that both your parents died before you were twelve; that in Sicily, in those days, young boys were sent to work on fishing boats or enslaved in the sulfur mines; that an aunt took pity and brought you to this country. As a young man you joined the Navy, became a radio operator, found a role that made you proud. I have a picture of you standing on the roof of your house next to your ham radio tower, wearing a kind of undershirt people used to call a wife beater; before that, they called it a dago tee.

I learned that those free VA hearing aids of yours were so poorly made that you had to shout to hear yourself; and that hoarding is often a sign of grief.

And from those letters, I learned that you felt both proud of and betrayed by your oldest son, the one who brought home steaks you couldn't provide, the one who showed up in your driveway one day with his wife and children in a brand-new red Cadillac, a car that meant *American* and *success*. You thought he was flaunting it. Where were the thanks for the life you had made possible? Where was the gratitude?

I'm not writing to say it was all a misunderstanding. I'm not writing to ask your forgiveness, or to chastise my mother, as she, too, is gone now. I'm writing because, as tempting as it is to embrace family lore, both the good and the bad, it's my nature to distrust the simple story, the easy explanation. And so, without a name to look up or a phone number to call, I went: to Sicily, to Palermo, with my wife and son you never knew, to an address I'd been given: Via Pasquale Prestisimone 26.

There was no listing on that door of anyone by our name (but your nose, your gestures: I saw them everywhere). As I searched for places you would have known as a boy, disguised by upscale gelato shops and souvenir stores and nearly a century of change, I wondered if those streets would have felt like home to you—and if you had yearned to see them again—or if they represented so much hardship and loss that you felt glad to have escaped. After all, you became one of those immigrants who didn't want your boys learning Italian; you wanted them to speak English, to go to school, to belong. In your tiny front yard in New Jersey, you planted an enormous flagpole.

As I walked through that city entirely foreign to me, I wondered what your childhood was like, and what you remembered of your parents, and how impossibly far the United States felt to a twelve-year-old Sicilian boy in 1910. I tried to imagine where you thought you were going, and what it was like to survive that journey only to be treated—upon arrival—as less than human. Most of all, thinking back to those poorly typed impressions on carbon that I strained to read, I wondered, if we had listened, what it was you wanted to tell your grandchildren—what you wanted us to know.

≈ To My Grandmother, c/o the Mush Hole

TSI KANATÁHERE (BRANTFORD, ONTARIO)

by Amber Meadow Adams

Your skin must be part of the swell of dust that washes us when we walk in. Your smell, one chemical note in songs of mold and dry rot, of flaked paint and mice and rust and old paper, slides into me on shy breaths. Strangers, us two, meeting in the dust we're made of. You, tota, are the grandmother I never met, and this is where you were born.

The Mohawk Institute was a school for teaching Indians, first of many like it in North America. Built on Kanyen'keháka— "Mohawk"—land, with Kanyen'keháka money. A nation perched on the hinge between British invasion and the old downbeat of Haudenosaunee diplomacy, we'd been spinning it for centuries: translators, talkers, bridgers, and builders. The school, at first, was just another stone to whet our edge. That was the 1830s, when they were recruiting teachers from good Loyalist families. By the 1930s, when you were there, the trust money was being eaten a mouthful at a time by Indian agents, the New England Company, and the Queen her very self.

They called that school the Mush Hole. Mushy gruel in the open hole of a broken mouth; mushy shit out the end of a wormy gut. A place for making the boys farmhands and laborers; the girls, maids and mothers. The good girls left to set nice tables for white families in Hamilton or Toronto. Were you a good girl? Did you turn the blade of a butter knife toward the silvered rim of the plate? Your other grandchildren show me photos of a skinny girl out of uniform, wearing a borrowed Sunday dress and standing at her father's bent knee. You were the ninth or tenth child of his third or fourth wife.

The architect renovating the school guides us up to the second floor. All the plaster and most of the laths down, and we can see the building's naked bones. They want to turn it into a museum. It has caged more children in its wooden hips and ribs than any of its offspring, than even its chain-link descendants now hold in Chiricahua and Tohono O'odham country. The architect complains about toilets and access. The building's monstrous and still shifting, its gables arched like raptors' wings. This man's nervous in the role of host, a flushed tourist showing us around our own ruins. He tells us about the times the building was set on fire. An anecdote, an oh-my-goodness trill in his voice, as if setting fire to schools were a meaty footnote in his ethnography. As if children routinely take the heft of their own lives in hand and choose death by burning.

He shows us the girls' dormitories. He shows us the head-master's office and family quarters. The Reverend William John Zimmerman, MA, was headmaster here from 1945 to 1950. You left in 1946. Drive 2,055 kilometers to Winnipeg where the Truth and Reconciliation Commission's files are locked away, and you'll find a catalog of ways they say Reverend Zimmerman forced sex on children here. I count the steps from his office door to the girls' rooms. Thirty, for a grown man. Forty, for a little girl.

I keep waiting to feel the trace of your hum. *Orenna*, the word they say means "song" in Kanyen'kéha but really describes frequency, oscillation, the way we fold and press and loosen the air around us. It ripples now in July heat, scattered by our shuffle-voices. I sift for your slender braid of air. Down in the basement, you scratch the back of my throat. We stand in a triangle formed by kitchen, mess hall, and laundry. This is the sharp-cornered heart of the place. I taste blood, mine and yours. Words rise in your voice: *Who the hell do you think you are, bringing me back here?* I'm a spy, looking through eyes whose fishhook slants I recognize from your pictures. They skim the frog-green tiles, the gas burners bolted to the kitchen floor in imitation of hearth fires. *Kahwatsire*, a hearth. A word that also means "family."

From the kitchen we look across the mess hall into the laundry. It's a big, sunny room with a locked door. In TRC testimony, this was a place for being raped. It's tiled white halfway up the walls, the only room with paint intact. Arsenic green, same color as hospitals and asylums of that era, thought to calm lunatics. Crank washers and manual wringers—did their noise drown screams? The teachers' dining room is next to the laundry. They ate food the children raised on school grounds. The children cooked and served in the dining room. What's the difference, tota, between rape on a full stomach and on an empty one?

Nobody can stand the laundry room for long. We are all—except the architect—the children of the children this place made. We go into the mess hall. From a high horizon of windows, you can see the field reaching all the way back to the trees and, under their wet veil, the railroad tracks. Some children ran. If you followed those tracks, tota, they would've taken you to Niagara Falls and the US border. Some made it, eating from trash bins and walking at night. Some froze. Some were caught and brought back and punished.

You never ran. You were born here. This was home. Even later, as a grown-up with children, you kept a scrubbed kitchen, ironed shirts to stand like soldiers on hangers, served meals with knives in place. You wrote a tidy Palmer hand, your English faultless, because you were taught well in school.

The architect's hair is dark with temple sweat and he's talking about bracing the building from outside. He throws a dirty hand toward the lawn and chokes for decent words. Remains, he says. There are little cupped burials of miscarriages and wire-hanger births on the other side of the window. Even malnourished girls were fertile enough to fertilize the earth with the eggshell domes of new faces. Your eyes and mine scan that gruff lawn growing crabgrass and chicory for the seed of an uncle or an auntie of mine, planted and still thumb-sized after sixty years. I wonder why my father's not here, too. Did you hide him inside you, tota, until it was too late for them to pull him out? Or did they decide this time the sin was all yours and demand your father come get you? My father, the size of a fist. The reason you finally came home.

The day's burnt and fallen, and we've both seen enough. When I walk us out, into the shade of my parked car, I try to pull us apart again by vomiting. But the summer grass doesn't absorb you. I brought a mask and didn't wear it, so breathed in too much of your dust. Now I can't get you out. You're in me, awake and building thunder that won't break the sky but only split the night in my head. I wanted to know why you were a stranger, tota. Why we could never speak. Now, you tell me, whimpering in the shadow of the Mush Hole, that pain is the song you left me to sing, when I had the nerve to step in and swallow you.

≈ CHEMISTRY

≈ To the Girl at the Riverbend

BAKER RIVER, NEW HAMPSHIRE

by Howard Axelrod

It was an excursion from an excursion from an excursion. And all the excursions were firsts. My first summer away at overnight camp, my cabin's first overnight at Baker River, and my first sojourn away from the group: my first walk down the river alone.

I was twelve; this was nearly thirty years ago. I've never written about you, never spoken about you, not in the weeks afterward to brag about with the boys in my cabin, not in the years afterward to seduce late-night friends with mystery, and not in the decades afterward to revive some lost feeling of youth.

But I must have stowed the memory in a kind of shoebox in my mind, one that has traveled with me through countless cities and languages and bedrooms, until I was ready to open it and try to understand. There's no reason why you'd remember me—unless that moment in the river helped you to consider your life later on, too.

That morning, my camp group had packed up our tents, eaten breakfast, and hiked upriver along the sun-bleached rocks in our sneakers. There were clouds of gnats, golden in the sunlight, odd piles of shipwrecked branches, and smooth lips of stone with their purls and eddies. Reaching the swimming hole a few miles upstream felt like an achievement. The water shocked and ached. Our towels laid out on the smooth slabs of rock; we swam, lazed in the sun, swam again. My one friend from home, Josh, had told me to bring a Walkman. He liked the Police; I liked Michael Jackson. We were just learning to be cool.

Before lunch, my attention wandered to the bend in the river. The possibility of being out of sight of everyone intrigued me. I wanted to see how deep the river was beyond the bend, but I also wanted to see what would happen to me there, how it would feel to be unseen, alone in this beautiful place.

When Josh put his Walkman back on, I meandered into the trees as if to take a piss, then waded into the water away from the group. The river was waist-high, the current a steady push on my legs. As soon as I turned the bend, you were there.

You held your palms just above the water, making small circles, as though casting a spell. Off to the right, there was a jutting rock, white water rushing around it, and two girls stood on its far side, holding their elbows, talking with each other.

To turn around would have looked strange, so I kept wading, nervous, not sure what to do. It wasn't until I was maybe ten feet away that you looked up.

"Hi."

"Hi," I said.

I came closer, glanced at your friends as though for permission to approach, but they ignored me.

"What are you doing?" I said.

"Making shadows."

With the current, the shadow of your hands looked alive, like silent creatures fighting to stand still. Your bathing suit was orange and black, like the colors of the Cincinnati Bengals, and your arms were deeply tanned, with little golden hairs. You were my age, maybe a year older. I had no idea what I was feeling, only that I'd never felt it before.

"To the fish, maybe it looks like an eclipse," I said, instantly regretting it. So uncool.

"Or maybe like kind birds. Birds who hover and watch."

Eclipse, kind birds—that's all I remember of what we said. Your eyes were green, luminous, like the sunlight in the shallows, the way it seemed to emanate from the sand. I knew how the beginning of a crush could set off flickering lights below my throat, knew how those lights could make my voice go quiet, knew how to calculate who I was supposed to be.

But what I felt with you was different. I was aware of a part of myself I'd never seen in a mirror or in anyone else's eyes. It was all around me—there in the current of the river, there in the flying shadows of our hands. It seemed time was moving through us, racing through us, and we were together standing still. Maybe we talked for five minutes, maybe ten, I don't know. It was a different kind of time.

Soon, voices upstream would call me back for lunch, I'd return to camp, switch to private school in the fall, have my first girlfriend, lose my first girlfriend, go to college, suffer a freak accident and lose vision in my right eye, graduate from college, live out of my car in the Southwest, cloister myself away in northern Vermont, and try to find something like that sense of myself I'd first found with you—a reflection that didn't need surfaces, an orientation I could trust beyond vision, a timeless self to start from.

It was time for lunch. We said goodbye. We never asked each other's name. As I waded back upstream, I felt heavier and lighter, and older, in the way only a young person can suddenly feel older, like you'd given me an important present, though I didn't yet know what it was.

Thank you.

≈ To the Stranger in My Family

BETHESDA, MARYLAND

by Kiki Petrosino

You were eighty-five the summer I lived with you. Mornings, we rose early, settling into the strange and ever-present hum that seemed to surround the condominium. That *hum*: part air-conditioning, part asphalt, part geranium-bright Cadillacs spinning down Westlake Terrace on their way to the capital. That summer, I learned to associate this soft, metropolitan drone with your lucky mid-Atlantic elder years. To me, your life was sunshine, breezes, comfort.

I was between worlds, having just graduated from the University of Virginia on a muddy Sunday afternoon in May. My parents, freshly divorced, had attended my commencement but refused to interact. I had two graduation dinners in Charlottesville, two photo sessions featuring me in academic dress, my sandals sinking into Jefferson's Lawn. My last days of college were rain-soaked and stormy, a dissolving kingdom. I'd already started to tell myself that I was a happy wanderer, a young adult who could find her home anywhere in the world. I imagined a family of my own making: long dinners with laughing friends, road trips to beautiful places. That summer, I'd finally packed away all the photos of my study-abroad boyfriend, a Florentine dental student who'd dumped me the previous winter ("I think you are not the woman of my future"). Now I was moving back to Europe, but to Switzerland this time: a shinier country. I'd be a schoolteacher there. I would build a life I could keep.

On Tuesdays at your condo, I'd roll up my bedsheets for laundering while you unfolded your *Washington Post* in the den. Sometimes, you'd watch the local news. One of the anchors reminded you of my grandfather. He'd passed away when I was a toddler, but I remembered certain things: the way he bent his tall body to fillet a catfish at the sink on Kennedy Street; a single, hand-in-hand walk through his early spring garden, where he'd pointed out the white look of a tiny alpine strawberry still on the vine.

Until that summer, Paw Paw was one of the only things we'd ever shared, and that was because you'd already chosen him, decades before, to be yours. So I offered you these few memories like foreign coins I'd been saving without knowing why. I always had the impression that you didn't necessarily like being a grandmother; there was something about it that puzzled you, as if you'd received the odd gift of a tureen with one more lid than necessary. We saw each other at holidays, mostly.

That summer, you took me in, keeping me out of my parents' post-divorce transitions. After breakfast with you, I'd take the bus from Montgomery Mall to the National Institutes of Health Metrorail stop. Then, I'd ride the Red Line train over to Tenleytown, where I worked as an unpaid intern for the local NPR station. I sweltered on these commutes, and quickly exhausted my cycle of office-suitable clothes. I couldn't afford new outfits; as it was, the daily costs of the Metrorail were digging into the remnants of my college money.

But I was silent about this. I didn't want you to think I was foolish for agreeing to work without pay. Having left your father's farm at the age of twelve all alone, you were a woman who made her own prosperity. The little Negro school in your rural Virginia neighborhood only went up to sixth grade and you wanted to go to seventh; just like that, you willed yourself to DC, leaving your girlhood behind.

For the first time that summer, you told me about the two uniform dresses you had to wear for your job as a nanny for a wealthy white family: blue for playtime with the children, white for dinner service. You and the cook would eat in the kitchen afterward, and then you'd study all night. This family had an indoor washroom that you described in detail—it was an urban luxury they forbade you to use. Do you see why I didn't think you'd have much sympathy for my money troubles?

But you surprised me one day, when I accompanied you to Sears. You pulled out two simple pencil skirts in my size: black, navy. "These will look nice on you," you said, and bought them for me.

That summer was our closest, our best time. In the evenings, you showed me photographs of your younger self, wearing mid-calf versions of the skirts you'd bought me for the office. And on the very last page of an album: a handsome portrait of Paw Paw, taken in his early twenties. You showed it to me, before quickly placing your hand over the image of his face. "Oh! I can't look at it," you said, and the sudden spark in your voice—the bright bolt of something with wings—told me that grief had surprised you in that moment. Grandfathers die, and mine had been gone so long that, for me, looking at his photograph was like visiting a national park or hearing a story about a solemn king. You were my first lesson in living memory, how it leaps and snaps. How it nips at you, unexpectedly.

"Sometimes I still miss my boyfriend," I confessed to you, in the condo hum.

"I know you do, honey."

That summer, we discovered that we liked each other. We didn't know it would turn out that way, or that another opportunity would never come again. But for those few months, there was an opening we both stepped through on our way to something else. When I left for Switzerland, you and my mother came to see me off at Dulles. And because it was the very last summer before 9/11, when our American universe still felt luxuriously unassailable, you waited with me right at my departure gate, and I didn't board my flight until the very last call. You held my hand in both of yours and—with that same surprised note in your voice, same bright flick of a wing—you said:

"I'm going to miss you, child."

≈ To the Man Who Spoke with His Hands

SOUTH CHINA SEA

by Ying Reinhardt

It was 10 p.m. when you walked into the dimly lit crew bar. The wooden door with a dust-streaked porthole in the middle creaked, and then swung back violently behind you. You were new; I hadn't seen you around the *Allegra* before.

I was on my own as usual, practicing an after-work ritual that kept me sane for the past eight months: Jägermeister on the rocks in one hand, a book in the other. In four days, I'd leave the ship and be truly free.

Around me were crew members in groups, cracking roasted peanuts and jokes with their fellow countrymen or their immediate colleagues. I had neither; I was a free-roving agent with too much time and not enough work. Without default cliques to fall back on, a vibrant social life proved to be a struggle. With the other Asian crew, I was mostly a perplexing subject to be gossiped about. My tapering eyes and round face are Asian enough but my ideas aren't. Failing to find common ground, they, too, kept their distance. The Chinese crew only slapped each other with amusement when they knew I could speak Mandarin but reading the characters eluded me. "What a strange one," they muttered.

When you took a seat next to me, I'd wanted to ask you a question that had been plaguing me, yet I'd no one to ask: How could one feel lonely despite working and living with 350 others in a 28,500-ton floating hotel? Something about you—with your disheveled darker-than-night hair and silver sideburns, clad in grease-stained white overalls—told me you'd know the answer. "Ciao," you bellowed, deep dimples appearing at the ends of your smile.

I watched you take the glass of iced Campari soda from the Filipino bar boy across the counter and bring it to your lips greedily. A drop of the shocking pink dribbled down your stubble. You wiped it away with your tanned, calloused hand and grinned, like a boy caught eating cookies that he shouldn't.

You deserved that drink, you said. The four-hour watch on your first day aboard the MV *Costa Allegra* was hell. Newer Costa ships were easier to deal with. A flick of a switch here, a press of a button there—all fixed, you mimed. Older ones like the *Allegra* still required engineers to coax the machinery to work while on their knees. But hey, smaller ones have all the charm, you said, laughing. I didn't think the *Allegra* was charming, though; I wanted to get the fuck out.

"You knowing . . . the *Allegra* . . . before . . . is a . . . *come si dice* . . . a—a—*" you looked up to the ceiling, reaching for an English word that was out of your grasp. Frustrated, you asked the bar boy for a piece of napkin, and using a ball pen that you unclipped from the pocket of your overalls, you traced out an outline of a ship carrying boxes

"A container ship?" I prompted. Jägermeister had made me bold, my tongue loose.

"Brava, container ship-pé." Your Italian tongue—not used to consonants at the end of a word—needed the additional vowel so that you could pronounce it.

I was pleased the first question you asked wasn't where I was from. Social interactions on board usually started from there and then went nowhere. No one had ever asked me beyond what I wanted for lunch. You were an aberrant to my neat conclusion that language and sex were the only obstacles to friendship on board.

In the first month of my contract, I'd learned that guys who talked to me only wanted to share my bed (or theirs). Italian men wanted to teach me the international language of *amore*. When I declined, their *brioche* stopped appearing on my work desk.

Slowly and patiently, you coaxed little secrets out of my heart. You were curious and I was happy to oblige.

You were forty-two years old but you didn't look a day past thirty-five. I was twenty-five, naïve and restless, my first contract as a crew lecturer on *Costa*. It was your fifth. You'd never met a crew lecturer, you said. What exactly was it I did?

"I teach the crew English," I said.

"Ah, an English maestra," you boomed. "Next time, you must teach me English."

You were the first I told that I'd wanted to write a book. *Perché no*? You said you'd want to read it. You were the first who wasn't surprised when I confessed that I'd wanted to travel further after this contract, that I'd wanted to fling myself to obscure nooks around the world. Most would have just asked, "Isn't this already traveling?" You knew exactly what I meant when I told you stopping by a few hours at a port didn't mean shit. *Zingara*, you pointed a finger at me. "A gypsy." In return—with your eyes, glittering like a reflection of stars upon the ocean at midnight—you said you'd like to do the same. Motorbike around Greece in early September. Like *The Motorcycle Diaries*, we chimed together. Your face crinkled into a warm smile.

"Where exactly in Italy are you from?" I asked. You drew a pizzalike shape on the napkin and said Sicily. Slowly, you started telling me about the love for your family, your dogs. You said you had a sister who was a Buddhist, a backpacker and a voracious reader—like me.

With our hands and snatches of several well-worn Italian verbs and adjectives that I'd learned from my time on the *Allegra*, I could surprisingly understand what you were trying to say, and you, me. After staying silent for so long, I was now gushing like a broken dam. As the *Allegra* knifed through the South China Sea in charcoal darkness, our easy banter continued well into the witching hour.

It's almost a decade since that night. The irony is, I still find myself in the same conundrum: alone in a sea of non-English speakers, craving a sense of belonging. I now live in a quiet village in East Germany, where people stare at me without comprehension when I try to communicate with them in my husband's mother tongue. Here, wild hand gestures don't help.

The Italian language and all those years working on Italian cruise ships are now dusty souvenirs—one of the many I'd collected in my heyday as a wanderer, one that I'm possessive of. I often find myself going through the archive of those days, pulling out a memory that reminded me that—if I could survive the crazy then—surely I could survive now.

Would you believe that, years later, I mastered Italian? I've often wondered how it would be to meet you in the present, now that I can speak your native tongue. What would we talk about? Perhaps about the book that I'd finally mustered the courage to write, just this year? Or about how committed I was to my wanderlust dreams, traveling to more than sixty countries since then?

Perhaps it would be of no consequence. After all, what brewed that night between us in the crew bar needed no common language.

≈ To the Taxi Driver Who Looped Back to Get Me

PARIS, FRANCE

by Irina Reyn

It was a warm October morning in Paris when you picked me up from the airport. Normally, I don't talk to my taxi drivers. I prefer cocooning myself in grateful, anonymous silence. But a transcendent flush of orange was pebbling the worn leather seats. A long-dormant French language was blooming once again on my tongue. I was in my early forties, my family and real life left behind for the moment. If there was ever a time to start yammering in rusty French to a Parisian, this was it.

I tentatively remarked on the unexpected heat. Once I felt I'd mastered weather, the other sentences started jigsawing into place. How did you feel about Macron's chances of winning? Recent strikes? Unemployment rate? You were forthcoming, polite, lied that my French was impressive.

October light streaked us with a tantalizing glow. You recommended the usual tourist highlights, and I was emboldened to confess I would be seeing none of them. I would only be here three days, I said. This was no time for the Louvre, for the Eiffel Tower, for Notre Dame.

What was I planning to do? I would eat pastries and hug my

old friend from college. She'd just gotten some hard news. I'd found out from afar. I wanted to look at her, touch her, ascertain that she would be okay. That was about all the plans I had.

You liked this itinerary. Too few visitors traveled to Paris just for bread and friendship. You asked my name. Your name was Samuel, which meant you were Jewish like me. What was it like being a Jew in Paris? What was it like being a Jew anywhere these days? I didn't ask any of those questions out loud.

"You want to eat bread?" you asked, taking us off-script. "I can tell you about bread." You rattled off bakeries near your house in some arrondissement I forget now. Eighth? Eighteenth? Subtext fell outside my linguistic abilities: Were you implying that we should eat bread near your home? *"Ensemble?"* I wasn't getting too many of those offers these days. I felt a whirring as long-buried inside me as the French language.

"I also like gelato," I said somewhat provocatively. "And a glass of rosé."

"I like that, too." We were at a stoplight and you swiveled around. You were handsome the way some French men are handsome, gruff confidence compensating for classical beauty. Your sideburns were almost fully gray, the rest of it a thick scrub of brown. You seemed around my age or ten years in either direction.

It was certainly pleasant to be idling in a traffic circle with you, watching anonymous passersby rushing to work in pencil skirts. Last time I was here, an alternate future was possible for me as one of these women, harried but unstressed in monochrome uniforms. Midlife seemed like an ideal time to contemplate a phantom life with you. This was the precise moment when women did things like this, took off with taxi drivers.

"Let me drive you back, too." As we approached my friend's building, you suddenly added, "I will take you to the airport."

"Okay."

The car took off and I remained on the sidewalk with my luggage. I felt a strange peace knowing you'd return for me in three days. It was comforting to know that somewhere out there—just a few arrondissements away—a person was willing to whisk me away.

Three days of bread and long intimate walks with my friend later, there you were, waiting for me outside the apartment building. Leaning against your car, then reaching for my suitcase.

"So, this is Samuel," my friend said. She exchanged some brief, fluent French sentences with you. Her smile of complicity reminded me of being in college when I'd introduce her to some guy or other and we knew that it wasn't really about the guy, but something far murkier having to do with desire, experimentation, one path abandoned for another.

When she'd first called to tell me the diagnosis, how far she'd sounded on the other end of a telephone call. Touching her, seeing her, made the present moment glow with worth. It collapsed all that distance. Now that I'd learned her prognosis—now that I knew she and I might stroll these streets together ten or twenty years into the future—I could exhale.

You opened the back door, shut it behind me. You slid behind the wheel.

"It's very good to see you again," I told you.

"And you." We smiled at each other, pleased with our little reunion.

Anything was possible now, me and you and your bakeries and our Jewish life together in Paris.

We rode to the airport, the breeze still warm but lined by an undercurrent of chill. You wanted to know what I'd done instead of the Louvre. You wanted to know the flavors of the gelato I ate. *"Cassis,"* I said. Blackcurrant. I didn't mention how we'd walked Paris until our feet ached, eyeing éclairs, polishing off the final crumbs of our cones by the banks of the Seine. Who could have known how satisfying that particular gelato would be, how precious?

I watched the same scenery unfold in reverse. I was starting to comment on it entirely in French.

"Three days is not long enough for Paris."

Your fingers were poised on the wheel. "I have an idea. Why don't I get off the road?"

"What do you mean?"

"Right now."

"And go where?"

"A *resto*, any *resto*. Let's have a glass of rosé and gelato. Just say the word."

You looked at me through the rearview mirror as if to say that what I'd learned in the past three days, you always knew to be true. This highway could be exited at any time.

≈ To the Woman Whose Shoulder I Slept On

NEW YORK CITY TO BOSTON

by Naomi Gordon-Loebl

You came down the aisle of the Greyhound like a five-foot-tall mannequin from the Army Navy store, olive green everything and a body-sized duffel in your arms that made your biceps jump with every step you took, the sunlight from the bus window illuminating the thousand fine blonde hairs on your arms.

"This seat taken?" you asked, and even though just minutes before I'd been celebrating my good fortune at having the only empty seat on the bus next to me, your appearance set off a tiny detonation inside me, the subject of my gratitude shifting instantly from the empty seat to you, the blonde, ponytailed soldier who was about to be my seatmate.

"Nope," I said, attempting to evoke nonchalance but probably hitting a note closer to drunk.

No matter. You were sitting already, having swung your duffel onto the overhead rack like it was a stuffed animal and lowered yourself into the seat next to me.

"I'm Julie," you said.

"Naomi."

Twisting awkwardly in our seats, we shook on it.

You were the type of woman I probably wouldn't fall for now. There's the military thing, which is the kind of political problem I might've fetishized at fifteen but cannot leapfrog my conscience on today. But it's really something else. You had that look—a tomboy with long hair, the kind of woman who would never wear a dress but would never consider leaving her legs unshaven either.

It makes sense that these were the first women I wanted. They were so visibly gay, so unmistakable in both their queerness and their womanness. I love these women now, but what I feel for them is not the desire that surges from just below my belly button, insistent and unwilling to be refused. I know now that I prefer them as friends rather than lovers; recognize the tug I feel toward them as affection, affinity, but not want.

But that is now. Then, you were everything: strong, compact, smelling faintly of soap. And you were sitting next to me, asking where I was going.

"To Maine," I said. "To visit my grandparents. You?"

It turned out that you were a soldier—no surprise there—on leave from Okinawa. You were on your way to visit your mother in Boston, which explained the charming accent I was too young, and too New York–provincial, to recognize.

"Boston's home?" I asked.

You shrugged, those round army-green shoulders coming up briefly around your face and then falling again. Me: already in love.

"For now," you said.

As the bus merged onto the West Side Highway, we began to talk. When I'd woken up two hours earlier in Brooklyn, I'd been dreading this long drive with its many hours of highway. Now, suddenly, it didn't seem so bad. You told me about the military, about how North Carolina made you homesick, but that you weren't sure for where. I told you about high school and the Riot Grrrls I hung out with—the antidieting pamphlets we snuck into glossy magazines at Barnes & Noble, the abortion clinics we stood outside of early on Saturday mornings.

"So," you asked. "You have a boyfriend?"

The question surprised, then annoyed me. I thought we had been engaged in the act of mutual seeing—and here you had misunderstood me so badly. But then I noticed the way you were looking at me. Your slight squint did not belong to a person who has asked a question; it belonged to a person who has advanced a theory and is awaiting confirmation.

"Nah," I said, as though this were obvious. My own theory-testing.

"Knew it," you said. Confirmation: your theory and mine. And then: "I didn't think those Riot Grrrls had boyfriends."

I smiled and something passed between us.

After a pause, I asked: "You, too?"

"Oh yeah," you said. "No girlfriend, though."

In my head, we were getting married. You didn't have to know that I had never kissed a girl, right?

Somewhere in Connecticut, I fell asleep on your shoulder. When I woke up, I noticed the weight of your head on mine. Don't fall asleep next to a stranger on a Greyhound, I thought. Unless she smells like this one.

The bus parked at Boston's South Station for a thirty-minute rest stop.

"Want to sit outside for a bit?" you asked, gesturing with your head toward the bus door.

I followed you out of the terminal, and we found a concrete bench to sit on. You pulled a can of chew from your pocket. Exclamation points paraded across the movie screen in my head—I had never seen someone chew before—but I tried not to gape.

"Sorry," you said. "I know it's disgusting."

"No, it's not," I said. Was it disgusting? Who knew? Who cared? You straddled the bench and pressed your palms into it. Your triceps formed horseshoes just below the sleeves of that green T-shirt. *Kiss me*, I thought.

"Hey," you said. "Want to be pen pals?"

It was something. You wrote down your address in a notebook, handed the torn scrap to me. I can see it even now: your round handwriting, the PFC before your name. I held onto that tiny rectangle of paper for a long time.

You had to kiss me, I thought. How could this perfect gay soldier who I had practically manifested onto my Greyhound in the first days of summer not be the first woman I kissed? We sat there, you and your biceps and your triceps and your chew, me and my silent pleas, like a thousand tiny riders on horseback sent from my brain to yours with a single request: *Kiss me, please kiss me.* It didn't occur to me that I could kiss you.

But we only talked, the conversation easy but my own dim awareness of the bus inside the terminal becoming less dim. I realized, slowly and then with abrupt certainty, that we would not kiss. I hugged you goodbye; we promised to trade letters. As I walked into the terminal, the bus was pulling away from its berth. No amount of waving my arms seemed to capture the driver's attention. I watched as the bus disappeared around a curved exit ramp, all of my belongings on board.

We wrote, but only a couple of letters. You never heard about the girl I finally kissed on a private dock next to the West Side Highway, a few miles south of where our bus turned north. But she heard about you.

≈ To the Source Who Kept Changing Costume

DHAHRAN, SAUDI ARABIA

by Keija Parssinen

You wore the wrong outfit to pick me up the first time—
jeans and a hoodie—so that my conservative host, whom I had
never seen in Western clothes, gave my father a look that said,
You're going to allow this?

My expat father did allow it, even though in Saudi Arabia we
were breaking the law riding in your ancient Suburban together—
an unmarried man and woman going for a coffee at the Italian
chain down the street. I was American, yes, but that wouldn't pro
tect him.

The King was supposedly more progressive than his forebears.
He had mostly brought the religious police to heel; we would not
be interrogated at the café, or whipped with a bamboo cane. Still,
you were nervous as a cat, on the lookout for bearded men in short
thobes, telltale signs of the Committee.

At the time, I was in grad school working on my first book. I
had grown up down the road in Dhahran, on the Arabian American
Oil Company compound, and had returned to refresh childhood
memories. The book was set in Saudi, and I planned to stay with

Saudi and Arab friends both on and off the compound. You were meant to help me with research.

The second time you picked me up, you went for the traditional look: black winter thobe, ghutra, and sandals. Again, this was wrong, for I had changed houses, was now staying with a liberalayeen family who watched *Grey's Anatomy* and sent their son to Tufts. When my host (wearing a Polo shirt and khakis) answered the door, his mouth quirked into a funny smile, as if he knew you were playacting for the American—me. He knew that men like you—like him—were more comfortable in jeans.

In a way, you were costuming. Earlier, I'd seen a photo of you wearing a black thobe on Facebook, at a Halloween party you had attended while at college in Arizona. You looked both handsome and ridiculous, smoking shisha and throwing up gang signs. And yet the photo was emblematic of where you stood, with a foot in two worlds.

Perhaps you donned Saudi national dress for Halloween as a provocation. It was post–9/11 America, after all, and you were politically savvy—were, in fact, the student body president of your university. I could see you relishing the chance to draw out the Islamophobes and then shock them with your American-accented English, slashing through their ignorance with jokes made at their expense.

But ignorance had the last laugh. You overstayed your visa and were thrown into an Arizona detention center. President Bush's neocons did not look kindly on young Saudi men, and—perhaps to atone for the security blunders that had allowed for the September 11 attacks—they came down hard on people like you. You had broken the law, yes, but your gravest crime was being an Arab.

Our second meeting was at a drab French place with screened-in booths that allowed for "mixed" dining (men and women eating together). There, you told me about your time in detention—how your classmates and professors had rallied in support, started a *Free You!* campaign that ultimately came to nothing.

In the end you were deported, not to Saudi, where you were born and raised, but to Yemen, your father's country, because in Saudi Arabia, citizenship is patrilineal. Your mother was Saudi, but you weren't a citizen, so you were shunted to Yemen. There you languished in prison for another year before finally going home. You were living with your parents when I met you, still not a Saudi citizen, unable to get a work and so frustrated and bored.

You see? I said. *Both of us grew up here, but neither of us really belongs.* You laughed. You told me how, as a boy, you had loved going to Dhahran, loved seeing the American girls like me, blonde ponytails bobbing as they made their way to the company pool like bright tropical fish in their colorful bathing suits. *Maybe I saw you! I bet I thought you were cute.*

The third home I stayed in was a company house in Dhahran. My hosts were a Saudi man who had grown up in Dhahran, an Aramco "brat" like me, and his Turkish wife. I took comfort in the cookie-cutter familiarity of the house, which was so much like the one I'd grown up in: the tan carpeting and slatted accordion doors, the cheap vinyl of the kitchen counters, the roaring air-conditioning unit.

It was January, and I was glad to be far from the frozen Midwestern college town where I had nursed break-up wounds since the previous summer. In the mild Saudi winter, I basked in the heat of your flirtations. *What if?* my loneliness began to ask.

I confided to the wife about you, and she insisted you come to the house. She had the maid prepare a feast of mezze and then left for an engagement. In the living room, you and I sucked on olives glistening with oil, then licked each other's lips. You told me how you were banned from returning to America for ten years, how it broke your heart because you loved *that goddamn country.* It was early 2008, and you were a fervent Obama fan. *Barack Hussein Obama!* You said, laughing. *What's not to like?*

What if I married you? I said rashly. *What if you got citizenship that way?* I was stone-cold sober, impaired only by the mad hope that seizes the newly intimate. I was joking, but also not. I saw us in ten years, me fluent in Arabic at last, the two of us moving back and forth between the countries we shared. We would return our respective countries to each other, and wasn't that a gift? I'd be your blonde American fantasy fulfilled; you, my passport to an authentic Middle East I'd never known from my compound childhood.

Later that night, we drove your Suburban down the darkened streets of the compound. We wanted to find a lover's lane where we could make out, and settled for a parking lot near the Dhahran bachelor quarters. Though the Committee wasn't allowed onto the compound, I was nervous about getting caught by security. We kissed for a while but when you asked for more, I said no repeatedly, imagining the humiliation of being pulled from the car by smirking or hostile strangers. Then I would be a cliché, the slutty Western woman, and you—you, with your tenuous residency status, your criminal record, your Yemeni surname. You would be far worse off, I imagined.

Despite all this, you grew insistent, pushing my face into your crotch, where I reluctantly took you into my mouth before letting you push yourself between my legs. I wanted to have sex with you, but not this way, where the threat of danger extinguished all desire. Still, I gave in, for the reason that so many women do: it was easier, and I wanted to please you.

I remember how you moved with fevered efficiency, your body illuminated by the cold light of the streetlamp. For a moment I didn't recognize your face, you were still so new to me that there were angles of you I hadn't yet seen.

You finished, then dropped me back at the house. In the bathroom I could still smell you, even after wiping away the wetness. Now, I wonder: Was it just lust driving you that night, or did you feel safe in that Westernized space, protected by its alternate rules? Was it the pressure of two years in prison, or the desperation that overtakes a body living in a place that punishes natural urges? Was it the knowledge that you might not touch a woman again for months, years even? Or were you just a man, like other men, who could not tell the difference between a willing woman and a body?

At the time, I didn't ask myself—or you—these questions. Already I was burying my sense of degradation, recasting it as a moment of sexual daring. We hadn't been caught. We had acted in defiance of Saudi Arabia's draconian laws. I did not know then— this was my first experience of violation, though not my last—that shame always takes root eventually, even in the hostile soil of a denying mind.

When I got back to my apartment in Iowa, the town lay inert under a thick crust of ice. We stayed in touch for a few weeks, talking on Skype, even having Skype sex once or twice. You couldn't reach me through the screen, I could close my computer on you at any time, and I wondered if maybe more relationships shouldn't handle sex this way.

On my desk was a petrified bird's egg I'd purchased in a Khobar shop before I left. I'd given you one, too. A symbol of fertility, yes, maybe. But also a small, hard thing that will never know life.

≈ To Father of the Baby with the Brain Freeze

TUCSON, ARIZONA

by Margo Steines

You were sitting in the courtyard at the Mercado, near the window where people line up to order tacos and jamaicas, on the hottest day I had ever walked into.

I was dressed inadvisably, in black sweatpants and a black shirt, so sweaty that my newspaper was damp and crinkly from where I'd held it between my ribs and my arm. In recent days, I'd been indoors for way too long. I was scared of the Arizona sun, but also I was just scared. I felt afraid to step into the unmarred sand of my speculative new life in the desert, a life that seemed, upon arrival, like a spectacularly poor fit. For the entire week since I arrived in Tucson, I'd only been inside my air-conditioned truck, my air-conditioned apartment, and the air-conditioned post office, where my belongings trickled over the Pacific from Hawaii in tattered boxes, a few every day for a week, until they stopped. I hadn't spoken out loud to another human for days—for so long that my voice creaked when I got to the front of the taco line and tried to order.

Earlier that day, I had built a giant sectional IKEA couch by myself. The instruction pamphlet pictured two cheery builder-people lifting and flipping and hammering in tandem, along with a smaller, cautionary image of a solo couch assembler with a line of prohibition through it: *Doing this alone is a bad idea.* I built the couch alone, frothing with self-pity and loneliness the whole time, and when I finally finished and sat down on it, I felt the strange emptiness I sometimes notice behind my navel, the one that twitches a few times each month, the one that demands answers to the question of whether I have waited too long to have a baby of my own.

In Hawaii I'd left behind a house with an ocean view and plumeria trees out front. In it I left behind a man who texted during dinner and thought my writing was in poor taste. He'd thought about coming with me, that man had. But I didn't want to clean anyone else's crumbs out of my couch, I didn't want to tiptoe in the dark around anyone else's sleep. I came to the desert for only myself, and after years of sleeping lonely next to someone else, I had nearly convinced myself that fully alone was the better way to be.

Then you. Sitting at a table on the other side of the mist machines, looking like a digital image covered with a hazy dream, or the Instagram-filtered cover of some terribly modern romance novel in which the men are muscled and sporty and tattooed but with an old, timeless beauty: full lips, broad chests, square chins, lush hair.

I noticed you as I walked back to my table from the counter, which I had approached to order my second round of tacos. I was hot and full and sad, face greasy, mouth gritty with corn chips. Your woman, sitting next to you, got up and walked to the bathroom, and she was perfect: lean and tough and striking, with leonine eyes and shiny hair, sleek and bouncy at the same time. I wanted to vanish, in that moment, through the tiny pores of the bricks lining the courtyard, to fully melt and dissolve into the wettish clouds of mist. I didn't want someone like you to see me like this: bedraggled, defeated, alone.

Your baby was sitting there with you, small enough that he was babbling the way very small children do, but big enough that he was eating ice. While I was doing my best not to watch you expertly place tacos into your beautiful mouth, he got what must have been his first brain freeze, from the ice, and began to wail. I don't know if you laughed first, or who caught whose eye, but when we laughed together, I felt a jolt of humanness come back to me, some lost piece startle back into place.

I looked at you then, fully, and you at me. We smiled wider than strangers can smile, you with your thick, dark eyelashes, me with a grin that started out guarded but gathered power too quickly to restrain. As you comforted your baby, as he shrieked *Too much ice!*, we both dissolved into laughter and looked at each other so deeply it felt like you had touched me.

Your woman came back to the table and I sharply looked away, unclear if I had done something wrong. But I also didn't want to share our moment with her, or with anyone. I wanted everything there: you; a baby; to be part of a tiny family of strong, gorgeous people; to eat tacos in the afternoon with a man who knows how to comfort small creatures. To smile, to laugh, to not be alone.

You left while I was still eating. I think you looked at me on your way out. I think maybe you tried to catch my eye, but in the wake of our moment I was superstitious, by then convinced that looking at someone else's man was a crime punishable by lack and sadness and broken eggs. I read my paper and finished my tacos and tried to will the thought of you out of my head, and I very nearly did, so much so that months later, when you said to me, *I think I've seen you before*, my response was as honest as it was untrue: *I've never seen you before in my life.*

≈ *To the Inescapable Teacher*

PARAKOU, BENIN

by Erica Cavanagh

You were the person I couldn't stop seeing in Parakou. It was your hometown. I'd be riding on the back of a zemi and think I saw you in your blue button-down passing around the corner on your red scooter. I saw you at marché buying new shoes, and by the rond-point, where a woman sold wagasi cheese, my hand jerking up to wave at you.

Did I say I would write when I left? If I did and failed, I am sorry. I failed to find a French translation of Hemingway's *The Old Man and the Sea* for you. I kept wanting to send you that. From our talks on the veranda, I thought you might like it, but my bookstore in the US said they couldn't get one. They say the Internet is more "connected" now. It's supposed to be easier to find things, and people, too. Still, when I had the chance, I didn't try hard enough to find what I wanted to find for you.

"Eureka! I found you!" you used to say, playing on the sound of my name.

You were my teacher. For ten weeks, you helped train me and fourteen fellow Americans for life in Benin. For ten years, I've taught Americans, too. I hope we thanked you; I hope I thanked you.

I think about our talks on the Gounons' veranda often. I see your legs hanging over the concrete railing, your thin ankles below the hem of your pants, and your broad shoulders leaning in. I hear your laugh. I hear you speaking to me under your breath.

When I returned to Benin for the first time in 2002 and saw the Gounons, they asked if I knew you were dead. I did. I'd gotten the news in a mass email, which seemed wrong, but that's how it goes now. The Gounons remembered how respectful you were when you visited me during that short time I lived with them in '97, how you'd always go around back and say hello to Maman before coming around to the front again to join me and the children, who were always playing some game in the shade.

In the beginning, I thought you were coming over to help me improve my French. We'd talk about the books we knew in common, like *L'Enfant noir*, *L'Étranger*, and *Candide*. Neither of us cared for *L'Étranger* much, though I liked Sartre's plays and tried to tell you their names, but didn't know the French translations for *No Exit* or *The Respectful Prostitute*. Sometimes my side of the conversation was like playing the game I'm Thinking of a Word, my mind reaching for the French that had yet to become a part of me. You often spoke with your hands, the top of your index finger bent inward from a machine accident when you were a boy.

I confessed I had not joined the Peace Corps because I thought I could fix anything; I had come to Benin to make friends—to watch, listen, care, and learn something different. You had a twelve-year-old daughter. Or was she ten? It seemed too personal to ask. We joked a lot instead. I can still hear you quoting from *Candide*: "Oh, but we live in the 'best of all possible worlds'!"—making it the punch line of our conversations about the despotic bureaucrats who stole donations from Beninese clinics, the American media spectacle and wasted millions over Bill Clinton's indiscretions, the Ogoni villages burned so Shell Oil could take Nigerian land and drill.

I think you were thirty-two then. You had a deep-throated, sincere laugh. Sometimes, when you looked at me, your eyes were so full of intent I could feel it right in my sternum and had to look off toward the neighboring maize field, the leafy stalks bathing in dusky light.

"I want to know you," you said to me once, and the heat rose up my spine. "I want to see you," you said, in case I had missed your first statement. "Do you understand?" I did understand, but pretended I didn't get it. I felt so wound up around you I didn't know what to do but wait it out until the end of training, when I would be shipped to a faraway village and rarely see you. I haven't known how to explain this, only that I needed to get to know you more slowly; I needed to know the language better and not be so new to Benin.

No one is guarded or unguarded for no reason. There is a game in the United States called tag, and this game teaches you that a touch can freeze you and another kind of touch can unfreeze you. Where I come from, girls are sometimes treated like a game, like that time two boys I knew pulled me away from a party, where music was playing and I was dancing. You're going to like this; this'll be fun, they kept saying, gripping my arm, and then they pinned me to the ground. That taught me not to trust myself or anyone else.

Remember the time you were walking me home and a storm was coming? The heavy heat was pressing down just as the sky boomed and darkened, thunderheads amassing on the horizon. Then the wind picked up and the clouds rolled in fast, the rain rushing toward us like a swift-footed army—which is when we looked at each other and, without saying anything, took off running toward the Gounon house. We'd almost reached the gate when the deluge hit and soused us instantly. The front door was locked; we knocked and knocked, but the rain was so loud that no one answered. I only had a key for my bedroom, a room separate from the rest of the house. I wasn't thinking I shouldn't be alone in my room with a man, I was thinking we needed shelter.

We dripped on the concrete floor, taking turns with my one towel as we tried to dry off. The room was small and spare. A desk, a wooden chair, and a mattress on the floor were the only furnishings, remember? And my mosquito net hanging over the bed as rain throttled the roof so completely it was thrilling. But we sat, you on the chair and I on the edge of the mattress, looking up at you and trying to seem so casual as you looked at me plaintively and turned shy suddenly, looking away at your hands.

Toward the end of training, when you started teaching us Bariba, your mother tongue, I sensed I would miss your voice and your hands. I remember you teaching us the word for God, "gúsūnɔ," and the many Bariba blessings that begin with that word. You taught us God, despite your doubts that one even existed.

When I am away from Benin, I miss the sounds. Do you miss the sounds? When I came back, I stayed for two months and had to write down all the sounds, as if I could keep them. The first night I arrived, I heard a storm in the distance and thought about the Bariba celebration for the dead, Gɔɔ Yiru, and how, every night during the monthlong celebration, calabashes are played, huge calabashes in lantern light played by the open hands of old women. The gift offered up to the dead is sound, so sound is what I must give you now:

I'm surrounded by mosquito netting on a full-frame bed. The swollen air knows the rain is coming. Taxi motos buzz by, and then the heavier, trundling sound of four-wheeled vehicles on uneven roads. The curtains, made from someone's old sheets, waft, three panels of them, blousing off of the glass-louvered windows like softly rappelling breath. The ceiling fan whirrs, but I'm turning it off so I can hear the storm coming. . . . And it does come: the throw and toss and sway of wind in the palm trees, and how the palm leaves, hitting each other, sound like the spray of dashing waves. In the distance, thunder growls like a waking giant, and in the darkness, lights flash.

That rainy season I learned another Bariba blessing: A kà nim n dosi, dear Idrissou. May you dream in water.

≈ To the Gambler I Met in Jury Duty

CHINATOWN, NEW YORK CITY

by Jenessa Abrams

In the courtroom, we sat on opposite ends of the same bench. Your arms were bulging out of your T-shirt, stretching the fabric, while the veins in your muscles strained against your skin. You looked like the kind of man who could pummel me. At the time, my boyfriend was the kind of man who patted me on the back and whispered: *it's okay—it's okay—it's okay* when I woke up from a nightmare.

When the judge asked: "Does anyone here believe only God is capable of judgment?" a woman rose.

She was seated behind us. Her hair was thick and dark. She wore a draped red dress that hung off her shoulders, revealing her collarbone. We both stared.

The judge craned his neck and his New York accent appeared: "For real?"

The woman nodded and started reciting what must've been a Bible passage.

"You're dismissed," the judge said, and gestured for the woman to be taken from us.

We watched her leave, watched the way her hips swayed underneath the silk. Watched her disappear behind the enormous brass doors. Listened to the sound of her gone. That's when we looked at each other. We shared something like loss.

When our names were not called, we agreed to leave together. Silently, with the flick of your wrist and the gentle nod of my head. You led me out of the courtroom and we walked like we'd always walked beside each other. You were twice my height and almost triple my weight. It felt comforting, knowing there was so much of you surrounding me.

In the elevator, you asked me if I was hungry. I nodded too quickly. You laughed and said: "Good." When we emerged into the daylight, I got a better look at you. You were stuffed into that T-shirt, but you had boyish dimples and an expensive haircut. I was wearing a satin blouse and a pencil skirt. That was back when I wore a full face of makeup and coiffed my hair to look like an adult. I was fresh out of college, under the guise that I understood—both the world and myself—so much more than I did.

"This way," you said, leading us into Chinatown. The streets were crowded with people pushing carts of groceries: thick stalks of lemongrass and cases of shiny red cherries. Buckets of squid and barrels of crab legs. The workers shouted across bustling food stalls, trying to lure in pedestrians. You shook your head hard enough for them to leave us alone. I knew almost nothing about you, which is its own sort of nirvana. The small window when we can still be anyone to each other.

You asked me about my life and although I'd been dating the same man for four years, I didn't mention him. Later, on the internet, I found out you were about to become a father, but you never said anything.

The restaurant was humming with families at round, communal tables. Red and gold tapestries hung from the ceiling. You ordered for us, not asking me what I wanted, which felt like you understood something essential about me. A waiter carried over a mound of soup dumplings. With a delicate hold on your chopsticks, you brought one to my lips and delighted in watching the moment the dumpling opened itself. Broth slipping down my chin. I sucked the pork out and slid my tongue against the dumpling skin.

When I asked what you did for a living, you blushed hard. You were a gambler. *But not the kind that's a bum.* You were a professional. You'd won a championship. Been on television. I nodded and this version of me was impressed with your dominance. You'd worked on Wall Street. Given that life up. Made double your salary playing poker in one night.

I told you about working from my boss's apartment in the Upper West Side. How we were a small nonprofit with dreams of making the world a little brighter. In reality, my boss and I huddled around her dining room table, having philosophical conversations with nightly goblets of wine. I told you how I felt like I was failing. How I was doing everything and how it felt like nothing. I told you I wanted to quit my job. You were the first person I'd said that to. It felt dangerous admitting that to you.

"If it's not making you happy, you should leave."

Why did I not tell you about the man I was living with? About his soft eyes and the kindness that was indented in his chin. About how much he needed me. *Constantly.* Why did you not tell me your girlfriend was pregnant, that she was honey-blonde and gorgeous, that you were about to start a family?

You looked at me with eyes that were hungry. For the first time, in a long time, I felt the force of desire; it startled me. It wasn't you. It was possibility.

You told me you wanted to take me somewhere and I followed. I would have done anything you'd asked of me. Down a nearby alley, you pushed open an unmarked door. The walls were painted lavender. The lights hung low.

We were in a massage parlor.

A part of me stumbled. Hesitated in the lobby. *Were you going to undress me?* I wondered if the skin on your hands would be rough or soft. The solid part of me turned back toward the street. The other part did not.

A small woman in a robe came toward us. She smiled and seemed to ask me something without speaking. Everywhere it smelled of coconut. I watched as you settled yourself in a leather sofa chair. Your enormity was both masked and more prominent there. The woman laughed and welcomed you by name. You looked like a child sitting on a throne. Rosy cheeks, goofy grin.

The woman spoke very slowly. She held one of my wrists with her left hand and began tracing my veins with the other. *I have my mother's arteries.* That's what I almost told her. They're prominent. You can feel them not quite fitting inside me.

The woman asked: "Where is it okay for me to touch you?"

I wanted to say: *Everywhere.*

Instead, I sat in my own chair and the woman knelt down and cradled the soles of my feet in her hands. Meanwhile, you started telling us a story about freshly printed money. The feel of it on your fingers.

"If you run your thumb along the bill, the ink's texture isn't raised and isn't flat. It's something—other."

You were so material. So of this world.

I thought about rising from my chair and embracing you. I wondered if the women massaging us would wordlessly flee the room. I wondered if you'd hold me gently or if you'd seize my hips with both hands. I turned to look at you.

You said: "Do you want something?"

I looked down.

The answer was that I wanted everything.

We sat in silence as strangers massaged our feet. Their hands worked their way delicately around our skin. Then they pushed harder, pulsing their fingers around our ankles. I wanted to ask what you wanted, but I was too afraid of the answer.

It was still light outside when I went home to my partner.

≈ To the Stranger from the Silver Hour

ROCAMADOUR, FRANCE

by Colleen Kinder

Of course we'd say hello: Nobody else was awake in
Rocamadour. Rocamadour! How tired and cheap the town had
felt, just the day before, as soon as my bus rolled in, so late in the
afternoon, when everyone cramming the main medieval lane was
waxy with sunburns. Parents looked ready to lance their kids. Kids
looked ready to beg for Slurpees. So I gave right up on the place,
went to bed at a geriatric hour. If there was anything to find in
Rocamadour, I'd find it at sunrise.

You must have had the same idea: climb the town at dawn. I
had just the slightest head start; I'd gotten up in a creamier darkness, a bracing crispness that injected me with more energy than
any shot of any coffee. Outside: a cold silence. This was another
town entirely. Bats sliced through the thinning night, gone before
I could be sure they weren't birds. A sphinx of a cat ran off, as
soon as my footsteps broke the quiet. I felt like a trespasser, stealing
through the town's older self, long before Rocamadour's cliffside
château inspired the Disney castle, dooming this town to cartoon
comparisons.

But at dawn, you can forget about animated princesses, and
instead you sense the ghosts of friars, of monks climbing as

many marble steps as it takes to scale a cliff. Because that's what Rocamadour is: a beautiful staircase of masochistic proportions, a ravine where pale stone chapels and steepled chateaus cling like stalagmites to the white rock. You climb until the turrets shrink to bulbs at your back, until the spires whittle to needles, until the spread of furry green trees reveals how much more to this valley there is. Quad burn. Lung rasp. Awe. How could there be more? There is more. The path sends you into a merciless switchback, each vertex marked with a Station of the Cross as if to point out, while you suffer: the Lord Jesus did, too.

The sun beat me by seconds, cresting its bald pink forehead over the distant ridge. I stood there, gasping, and watched what I'd just told my students to never bother capturing on camera: sunrise.

It amazed me: the speed of the sun's helium lift. Sky just kept spreading between the sun's belly and the fur of that distant tree line. A student of mine had just written about early dawn—"the silver hour," Hayley called it—those rare minutes after darkness dissolves, while the only light is a borrowed glow from whatever lies east. The sun's out—somewhere—but hasn't had the chance to warm the stones beneath your feet.

And along you came: an ascending blotch of tomato red. Your T-shirt was red. Your shorts were red. I know your shoelaces were red because in just a few moments I would mention them, desperate for a thing to say, to sprinkle into our stillness, our up-closeness, like a schoolgirl, about to blush. *Your shoelaces are red.*

You were cute from far away, and then up close: a silver fox who didn't reek of dad. Mind you, I'd been shepherding college students around southern France for two weeks straight, urging them to write, to squeeze the place for all the juice it lent. I'd pointed to the things people love to call *indescribable*, and said, "Describe that." Your grades will be based on the ferocity with which you describe that: lavender breeze, fig seeds, the sag of those sunflowers' necks. Rip up the postcard, and write what you see.

My bonjour must have startled you: I bellowed it. I had way too much exuberance to keep to myself. What is it about the early morning? Why does it change all the rules? I've wondered this on so many mornings in so many places, but you, dear Frenchman—so willing to give away your day's first smile—are the face of my theory now: The dawn erasure of everyone else is bound to pull two strangers together. They become a pair, a secret minority, an *us*.

You spoke English, so we touched on all the basics, standing there on the slope, Rocamadour so tapered at our backs. Bordeaux was your home; Brooklyn, mine. My students were fast asleep down below; you mentioned no one. Driving through on a work trip, you'd paused here on a whim. Somehow, I smelled aloneness on you. You felt like a man alone in a loveless time.

Skittish, I said something goodbye-ish. *Well, enjoy the day . . .* And when you did not move, when you held there like a statue, I knew our imaginations were in lockstep. You wanted to kiss me, too.

Sometimes on dates with men I've just met, when the possibility of a kiss abides, the *longer* it abides—the deeper we retreat behind the curtain of that live moment into the closets of our minds where scenarios of possible first kisses play on loop—the more impossible it feels: that we'd just do it. Find some way to broadcast permission or complicity, send the word *yes* to the fronts of our eyes.

With you, it was the reverse. With you, it felt like a why-not, a how-could-we-not? Because Rocamadour was a fiction so far below, because everyone who might see us was tucked under the terracotta shingles of those miniatured roofs, because my students had been making me feel so *old*, and to kiss you would feel like a love song to maturity, a celebration of the gumption I never had at their age.

I bought us some time, blathering. I told you it was my Jesus Year. I can't believe I told you it was my Jesus Year. I'd just turned thirty-three, a year that found me wanting to *place myself* in the scheme of my own life. When a friend pointed out that thirty-three was the age Jesus was crucified, I latched onto it like a milestone as well-known as the Sweet Sixteen: the Jesus Year.

Teaching only deepened my obsession with age thirty-three. I felt recast as a mother hen, ever aware of my age in the company of students. My kids didn't think twice about coffee at midnight or a fourth glass of wine. I watched in envy of youth but all the while cringing at what a fledgling adult would put herself through. That summer, I felt like a revised and improved human being, my core sinewy with things a person can only learn by living her own life out.

Which brings me to you. Because to meet you, I had to spring out of bed at like 5 a.m., and before that, go to bed at like 9 p.m., and prior to, become a person who prefers a mint-fresh morning to a wine-drenched night.

Now, I just had to look up. I just had to look up and not immediately down. I had to lift my eyes from your feet, shut up about red shoelaces, *shut up*. And because a younger me would have scampered off fast and regretted it faster, I felt dared. It was 7 a.m. I was in France. I was thirty-three. The sun was up. Bells had rung. I looked up at you, and did not take my gaze back.

It was good, fast. Not great, but ardent. The relief that we were just *doing* this, both so surrendered, pressing into each other's lips and palms, finding the rhythm of tease and press, slow then breathe. The thrill of just doing this! Traveling fingers across each other's necks, reaching back for the railing when feet couldn't hold our press. I could feel you love every new thing I did, every next province of your skin I touched. Breath to the neck. Soft bite to the ear. The bottom ridge of your hair was easy to grip, satisfying. I went up into the sleeves of your T-shirt and appraised my favorite part of every man: the breadth of a bare back.

Hickey, I worried, because I had students to teach. A steep mile below, I was a teacher. You kept slowing our kiss and trying to tease out my tongue, snake-charming. Was there something about France to read from your kiss? *French kiss*, I thought—a style I've never been certain about. I know just one thing about kissing: that I kiss best when I believe I'm driving a man wild. You helped, finding the clip of my bra, pressing it free, realizing I was going to let you go anywhere, so long as clothes stayed on. At some point—I remember this well: one of your legs trembled.

"I have to *go*," I said: a sultry whine with no resolve whatsoever. "I have to meet my students." You nodded and went right back at it, tucking fingers inside the lip of my jeans, finding the small of my back.

And then there were footsteps. The patter of feet. Someone was coming and he was a priest. Please don't forget this: there was a priest—a full-on, Franciscan-frocked, rosary-bead-belted man of the cloth. He bonjour-ed and we bonjour-ed and as soon as he disappeared down the path, our cheeks let out all their laughter. This was all happening. Thank you, Father.

"I have to go," I tried again, invoking students like that word could break the spell. Every time I opened my eyes you looked older. Still not like a dad, but a person in their next era, the one ahead of mine, one I couldn't possibly know until I reached it myself. You could look at me, into me, and know what I didn't yet know, like I could glimpse things my sleeping students had ahead of them still.

It took a while to walk away, to re-estrange. Our bodies fell into a kind of slow dance, pushing apart and coming back. You lifted my arms over my head, with my palms clasped together under yours. No one else has ever done this to me. I felt like a figurine, the spindly ballerina in my girlhood jewelry box. We stretched the moment as far as we believed ours could stretch. The mesmerizing thing about sunrises isn't their palette or hue, but their speed. As soon as one begins, it looks so adamantly about to end.

"Thank you" was the last thing I said to you, meaning it. There was no way to know what this silver hour meant to you, so I spoke for myself, thanked you for conspiring to go ahead and kiss. I'm guessing it was about even, what each of us gave and what each of us got, and I've traveled enough to know just how rare that is.

Down in the town, I walked into the clangor of hotel breakfast. Spoon clicks, bowl scrapes, juice pouring. My students sat at a table littered with croissant flakes and honey packets, their eyes puffed with reluctance to the new day.

I could still smell you, when my fingers got close to my face. I sensed the scary ease people having affairs must feel when they slip back into family meals, among innocent people who have no idea. Anyone looking for clues would have found them. I felt a looseness around my chest suddenly: my bra was hanging free. In the hotel mirror, I'd note a missing earring: the glass slipper of our Rocamadour tryst.

But no one was looking for clues, and I admit some disappointment. My students were talking literature—the rare works of fiction that had taught them something real and applicable to life. I brought up a short story I'd read when I was exactly their age. The author's name was foggy; the plot was not.

A man's headed home from a business trip, on a plane that starts to fail. People scream. People pray. As the man sits there, realizing his life's about to end, he swells with love for his wife and children. The plane crashes, but—to our and his surprise—the man lives. He can just go home. So he does, ready to embrace his family with newfound force. But our hero opens the door to a wife who's pissed he's late. She thrusts a kid into his arms and chases after another one. He's stunned, muted by the avalanche of the mundane. So *soon*. He never tells his wife—or at least he doesn't by the story's end. Only when I retell this tale in Rocamadour as a teacher do I realize what an allegory it is for anyone who travels.

You can't bring the crackle or the soul-swell or the revelation of the journey home. No one has the time; no one really cares. The ordinary won't expand to let the extraordinary through the door. This reality used to sting me, but, many journeys later, I know it as something the traveler has to get over.

I look across the table at my students—young writers to whom I want to give so much—and realize there's a caveat. The traveler has to get over this, I tell them, but the writer does not. The writer is *the one who does not*. She can't bear the journey ending without a telling. She sees the futility, but again picks up her pen. She writes to a man who will never read, but says it anyway:

Where we met, on that switchback, ten steps down from the peak of Rocamadour, was the silver hour of the rest of my life. Thank you for helping me mark it.

≈ GRATITUDE

≈ To the Pharmacist on Futong West Street

BEIJING, CHINA

by Monet Patrice Thomas

You may remember me, I'm guessing, because in the year I lived beside the famous Wangjing Soho I never saw another Black woman in our neighborhood. Once, there was a young Black man crossing Fu'an Lu on a steel-gray fixie bike and we nodded to each other. And, of course, there were so many white men of varying ages on scooters, in smart cars or Range Rovers, in business suits or cargo pants. I had run away from home and heartbreak to teach English to children in your country and I didn't know my head from my foot, which means I was lost. You may remember me, because I never had Google Translate ready, was always rummaging in my tote for my phone. I'm sorry I never knew how to be easier to help.

You must do a brisk business being near that busy intersection with the grocery store on one corner, the coffee shop its opposite, and you staring across to the Soho complex with its thousands of workers. I passed you every day on foot when I wasn't late for work or on a yellow Ofo bike I rented for one kuai. You may have seen me. I was either disheveled or well put together, but always running for the bus or huddled under an umbrella, my face obscured by a pollution mask. When the liquor store next door to you reopened after months of construction, I would go in every week for a bottle of Jameson, so you probably thought I drank too much. You're right, I did drink too much.

Do you remember the first time we met? I wasn't alone. My lover of one month was with me, tall and confident, and it was him who showed you a ready picture of Tylenol Cold + Flu on his phone, asked in Chinese: *How much?* Then he paid for my cold medicine. Or you may remember him because he came with me again, both of us hungover and wearing sunglasses indoors. I needed a Plan B, fumbled through typing "emergency contraception" into the translator. And you glanced down at the screen, brought forth a small box from beneath your glass counter and punched in the price on your jumbo calculator, so cheap I thought it was wrong. You were so brisk and nonchalant, as if you were selling me a handful of rice and not autonomy over my own body, that I didn't feel ashamed. I paid that time, because women always pay for these things, one way or another. That's true everywhere, right?

You were never nice. Or not what Americans consider nice. No politeness from you. I mean you never smiled or said thank you. When I had sore muscles and needed Tiger Balm, you sold me the most expensive brand; I only learned this later, when I bought more at a store close to work, but I don't hold that against you. A business has to make money and there was nothing I bought from you I couldn't afford. I traveled alone around your country to small coastal towns like Beidaihe and big crowded cities like Shanghai, met people like you who were helpful, though never enthusiastically so, which became to me the best sort of kindness. I learned the lack of a smile did not denote disrespect or incivility. You helped me understand.

At thirty-one, would you have guessed, I knew better about a lot of things. In China, I was too old to be single and career-less with no plans for the future. In America, certain women can wander a little longer, particularly when the combination of their education and adventurous personality is buffeted by the privilege of money or connections. We are, in a way, exempted from most societal expectations. But I knew even I could not wander forever. In my last weeks, I wished I could've told you how scared I was to go home, how it seemed there was nothing and no one waiting for me. My only affliction was loneliness, so I came in to your shop for nothing, except to be seen. I bought lip balm or Band-Aids I didn't need. I practiced my "thank you" and "goodbye" and went back out into the polluted nights without a mask like a true Beijinger.

I know I was often a real nuisance. Never ready. Couldn't understand numbers between seventy and ninety. Didn't know how to describe what hurt and how much. Near the end, you never looked happy to see me when I parted the plastic curtains in the late evenings, the sun low over my shoulders. I was coming in every day because I didn't know how to say goodbye. I just wanted you to know that when I entered your dim world of medicine, I was always so happy to see you. And so thankful.

≈ To the Woman Who Spared Me an Orange

OAXACA, MEXICO

by Sarah Menkedick

I was scared of everything then. The chipping clay pitchers that held atole. The grayish-blue smoke from the fireworks. The bugs. Still, even as early motherhood plunged me into full-body, full-time fear, I wanted my baby to know the wild openness of travel: bus rides deep into the mountains, a tiny village down a dirt road, turkey calls, coffee and beer at shared tables with strangers. This part of me kept poking her head above the waterline of the fear, trying to swim.

Like most mornings tucked in the folds of these Oaxacan mountains, the morning that you and I began our trek was acute with sunshine and cold. I strapped my baby to my chest and, with my husband, took a hike up the mountainside toward a neighboring village. There was a shrine on the mountain's crest: a little box, painted white, with a virgin on top. Inside were pennies, candles, flowers. I prayed. I felt so vulnerable to any energy, any ritual. A whimsical deity seemed to threaten to lift or destroy me at any moment. Desperate for ballast, I could have joined a cult. This desperation had its dark side, but its light side was a keening sense of connection, one I miss now that my life has settled back into more ordinary emotion. Now, I wedge shoes onto tiny feet and sweep out the door, and when I startle a jay or catch a snippet from a poem on the radio, I hardly notice.

You came shuffling downhill trailed by an old man I presumed to be your partner, both of you carrying mesh bags of goods on your backs. You must have been sixty, seventy, eighty years old, your face brown and crumpled, your gray hair in long, sweeping braids. You said "Buenos días" lightly, carrying this load kilometers up and down mountains, just traveling from one village to another, and we said it back, we who'd hiked up here as vigorous recreation because our daughter woke up before 6 a.m. I watched you step down the vertiginous trail in your jellies, those thin plastic shoes I used to plead for when I was six. Descending, your burden on your back, the ravine tumbling deep below you into stark shade, you lifted me out of myself in awe.

We carefully picked our way down. The village grew hot. The loudspeaker blared announcements of ceremonies and games. We wandered, joined friends, ate. The baby became tired and fussed in her carrier. My husband and I, the only ones with a baby, the ones proving we could still do this, proving, proving, *everything has not changed so much*, were forced to head back to the adobe house for a nap. Along the way, we ran into you.

You clasped the baby's hand and grinned. You didn't speak Spanish or English, but Chinanteco, and we couldn't understand you. You reached into your bag and gave us an orange.

I felt the swelling, the sadness and the fear and the gratitude and the love, surging into me like a newfound spring. As a new mother, the boundaries between me and the world had dissolved. The sturdy me, who'd so confidently navigated and made sense of the world, had vanished, and I lurched between terror and a reverent sense of oneness.

I took the orange. You had very little—you walked miles to sell what you could—but it was no big deal for you to give it to me, nor was it a big deal for me to be in that bright village on that day with my baby and take it, and yet I felt right then that it was everything. A reminder of the simplest, most basic goodness. Behind all the fear I felt for my life and my child, this: an orange. Passed from woman to woman.

The intensity of this period diminished, returned to what we consider normal. But like a receding tide, it left gifts on the beach, moments marking my unbearable vulnerability. I think of them from time to time. I think of you, reaching into your bag, reminding me: Here, it's just this. An orange. I think of how, amidst all that longing and dread, the essential would suddenly emerge, unexpected, soft and corrugated and citrusy, carried all the way over the mountain just to be given away.

≈ To the Driver I Followed

INTERSTATE 40, NORTH CAROLINA

by Matthew Olzmann

At some point, that night, you probably thought I was a cop.
My headlights behind you for a mile.
Then five.
Who knows how much farther.
You slowed down, I slowed down.
You sped up, just a little; I sped up, just a little.
Truth is, in that storm, the taillights of your truck were the only
thing I could see, the only way I knew the road was still there.

There was no other light. No street lamps. No other cars on
the highway. We were miles from any city. Just the Blue Ridge
Mountains. And even those I couldn't see. But I knew they were
there, and I knew deep ravines opened all around us. My headlights
barely seemed to cut through fifteen feet of night. I couldn't see the
exits until we were passing them. My windshield wipers were just
swishing around darkness mixed with unrelenting rain; it was like
using your windshield wipers to repel a waterfall.

I wondered if it was easy for you, weaving through rain. You
seemed to understand the dark, anticipating each turn, as if you
had memorized the shape of each mountain, as if you had lived
with them for a long time.

When people wake in the dark of their own homes, they can navigate the obstacle courses of their lives without reaching for the light switch. They know where the sofa is, the corner of that little end table that waits to gouge an unsuspecting kneecap or shin, and the single stair just before the dining room. Without knocking the vase from the nightstand or tumbling over a cliff, they arrive in the kitchen, reach into the blackness, find a handle, open a refrigerator door. Then there's a light. Then they make a sandwich.

I wondered if this dark was like that for you. Maybe you lived among these peaks and valleys all your life and knew, by heart, exactly when the road would plunge or whisper in a new direction. This dark was new for me, complicated and unfamiliar. I was driving toward a new job, a one-year teaching fellowship at a small college in Swannanoa, North Carolina. My wife was already there, and I was bringing our last carload of supplies from Michigan. I had no idea what was ahead of me.

What was ahead of me, I learned later, was a tiny attic apartment in an old stone house where my wife had already unpacked several boxes of books. A teakettle on the stove. A welcome mat by the door. What was ahead of me was a life where I would sometimes get lost among the trees and emerge to find women playing banjos in a clearing lit by fireflies. The burn of homemade moonshine. An evening or two on the porch of a weathered farmhouse, watching the shadows of the neighbor's cows blur into the shadows of twilight. Discussions of poetry and essays in small classrooms with students who spent their free time tutoring children, building community gardens, and volunteering at homeless shelters.

As the rain stopped, you took the next exit, and I kept going.

When it's not raining, you can see little lights between the trees in the mountains. Houses. Perhaps one of them was yours. There are many stretches of highway on I-40 between the border of eastern Tennessee and Asheville, North Carolina, where, even on a clear night, you can't tell where the mountains end and the sky begins. The lights of the houses hover above the Earth, like new stars hung strangely low on the horizon. Like the old stars, these new ones form little clusters—constellations—shapes that travelers might recognize as stories, from a past life or new one creeping closer, luminous, and waiting to be known.

≈ *To the Man Who Sold Me Shoddy Film*

HARAR, ETHIOPIA

by Meron Hadero

I met you on my first trip back to Ethiopia, from where my family had emigrated during the dictatorship, when I was two years old. It was 2003, and I was traveling to Harar, where my maternal grandparents were born and my mother spent happy vacations as a girl. I was with my mother and sister, hauling luggage full of clothes, gifts, one book, a beloved old Pentax K1000 manual camera given to me by my father, and not enough film. So I bought more from you.

A friend who's a photographer later looked at my stack of black-and-white pictures and said the film looked somehow off, was possibly expired, or had maybe been exposed to too much heat. Either seemed likely as it was sweltering that visit, and expiration dates are easily fudged in the long-standing tradition of "Tourist bela," or "Eat the tourist." This is to say, you sold me bad film in Harar, perhaps willing to risk cheating me out of these memories, but I realize you did me a favor.

I had nurtured such romantic visions of this journey, let them take shape as the plane passed over Egypt, with its shadowless desert and the Nile stretched out below. The river played, separating into two, coming together again (an eye), splitting apart and merging like knots on a plank of wood, like the history of two hesitant lovers dancing toward and away from each other. When we approached Addis Ababa, it was night, a full moon, a new sky. That's how I think it went, at least. I've taken the trip often since, and my memories of these flights blur together now. But there's always the same progression: the desert, the river, nightfall, back again.

We only met briefly, and I can't remember the details; those days have since become diffuse around the edges. Were you one of the vendors who teased me about my fumbling accent (and how I looked like I should know better)? Or one who offered advice about where to eat? Did you try to set me up with your son or cousin, or ask me what it was like over in the US? Now I realize that all I have of you are these photographs. You are in none, but yet there you are.

The whites in the photos glow a bit more than they should. At times, the grays recede into some flattened dimension, like they're painted onto the paper with no relief. The effect is to both subtly highlight and hide what's happening in the photograph. A gharry looks as if it's drawn by an electric white horse. A rock wall in front of an unassuming stucco house appears half-crumbling, half-lit. Somehow this feels okay—even true. I'd always been told about this city through the distorted lens of our diaspora, which cast it in the light of a wistful nostalgia, but also reduced it, too, since the terrors of the dictatorship were not as freely recounted as childhood summers in the enchanted city of Harar: haloed, ever-bright.

When we reached Harar on that first trip, family I didn't remember approached us shouting out guttural ululations. We hugged and kissed in a dizzying dance until they turned away, faced the wall, fell to their knees and thanked the Lord that we, who had left during the country's darkest days, were here again. We spent much of our time at the *mesob*, the table. When we were not eating, we were sipping tea or coffee served in delicate cups that fit into the curve of my palm. We'd go house to house to visit relatives. We saw the old family home and, on the way, encountered a funeral tent where a relative realized he knew some of the mourners. We visited empty plots of land to imagine how things had once been, to understand what remained and what no longer was.

Is it familiar? someone asked me, half joking, half not. There is probably no better answer, no better way to capture that experience, I realize, than through photographs that looked a little magical, slightly askew—fallen out of time or forgotten too long in the sun.

≈ To Sandals Man

AN AIRPORT TERMINAL, CENTRAL CHINA

by Craig Mod

Sandals Man, we first met at an airport terminal in the middle of China. You, recently graduated, unemployed, traveling alone and aimlessly with a well-worn canvas backpack, bright teeth, making friends and chatting up everyone with whom you crossed paths.

I was traveling with a woman when we met. She made me better than I could ever hope to be on my own—I felt that as soon as she and I had been introduced, just a few weeks prior. She, recently divorced, though only twenty-nine years old. Me, recently disentangled from my own long-term mess of a relationship, already twenty-six. Both our hearts similarly raw. She stood beside me and suddenly I was kinder to the world, and the world itself felt somehow less jagged.

The impromptu trip was a naïve attempt to cleanly disconnect from our past lives. Forty days on the road together. We had time but no money, a circumstance fraught with catastrophic potential; two people who hardly knew one another intertwined through decidedly nonluxurious backpacking.

We were waiting for our flight in that Chinese airport terminal. It was depressing—the terminal—but she wore bright blue linen pants and sat twisted into a pretzel across from me. A yoga teacher, pretzel was her natural form. I made a face at her. She blushed, stuck out her tongue. An announcement was made in crackly Chinese over the intercom.

You stood behind us in line. Tapped my shoulder. Said, "Nice sandals." We had the same ones. Black Chacos with soft nylon straps and thick Vibram soles. I had traipsed across Cambodia in them; would later go on to hike up a glacier in the damn things. We laughed about how one could love a pair of sandals so much. Had my traveling companion not been there, I may not have been so friendly. But she was, and so we shared a strange moment of connection as we walked across the tarmac in the dim morning light. We continued chatting aboard the tiny Lhasa-bound prop plane and said farewell when we landed.

That farewell was short-lived, and weeks later we met again at a hostel. "Sandals Man!" you yelled across the tiny, dark lobby. We had forgotten your name, and you didn't offer it. We were too embarrassed to ask. Sandals Man, that's what we ended up calling you later, recounting the journey for friends.

The circuits had returned us all once more to central China, some nameless city, extruded from dirt and featureless. Backpacker circuits seem large, but are narrow, claustrophobic. Stick it out long enough and you are bound to meet again. We met in this place—a place that, after Tibet, felt so totally empty and without soul. So much so that we were reeling with an eagerness to leave, to head anywhere else.

But since we were all stuck in that sorrowful city for a night, we did the next best thing—we drank ourselves silly.

The three of us made our way from bar to bar, finishing at one with high ceilings that served only hard liquor. Those were my drinking days, my ablution-through-alcohol days. We ordered shots of tequila—always a ridiculous order. But it was the last drink of the night, so why not. This is how one drinks in a sad city.

We threw the shots back. When she excused herself to the bathroom, you turned to me and said: "You *really* like her." You made real what I was too afraid to say myself: Without hesitation—saying these words for the first time in my life—I responded with a lucidity that cut through all the alcohol of the evening: "No, I *love* her. She is the one."

It sounded inane, but it wasn't, not to me at least. I felt my heart swell. The one. What a phrase. Was it true? It was. You looked shocked. I smiled to dial down the gravity of what wasn't intended to be such a weighty statement.

"Yeah, man," I said, feigning folksiness, "she's pretty great."

"Well, then!" you said. "We need to drink to that!"

And drink we did. Another shot. Blessed my declaration with more alcohol. She returned and sat next to me and I felt for the first time the desire to hold someone so tight as to fuse with them. I hadn't felt that before, didn't know it existed in the wardrobe of feelings—though I've felt it many times since: like learning a new word, suddenly, it is everywhere.

Between that memory of her as an airport pretzel and that moment you extracted my confession, much had happened. She and I were of weary hearts, still, and although we tried to play it safe, tried to keep a distance, in the end we gave in to almost all of our impulses. Somewhere in the middle of that jumble, it seemed, we had fallen in love.

Though she made me a better person, kinder certainly, the worst of my demons still lingered. I'd go on to ruin the relationship with her over the course of a few more months. It was mine to ruin and ruin it I did. That loss became an inflection point in my life. I used it to sober myself up, to begin running marathons, to start doing the work that I thought I was supposed to be doing. All of it a penance; anything to justify having messed up so unequivocally.

In that instant at the bar with you, there was a trueness and tenderness to my love. You saw that. It jolted us both. You were there, Sandals Man. Your presence was like a countersignature on my proclamation, pinning down those emotions, allowing me to return to that moment, to believe over the years that I hadn't imagined it all. To remember that somewhere in the middle of China, for a fleeting moment my heart was capable of opening, and I wasn't quite alone.

≈ *To the Driver Who Was Not Godfrey*

KAMPALA, UGANDA

by Raksha Vasudevan

When you stepped out of the car, I was struck by your big, liquid-dark eyes, the crispness of your pink button-down shirt.

"Madam, please, I insist," you said, prying J's mom's suitcase away before she hauled it into the trunk herself. The look of offense on your face made J and I smile.

On time, the sky-blue sedan gleaming, lemony air freshener scenting its insides—we seemed to be in good hands with you as our driver. So, on Christmas Eve, the dry-season sun baking Kampala's red soil into hard yellow, J, his mom, and I set off on our weeklong trip across Uganda with you.

But once we started driving, you said little. Nothing, in fact. I was surprised: my friend who'd recommended you had warned me you'd talk our ears off. But with us, you barely spoke, eyes fixed ahead at the deadly still traffic of Jinja Road, jammed with families escaping the capital for the holidays. Hawkers selling roasted g-nuts and cold sodas wove between the unmoving vehicles. From a matatu van in the next lane, a woman stared at us. Our "family" must have looked odd: J and his mum, milky white. Me, Indian. You, Ugandan. From the beginning, we were a strange galaxy in that car: planets orbiting each other but always worlds apart.

You switched off the engine, resigned, and leaned back in your seat. With your slight potbelly and balding head, you looked like someone's dad—maybe that's why I felt an immediate affection for you. Growing up mostly without a father, I latched onto potential substitutes.

Maybe that's also why, later on, learning you'd lied to us stung more than it should have.

Once we got on the highway, you floored the accelerator.

"Slow down, Godfrey!" J pleaded, gripping the handlebar. Outside, fields of plantain and pawpaw blurred. But you didn't react.

J's mother, a delicate-looking divorcée with a neat bob, squeezed her eyes shut. Not for the first time, I wished—imagined she was also wishing that J had returned to London for the holidays instead of talking her into coming here. Knowing her first trip to Africa was in part to meet me made my stomach twist. In the last few days, doubts had trickled endlessly through my mind: Why, lately, did I want to turn away from J's smiles? *Drip*. Did I even want to meet his mother? *Drop*. Should I go on this trip? *Drip*.

The faucet of misgivings continued dribbling as I packed my bags. It was too late to change plans: the lodges were booked, safaris paid for. So, I went.

Now, in the car, I did the same as J's mom: settling back, thighs sticking to the faux-leather seat, I closed my eyes.

The trill of my phone woke me. Hours must have passed: we were winding through a valley, jade hills of coffee trees wrapping around us. The air was cooler here, a world away from Kampala's dusty heat. I dug my phone out of my purse: the caller ID said "Godfrey."

I glanced at you in the rearview mirror: you were looking ahead, eyes pinked by the wind blasting through your window rolled all the way down. Your phone was nowhere in sight. Puzzled, I answered my phone.

"Hello?"

"Hello, Madam Raksha!" a man chirped. "This is Godfrey, the driver."

"But . . . Godfrey is in the car driving us right now." (In the mirror, your eyes flickered back toward me.)

"Oh no, no, that is my colleague!" the voice on the phone said. "You see, I got a last-minute job: UN convoy to the north. You know how well the UN pays, Madam! I couldn't say no. So, I sent my colleague in my place. It's all okay, yes?"

I was so disoriented I don't remember what I said. Maybe "fine." Maybe I just hung up. I tapped you on the shoulder. "Why didn't you tell us?"

You, Not-Godfrey, just shrugged, eyes once more fixed ahead. Before us, a truck loaded with longhorn cows swerved. The cattle, the three of us—we all stared at you, all baffled and alarmed.

"What's your real name?" I tried again.

"You call me Godfrey. It's okay, it's okay."

J, his mom, and I looked at each other, unsure how to proceed. Maybe you thought your real name was too complicated for mzungus. Or maybe you just didn't want to reveal any of yourself to us.

"Alright," J nodded. "Godfrey it is."

I looked at J, chestnut hair curling at the nape of his neck, his broad, straight nose, his pointed chin. How could he not need to know the truth? We'd been dating for almost a year; at twenty-seven, it was my longest relationship. Yet, I was still learning him; but did I keep wanting to? I looked away, at the roadside market we were passing, pyramids of avocados and tomatoes precisely arranged on wooden stalls. Those displays looked so balanced, so sure of themselves.

Over the next days, you drove us south, to Lake Bunyonyi, pointing out kingfishers hovering above the water. We watched them dive and emerge, fish writhing silver in their tweezer beaks. You drove us to Bwindi Impenetrable Forest, hiking with us in your penny loafers to find a family of gorillas. The silverback, four-hundred-pounds huge, was at once the most alien and human thing I've seen: its fingers and nostrils and penetrating eyes astonishingly like ours—like what we once were or could be.

At these sights, J's mom often cried, overwhelmed. J smiled, sometimes reaching for my hand. When my fingers remained limp, his smile faded.

You seemed to notice these moments, sentimentality verging into sadness. You must have wondered what drew J and me together. If you'd asked, I'd have told you that we had a lot in common: both foreigners, both working for international nonprofits. Those things were enough, until they weren't—until moments like this, when their hollowness rang loud. You always spoke up just then. *Look, a Ugandan crested crane—do you see? Look, a moringa tree—the powder is popular in the West, isn't it?*

I was grateful for your interventions. J was, too, I think. During the drives, he chatted away, trying to entertain, take care, control: *Mum, are you too warm? Godfrey, what are your kids' names? R, how's your book? Sure you won't get carsick? Sure you're alright?*

"I'm fine, J," I said over and over until once, I almost shouted it. "Okay," he muttered.

You looked at me in the rearview mirror, big eyes curious, but said nothing. This time, I was grateful for your silence. When I turned back to my window, baboons peered evilly back at me, stalking the roadside. I felt like one of them: menaced, menacing.

As the miles and days wore on, the vapors of doubt wafting around J and I crystallized into something else, sharp and painful. At night, lying next to him under a gauzy mosquito net, our bodies unconnected ("too hot," I said when he tried to reach for me), I could no longer pretend uncertainty—not to myself, anyway.

And then the car got stuck. New Year's Eve, the last leg of the trip, we were headed to Lake Mburo National Park. Tomorrow, we'd awake early to ogle zebras and hippos. But first, we had to get there. It was already dark when we turned onto the rutted dirt road. At some point, we must have taken a wrong turn, the road indistinguishable from the coffee-colored earth.

"You sure this is right, Godfrey?" J asked. You didn't answer, just kept inching the car forward around the holes. Until suddenly, we dipped. Just as suddenly, we emerged—almost. The back wheels were trapped in mud, spinning helplessly even as you floored the accelerator, again and again.

We got out, shivering under a black sky shattered with stars. Wild fig trees and acacias dotted the landscape like skeletons. For the first time that week, wonder washed over me. Finally, a moment that wasn't curated—where *we* didn't have to be curated.

"Goddamit!" J was standing by the car, boot-deep in mud, anger twisting his face. "Are you even a real driver?" he shouted at you.

This whole trip, he'd been so careful, always trying to strike the right note, trying to plan and birdwatch and safari us into happiness. No longer. It shouldn't have been at your expense, but I wish he'd broken earlier.

You didn't answer because you were rolling up your shirtsleeves and pant legs, readying to push the car out. What else to do? We joined you, sinking and slipping in the viscous ground, pushing, pushing until—it was out! We high-fived, panting and smiling at each other stupidly, our pants and shoes ruined with mud.

"Good job," you said, grinning. I felt like a kid who'd won her father's approval. It was the happiest I'd felt that week.

After the trip, after returning to Kampala and saying goodbye to you and J's mom, J and I finally ended it. I wanted to call you then, thank you for helping us navigate that week of delusion. A whole week of J, his mom, and I pretending to be things we weren't: untroubled, a happy family, a unit with a future.

At least you, not-Godfrey, were honest about your pretension.

≈ *To the Waiter Who Left Me a Tip*

BEYOĞLU DISTRICT, ISTANBUL, TURKEY

by Michael Agresta

When I traveled to Istanbul in 2013, I planned to spin off a spec freelance essay about visiting a new and totally unique literary museum. This is not that essay. I never finished it.

The reason I couldn't finish the essay: Sitting down to write it after returning home, I couldn't locate anything like an epiphany or heart of the matter. I wasn't comfortable putting my experience in the first person, because not much had happened to me, and I didn't want to fudge it.

Likewise, not much happened between you and me. We didn't have a heart-to-heart. You didn't show me the truth of your country, or mine. We didn't talk long. But you did hold open a door—like a waiter, with your foot, hands full—to help me pass through to a back garden I didn't know was there.

I had been reading Orhan Pamuk's *The Museum of Innocence* for the past ten days or so. On the plane to Athens. In the first bleary nights of jet lag. In spare moments through a strange weekend on Mykonos, celebrating a nonwedding that had been cancelled after our plane tickets had been bought. On the ferry to Samos and Kuşadasi. On an overnight bus to Cappadocia. In a restaurant in the vicinity of Taksim Square, after getting accidentally tear-gassed.

Still, somehow here I was, on my last full day in Istanbul, and I was still eighty pages short of finished. I wanted to be done with the novel before going to see the museum, also called the Museum of Innocence, also not far from your café. You understood exactly what I was doing. Ordering a third çay, pushing through to the melodramatic ending. You didn't try to hustle me off my table. You let me finish. Treated me respectfully, as a pilgrim—if with some bemusement.

At some point, I took a break to rest my eyes, by which I mean look at my phone. You came by to check on me. Asked how I liked the book. It's good, I said. Yes, you said. Pamuk's very good. Maybe you learned my language in the UK, or from an English person. "Very good" meant not your favorite. I asked what you thought of him winning the Nobel Prize. You shrugged.

I could suddenly imagine the gravitational interference, for an Istanbul literati, of living or working in close proximity to Pamuk's new brick-and-mortar museum. Pamuk has become, for a generation of Western readers, the face of Turkish literature. There may not be another native son or daughter Nobel winner for fifty years. That's how international literature works. There's not that much room.

Pamuk, to his credit, set out to do something purposeful with his good fortune. He sat down to write a book-length historical fiction—set in mid-twentieth-century Istanbul, capturing the glamour of the old Bosporus high society and the film-industry demimonde of that era—and planned, at the same time, to curate a permanent museum, supposedly presenting the private treasures of his fictional male protagonist, an obsessive who collected mementos of a passionate love affair. Both book and institution would be called the Museum of Innocence. So a dedicated traveler like me could plan two simultaneous journeys through Pamuk's world—one along the imaginative pathways of reading, and the other over land and sea to the street where your café is located.

The novel is good, fun reading. The museum, as I would discover after our brief conversation in the café, is interesting but not an overwhelming success. It feels too cute, too clean. I don't know what I wanted to be different. Musty stacks of photos I could pick through? A deeper game of hidden meanings? A secret room at the top of a dingy apartment staircase, discoverable only by those who read the footnote on some random page three-quarters of the way through the book, instead of a well-publicized cultural institution with a gift shop? The Great International Novelist himself, sitting there waiting to give me, his devoted reader, a kiss for having traveled all that way?

I like reading books in translation. Maybe it's because I want truths and visions to feel a bit more out of reach, a bit more reflective of the efforts we make to track them down. Unfortunately, literature isn't always the adventure I want it to be. But sometimes it is, often totally unexpectedly, and that's enough.

After politely pooh-poohing Pamuk, you gave me two alternate recommendations, your must-read Turkish novels: *The Time Regulation Institute* by Ahmet Hamdi Tanpınar, which I haven't tried yet, and *Memed, My Hawk* by Yaşar Kemal, which I read a few months after our conversation. Of course I had no way to tell you then, so I'll tell you now: I loved it.

Memed has the rare clarity of a novel that comes spilling out of the lived experience of peasant life—a worldview sensually tied to mountains, rivers, and terrain. I can think of a couple of similar experiences in my reading history, all fantastic discoveries for an untethered American like me. One was *Deep Rivers* by José María Arguedas, also a recommendation by a stranger while traveling through Arguedas's country, the Quechua-speaking Andes. Another was *Ashes*, by Grazia Deledda, from Sardinia, written in 1904. I read that one not on the advice of anyone I met in person, but because it was on Lenù's high school reading list in Elena Ferrante's *Neopolitan Novels*.

I mention all three of these novels together because they're united by a sense of culture-woven intimacy with the natural world, employing timeless story elements like hidden parentage, good-hearted bandits, and urban miseducation. Today, when I read in newspapers about the Kurdish people, viciously repressed in Turkey, at risk of genocide in Syria, scratching toward nationhood in Iraq, I think of *Memed*'s protagonist, and his simple, tragic heroism.

Books remind me of other books. People remind me of other people. Specifically, you remind me of the young Mexican couple I met in Morelia when I was twenty-two, who told me I absolutely had to read *Pedro Páramo*. They remind me in turn of the thirty-something couple I met in Spain not too long after, who sent me gothic folk tales of the area where they lived, around Brest in Brittany. Or the American retiree I spoke to once at a ruined castle in central Austria, around a cooking fire at night, who told me about reading *The Man Without Qualities* as he traveled through that country. I have not tackled that doorstop yet, but I remember thinking that's how I'd like to travel as I got older and knew better which books to read.

I don't require deep intimacy from my comrades, those also reading their way across the world map. We're all on solitary missions, leaked out to us one cryptic cable at a time. The best for us is just to exchange notes when our paths cross. That afternoon in Beyoğlu, I had come a long way, to the threshold of what I'd hoped would be one of the more exciting reading adventures of my life, but it turned out that my conversation with you was the part of that day that had life in it, that pushed me on—toward a destination I'm still not sure of, feeling my way by what makes a spark, turning away quickly from what doesn't.

I don't travel that way so much anymore these days. I tend to have firmer itineraries, work to do, little time to waste. But I'm still reading that way, when I can. My hope for you, friend, is that you're still doing the same.

≈ To the Doctor I Never Thanked

TARRYTOWN, NEW YORK

by Aria Beth Sloss

My daughter was eighteen months old that day. Her first food was fish skin, blackened and reeking of the sea—augury foreshadowing her fearlessness, her love of swimming, her appetites. Her father is a chef. We'd been at his restaurant since morning. Our daughters played in the old grain silo, filched cookies from the pastry kitchen, drew a dozen inscrutable pictures. After lunch, my younger daughter went quiet. I sent the four-year-old out into the November afternoon to pick carrots in the greenhouse and took the little one, my baby, to sit by the windows opposite the bakery. It smelled like bread, sunshine, cold.

Was this when you sat down? Three o'clock, three-thirty, a late lunch, the sun already plunging into the hills. The restaurant white-linened and hushed, miles from anything. A doctor on her Sunday afternoon out, just recompense for all those days spent saving people's lives. My father is a doctor. He loves creature comforts—a good meal, a warm bath, a nice crème brûlée. I have always envied him the brute physicality of his work, concrete in all the ways mine is not. Sometimes I wonder what I've done with my life, choosing to traffic in a thousand shades of gray.

Imagine: we sat no more than a hundred feet from you, a single wall between us. My daughter made a solid weight in my lap. At our checkups I feign indifference to her stats and then furiously text my husband when the nurse leaves the room: *99th percentile!! She's a beast!!* The beast has astonishing eyes—clear, thrilling blue; they peered up at me as I sang under my breath, rocking her. Her eyelids drooped, closed. I smoothed her curls and my palm passed over her forehead: burning.

Listen, I am not one of those hysterical mothers. I was raised to treat anything less than cancer or gunshot with aspirin, fluids, rest. I understand the body *wants* to heal. I held my daughter. I sang.

And then what?

To this day, I couldn't say. Something shifted. She made a noise; her body stiffened. I felt a stab of worry, a blade sliding under my ribs. I caught the eye of a passing server: "Sorry," I said—*sorry, sorry,* why are we always sorry, we women? Why the shame at taking pride in a healthy child? Why the endless excoriation of my choices?—"Would you mind asking my husband to come out here?" The doors to the kitchen swung open and shut. Once, I watched my father put my older brother, screaming, in a tub of cold water to lower his fever—106, I remember. A hard cure, but it worked. I felt my daughter's strong legs under my hands—the muscled calves, the feet that had once, from inside me, kicked and kicked.

The doors swung open; my husband walked toward us, wiping a hand against his apron. It's possible he'd just plated your next course, arranged a few spinach leaves just so. His job, too, is physical, demanding. I am surrounded by men doing important work. "Something's wrong," I said. "I can feel it, something's—" Against my chest, my daughter's body convulsed. My husband took her as her head jerked forward and back: she threw up. Oh, the relief! For one bright second, everything shimmered back to normal. Just a puking kid! That second flared, disappeared, leaving a little contrail of okayness. She went stiff again in my husband's arms and I heard her breath stop. "What's wrong?" I asked, my voice spiraling up. "What's happening?" Later, we would be told she'd had a febrile seizure, a usually benign phenomenon, which—coupled with a virus—had caused her to aspirate her own vomit. In the moment, all I knew was that she stopped breathing. Her face paled to a horrible white, then worse, passed into blue.

Do you have nightmares about your work? My father does: patients accusing him of misdiagnoses, sawed-off limbs, lawsuits. Since I became a mother, my nightmares have swelled with silent accusations: our house is being burglarized, my children have been kidnapped, our car hurtles toward a tree. I reach for my phone to dial 911 but my fingers jam the keys, my *help!* sticks in my throat. In every nightmare, I come up short. Catastrophe blows in and I crumple. I fail to keep us safe.

As my daughter turned blue and life began to leave her—a cliché, I know, but there's no better phrase to describe how I watched what makes my daughter *her* drain from her body: her ferocity, her humor, her tyrannical enthusiasms—I dialed 911. I kept punching the numbers with my finger, but the call wouldn't go through. The price of "bucolic" is no cell towers for miles, trees on all sides. I hurled the phone across the room. I heard a terrible noise, an unearthly howl, and understood it came from me. The only other time I have been an animal the way I was an animal that afternoon was when both my daughters were born.

My husband began the Heimlich. We didn't know she was choking; it's possible he guessed. I think it was just that something had to be done and so, being him, he did it. I was on my knees as I watched my daughter's face darken, dusky purple now, awful, otherworldly. Behind and around the three of us, a blackness crept up. It was thick and oily and I saw how easily we would all three slip in. My other daughter, too. A four-year-old girl, out picking carrots, who would come back inside to find everything changed.

That must have been when someone went to find you. Maybe the manager, the server, whoever it was, ran into that elegant room and yelled, *A child is dying!* I cannot imagine it any other way. People cutting into wide ribbons of pasta, spooning delicate broth into their mouths. My daughter could not breathe. Something had to have signaled that it was the end of the world.

And then: my husband squeezed, she coughed. Something dislodged. She opened her mouth and a shard of half-digested fruit dropped onto the floor. She made a sharp sound, a cry. I fell sideways; someone caught me.

That was when you arrived.

I saw how swiftly you moved: You knelt beside my daughter, still in my husband's arms, and began pounding her small back. You didn't ask permission. You raised your hand and drove the flat of your palm against my daughter's back again and again, the way the video I had once watched, years ago, had showed. The way I'd been certain I would never forget.

"She's okay now," someone said, maybe my husband. No: he was crying, too. Someone else. "She's going to be okay."

I remember your face in that moment. I looked up through my tears and saw you: dark hair, small earrings, a swipe of color across your lips. A doctor but also just a woman out to lunch. Possibly a mother, too. I sagged on the floor. You held my gaze: "Are *you* okay?" You watched me even as you took my daughter's pulse; it was your job to measure life's visible contours, to make sure all the important points matched up. It was not your job to make sure I was okay.

The ambulance arrived. EMTs swept through. I stood, still shaking. I stayed a long time with one foot in that blackness, what I'd glimpsed beyond the edge. I did not reach for her—that has stuck with me. That when the worst was over and I understood my daughter would live, I didn't lift her from my husband's chest and hold her warm body against mine. For weeks, I would look at my children and feel nothing. It seemed possible, given my failure, that I could not be a mother anymore. I had not done my job.

Someone showed you back to your table. You finished your lunch: a day's work. When I thought of you, after, I thought of how your competence had shamed me. But it is your kindness I think of now, years later. Your question; your hand on my shoulder as you stood, brushing off your knees. You were accustomed to the world cracking open, the proximity of the divide: life, death. But you saw how that moment blew my small universe to pieces, how it stunned me—for a little while—into wondering who I was. What it meant to be me: a mother, a writer. I had to remember.

I never got to thank you: a doctor, but also a human. Thank you.

≈ To the Woman Who Walked Beside Me

YONKERS, NEW YORK

by Sarah Perry

It was indigo dusk as I began the fifteen-minute walk to the 4 train. I'd spent a long day looking for my lost cat, and was so sad and worn out that I didn't immediately notice the car that came along and drove next to me—slowly—matching my pace for too long. It was a low coupe with impenetrable tinted windows. I was on a desolate stretch: the car the only car, and me the only person. I stared straight ahead; it gunned away.

Evenings like this are the reason mothers worry, why they call, keep tabs. Their anxious questions are meant to train you to see threat and avoid it. I'd never had a mother tracking me from afar. I'd lost her when I was twelve, the age right before independence. But the nature of her death—a murder—had made clear to me the danger of men.

The car rematerialized beside me. Again: slowing, coasting. This time I nervously looked at it sideways, thinking it somehow unwise to show my face. If I didn't put my face in this story, it wouldn't be my story. In New York City there's often a tragedy running along beside you that you don't want to enter. You stay in your lane, don't make eye contact, step back from the edge of the platform.

I walked and prayed I wouldn't hear the window roll down, the door pop open so I could be dragged through it. There was still no one on the street, just closed shops under sallow streetlights. I felt intensely aware of my smallness. Could I fight off a man who picked me up by the waist? Probably not. The whole thing took on an aura of inevitability, fate. I'd just moved to this city, I was broke, no one knew where I was—it seemed like just the moment when a person disappears. As the car sped away the second time, my body heated up with fear, convinced it would return.

But a block or so away, I saw you. Wearing a long, billowing skirt and a knit cardigan, you were red-haired like my mother was and middle-aged like she now would be. My voice pushed out of me before pride could suppress it. "Excuse me!" I said, the instant you entered earshot. "I think—someone's following me. There's this car that keeps driving up. Can you walk with me, please?"

I was ashamed to do this. I was used to being on my own, to protecting myself. You were another woman—also a potential target—but you were older and solid and there would be two of us. You had been walking the other way but immediately nodded, sharp and determined, and turned around to fall into step with me. You looped your arm under mine and I've rarely felt such relief.

"Where do you live?" you asked. You had a bit of what was probably a Russian accent. I said I wasn't sure if I was being stalked but I didn't want to take chances. "Of course," you said, in the voice of a woman who also knew what men could do. "You did the right thing," you said, and patted my arm.

You were so ready to take care of me that I've always wondered whether you had a daughter my age. If maybe you lost her, or had to leave her behind. If she ran away, or met a terrible end. Your help had a ferocity to it, an inner urgency. I could feel it through your arm.

I've been in New York City now for a decade, have experienced, so many times, moments of intimacy with people I will never truly know. I've called 911 for strangers, sent my voice under bathroom stalls to ask sick women if they need help, redirected overwhelmed tourists, talked to a lonely father on the train who radiated more sadness than I could bear to ignore. I have scanned the street for adults who look like the child who seems to be alone, and I have checked the ears of feral cats for the telltale notch that says they've been neutered, that a volunteer group is looking out. And I have imagined my lost kitty eating on the back porch of a little old lady who eventually coaxes her inside from the cold.

As we walked along, briskly but slower than the pace of panic, you asked where I was born, kept me chatting so we'd look normal. We didn't see the car again. We approached a gas station, and there was a taxi parked there. "You have cash?" you asked me, and I did. I forgot all about the train, put myself in your hands. I waited while you leaned into the driver's window.

"This is my daughter," you said, sternly, with the pride of an actual mother. "She lives in Manhattan, Upper West Side. You get her home safe."

You fixed him with a long, level gaze, pushed a twenty at him. I wanted to protest but I already knew your will was stronger than mine. The driver nodded, a universal New York okay-sure-whatever nod. You repeated. "My daughter. You take good care." He nodded again.

I stepped toward the car and you enfolded me in a hug that felt real. I relaxed into you. I hadn't been hugged by an older woman in years. I thanked you, and said—because I wanted to play along and please you, because I wanted to say it to someone, because my mother had been dead then sixteen years—"Goodnight, Mom. See you soon."

I sat quietly in the back of the car on the way home, watching the very last of the sky's glow fade to black over the Hudson, making my way to my bare, whitewashed, high-ceilinged room. When I got there, I wished I could call my mother, to tell her about you. She would've been so grateful.

≈ *To the Drunk Mr. Flunchy*

AVIGNON, FRANCE

by Gregory Pardlo

We all knew you'd been drinking from the way you cake-walked toward us, following footprints and dotted lines only you could see diagrammed on the floor. Swearing and spitting, you swung on a weary commuter who'd crossed your path. The poor guy's glasses slid across the marble.

Lanky as a Giacometti and more shabby than chic, you didn't look the type who'd slipped through the social safety net, but I couldn't explain you away as an over-sodden hooligan either. Had you gone off your meds? The janitor, oblivious, buffed the floor in his mini-Zamboni. But to me your rage was spellbinding; it cemented me in place, right there along the gift shop wall, where I'd plunked down with my girlfriend Ginger—and her mother. The three of us were awaiting the midnight train to Arles, and awkwardly avoiding the subject of my marital status.

Technically speaking, I was still married when the three of us embarked on that trip across France. When Ginger and I started dating, I mentioned it casually, with a giggle, as if it were a bit of stray gossip I had on myself. To my mind, divorcing "The Danish Wife" was just one trivial, outstanding task on my list of grownup things to do some day. The Danish Wife and I had been separated for five years. I'd say things like "only in the eyes of the law" and "we were kids then," but on this trip, my old excuses weren't cutting it.

Ginger pressed, wanting to know, for example, why I couldn't use The Danish Wife's name if I did not on some level still love her, preserving her in cold abstraction. The question only made it more difficult for me to use The Danish Wife's name (it's Maya—there, I said it), and was *Maya* refusing to grant me a divorce? What exactly *was* the holdup? What was I holding on to?

Ginger's father (a man rarely referred to by first name) had not abandoned their family decisively, but over years of studied neglect, an infinite sorrow that could swallow in its negative space all expressions of affection the two sisters or their mother might receive from any man, recalled or anticipated. Ginger's mother had emigrated from El Salvador to New York City in 1965 and later arranged for her beloved to join her. Eventually, he did and together they had two children within as many years—Ginger and her sister. The couple broke up shortly thereafter, but Señor Romero continued to live nearby in Brooklyn. The insult of his proximity served only to bond the three of them that much more surely, each of them committed to protecting the others from various wolves at the door.

Ginger and her sister were used to the glare of their mother's panoramic surveillance. It united and somehow fortified them. What I called "codependent," Ginger called "mother love." Before she met me, Ginger had taken her mom on several trips—the kind of tribute an immigrant mother who raises two girls in a tenement apartment on her own deserves. When Ginger told her mom that "we" were going to France for two weeks, her mom naturally counted herself among that pronoun. Ginger wouldn't dare correct the misunderstanding.

With the addition of her mom, Marina, the romantic getaway with my girlfriend began to look more like a corporate retreat with a cubicle-mate and a gnomic sexagenarian boss. The night we arrived in Avignon, as per routine, we booked a single with a cot. Guess who got the cot. Throughout our travels, Ginger maintained that because her mother had zero experience with French, she would need her daughter to translate the environment for her. Was it necessary to lay out the history and distinctions of "macarons" versus "macaroons"? It would seem so, yes. Less important, apparently, was the fact that I understood very little Spanish in general, and none of it in their Salvadoran accent and velocity.

I brought up the rear with all their shopping bags as we traipsed between stores and museums. From a scorned remove, I watched the two of them, five-foot-three Ginger towering over her mom. Occasionally, I'd try to edge my way into the conversation and offer my own mundane observations, usually to discover either that they'd already noted that particular detail or that Ginger found it unworthy of translating for her mother. The two pantomimed gleefully behind their firewall of language.

By the time we got to that train station in Avignon, Marina had already proved just how irrelevant the size of her body and her English vocabulary were to the exercise of her authority. At lunch, when her daughter got up to use the restroom, Marina wasted no time. "You're married," she said gently, as if to assure me, as if I were an injured animal and she a no-nonsense frontier veterinarian, soothing my brow.

"I'm married," I repeated, surrendering with a sigh the full weight of the fact. Admitting it felt like confessing to store security after being shown a video of myself shoving lunchmeat down the front of my pants. With Marina, there was no point attempting further misdirection. I felt stripped of some important mask. I remember exactly where we were sitting: at a fast-food joint called Flunch. We'd called it "Mr. Flunchy's" mistakenly at first, and then deliberately. A shared joke. We were bonding. The food was awful, which set the joke running: every negative experience from then on was Mr. Flunchy's fault.

And then you loped—seemingly out of the ether—toward the three of us: Mr. Flunchy incarnate. Mr. Flunchy out of a horror movie sans music and fog. Or a rehab center. I'd been busy sulking, packaging every inconsideration, every exclusion and careless inattention I'd suffered that day into a hefty grudge that would offset the weight of my guilt over not having dealt with my marriage. Now, I gawked. You were almost seductive, the way you inhaled the vacant space between us and made me feel like I was the only person alive. Before I realized how close you were—that you were no longer somebody else's problem, that you were mere feet from swinging at one or all of us—Marina leapt to her feet and started screaming at you as if she were scaring off a bear.

You tucked your face into your shoulder. You turned sullenly. You could barely lift your feet as you shuffled away, and a cold light drenched the crimeless scene like so much soapy water.

I divorced Maya as soon as we got home. That was twenty years ago. In the years since, whenever Marina has caught me being selfish or slipping into the well of my ego, she's threatened to let you, Mr. Flunchy, get me. Now that Marina's health is declining, I find myself replaying that night in the train station for reassurance that I could have, would have, protected my future second wife and mother-in-law if Marina had sat tight another two seconds. Three seconds, tops.

Last year she needed a quadruple bypass. Doctors installed tiny springs to prop open her arteries. Only recently, after she complained of fatigue, her doctor found a new clog had developed downstream from one of the springs. She's not afraid of her death, but I am. I'm afraid of losing the shape of what I refer to most meaningfully as "we."

These days I'm thinking about the perimeters of care, how we can believe they're predrawn, by bloodlines, or choose to draw them ourselves, to accommodate new bonds or affinities as well as to affirm old ones. An immigrant and single parent, Marina had to draw and redraw those lines daily. Sometimes I forget even that I live in a body, and that my body is a thing in the world. Then some Flunchy comes along, challenging me to consider the bounds of my personhood, singular and plural. It's painful to admit—now that I'm present to the fact of her mortality—that I only recently realized I've been on the inside of Marina's perimeter since the day you put me there.

≈ WONDER

≈ *To the Seller of Breadcrumbs*

BUENOS AIRES, ARGENTINA

by Cutter Wood

This was in Buenos Aires, August of 2012, the afternoon of the 17th, my notebook says. A Friday. I must have been coming home from work. It was raining half-heartedly and I was trapped on a crowded bus, which was trapped in traffic. The fogged windows made the outside world nothing more than a blur. A man slapped his knee with a newspaper like a character in a play. Another struggled to dislodge a knot of phlegm from his lungs. A little boy in an orange Digimon cap stared up at me from his mother's lap. She tapped two red fingernails against the slick glass. I looked out the door at the next stop. The rain seemed to have lightened. I decided to walk the rest of the way home.

I hadn't gone far when the sidewalk darkened and the trees began to shake. I looked up in time to see a curtain of rain sweeping up Calle Piedras. The only thing to do was duck inside the nearest grocery.

A child, hidden beneath a vast black umbrella, stepped in at the same time. Only when the umbrella tipped and collapsed did I see it was not a child at all but an old woman, bent nearly double with age. She wore black shoes, black stockings, a black coat of heavy serge, and covering her hair, knotted beneath her chin, a perfectly crisp white handkerchief. Her head hardly rose above the cashier's counter. She stopped to inspect a little rotating display where clear plastic bags of breadcrumbs, or *migas*, had been hung on clips. I turned left, figuring I might as well get a bottle of gin.

The whole world has breadcrumbs, but only Argentina understands them. Though the country is known for its pampas-fed steaks, the dish that anchors both the Argentine diet and soul is the breaded chicken cutlet, la milanesa. It's the country's culinary bulwark, and anyone who has lived in Argentina for any length of time has at one point or another been confronted, late some winter evening, by an oblong plate garnished with a few wedges of potato, a piece of lemon, and two slices of tomato, or perhaps wholly barren save the entrée itself, la milanesa, its beige, armorlike crust fracturing beneath the fork to reveal a feeble puff of steam and a slab of chicken hammered into pale submission. Without the milanesa, and without the breadcrumbs that make it possible, Argentine society would still exist, but it would be a different, maybe sadder, place. "Hacemos buenas migas." This is what two people say in Buenos Aires if they get along well.

When I returned to the register with my bottle of gin, she was still there, now holding two bags of migas in her hands and comparing their weight. At last, she committed herself to a bag, swiveled slowly, and with me following a step behind, she went back the way we'd come and placed it on the counter.

You were busy ringing up other customers, and you didn't see the old woman at all. With an abrupt jerking of your arm, you beckoned me to step forward, and only when I gestured with my bottle of gin did you look over the counter and see that crisp white handkerchief, the gnarled hand still holding onto the bag of crumbs.

There was no change in your face at this sight. I wasn't surprised. I'd been in your grocery before, countless times, and you were always like this, always far away. You wore a smock with blue and white stripes. You kept your hair in a smooth black bob. You weren't young, but you weren't old. I had seen you upbraid the children playing out front with such ferocity that everyone in the shop stopped breathing, and even then, your expression never shifted.

But now here was this woman with her bag of migas. She pulled an old soiled handkerchief out of her pocket, unwrapped it, and began to count coins out of its folds. It was like something out of a fairy tale, an old woman with coins knotted in a handkerchief. She reached above her head, pressed each one down onto the stainless counter with a tinny snap, announcing the numbers quietly as she did, one centavo at a time. You looked away and seemed to recede, to go back to wherever it was your mind was living while you worked, though you couldn't help but count along, and at that final snap of metal on metal I saw your eyes flicker. You knew the woman didn't have enough.

The old woman began to count out her centavos again, more slowly now, one by one, but you cut her short, sweeping the coins into your palm and pushing the bag toward her. *"Tómalas,"* you said. "Just take them." No smile crossed your face as you pressed the bag into her hands. The old woman's thanks were heartfelt and profuse, but you didn't have time for them. You waved them and her away. If anything, you were impatient to be rid of her. Her very presence seemed to cause you pain.

It was no grand gesture. You sacrificed ten cents, maybe twenty, in the act, but I remember it often. I see a car abandoned on the shoulder of the road, a mattress laid out beneath a rusting bridge, and I feel the world might collapse beneath the weight of its own indifference, and I think of you.

Later that afternoon, sipping maté in my landlord's kitchen while the rain fell in the courtyard, I recounted what had occurred. My landlord sipped, clucked her approval, sipped. Then, in a raspy voice, she began to imagine that old woman's life—the ancient furniture, the broken radio, the windows of the apartment dimmed by lace, and the breast of chicken waiting on the kitchen counter for its crumbs.

"She just wanted her milanesita," she said, shaking her head, and then she fell silent. We both did, thinking about a world without you in it.

≈ To the Woman on the Park Bench

CENTRAL PARK, NEW YORK CITY

by Aviya Kushner

It was the second day of Rosh Hashanah, the Jewish New Year, and I was doing it differently than I ever had before: I checked into a hotel in midtown Manhattan and anonymously went to synagogue in the morning and art galleries in the afternoon. It had been a long year; I had suffered a brain injury, lost the ability to read and recently regained it, and was seeing the entire world again. It felt strange, transgressive, to be able to make out letters. I had crossed from the land of the illiterate back to the land of the literate, and I was lost.

On that second day, I walked to Chelsea alone and did my own kind of praying in front of huge canvases painted by a pregnant woman from Brazil. I was bone-tired, still sleeping way too much after a hit to my brain, and I tried to ignore what my grandfather's neighbor liked to say: whoever sleeps on Rosh Hashanah, his luck sleeps, too. The park beckoned. A compromise: a rest, not sleep. I stopped and took off my heels.

That's when you walked in, wheeling a grocery cart. There were only two benches, and you sat on the other. You had thick, white hair, and were clearly old—but you didn't look defeated by life. For a few minutes we watched the birds. I wondered if I should wish you a happy New Year, but I wasn't sure if you were Jewish. "Good afternoon," I settled on, finally.

You asked me if I had gone to synagogue that morning. "I did and I left," I said, and you laughed and told me you did not go at all. You pointed to a church across the street and said that it was a synagogue now, hosting services, but you were done being involved with communities and went shopping, waving your hand toward your cart. You were ninety years old.

"What do you do?" you wanted to know. "Nowadays all the girls do something. It wasn't like that when I was your age."

"I write," I said wearily. I wondered if I should tell you I was worried I would never write again. "And I teach."

"Well then, you would understand this. I won a scholarship in a contest judged by W. H. Auden," you said, "but I had to give it back."

"Really?" I said. "Why?"

You explained that your father died young and your mother could barely support the family. The poetry scholarship was for tuition and not living expenses—certainly not your mother's living expenses. Who would support her? No one, that's who. You wrote Auden a letter and thanked him, but turned the offer down.

Instead you worked in a factory owned by a family of German Jews during WWII. There were two sisters who worked there, from the owner's family, with long, stringy hair that covered their faces, and they seemed impossibly old to you, even though they were only in their early forties. You were eighteen. The men they were engaged to were killed in the First World War, and after that they were spinsters.

You were terrified that you, too, would be left man-less after a war ended, so you corresponded with your high school boyfriend even though you didn't love him. "He was interested in me for sexual reasons," you said. I thought about asking what "sexual reasons" were when you said, "I think he liked my breasts."

You married the high school boyfriend, but he did not understand the poetry part of you. You had three children. You couldn't take it anymore, got divorced. You were forty-five, sure your marrying days were over. You joined two groups—Zionist Singles and Parents Without Partners. "The Zionists were all attached to their mothers," you said.

At Parents Without Partners you met an elegant, wealthy man who read a lot and had a beautiful apartment on Fifth Avenue. Slowly you realized he was not like other men. "He was gay," you said. "We didn't know such things in those days. But I realized he did not want me sexually."

So you left him and worked as a secretary and one day when you were wearing your gray dress you saw the president of the university waiting for an elevator with his assistant and you said, "What an honor to be your assistant." Months later, he tracked you down and hired you to be his assistant; "all because I said something in the elevator." Even though you did not have a degree, you made fifty thousand dollars a year and bought the co-op—you pointed to it—where you still live.

Then you returned to Parents Without Partners, where a man ten years younger approached. He persisted, said if you dated him he would make you happy. You agreed to try. Then he promised if you married him, he would make you happy, and that's what happened. "The happiest twenty years of my life." Then he died.

Somehow all this soothed me, made me think that the year ahead would be full of good surprises. My luck would not sleep.

After all, you had survived the post–World War II man shortage, and had made it through two wrong guys and one right guy. I had survived severe postconcussion syndrome, and my brain had made it through its own war.

I would be okay, I realized. But you were still talking. And still fending men off.

Now a retired military man—younger, in his early eighties—wants to take you out. You met when you let him stay in your two-bedroom co-op when he came to visit his sister, your neighbor, who doesn't have an extra bedroom. He was so grateful that he kept calling.

"What do you think, should I give him a chance?" you asked.

Of course I said, "Of course."

You wrote down your name and number and told me I should stay with you sometime, right there across the street, and to my eternal regret, I cannot find the piece of paper.

≈ *To My Steadfast Danish Soldier*

COPENHAGEN, DENMARK

by Julie Lunde

There's a picture of us from the first day we met. My sisters and I, just a few months old, are parked a few feet from your sentry box, distributed among two strollers—a single and a double. You must have relaxed your rules that time, surely unthreatened by a set of infant triplets; we're closer to you than normally permitted.

You're standing at attention in the photo, looking just as you always do. Dark blue tunic. Bearskin hat. Red station hut barely containing the hulk of your silhouette.

Shortly after that picture was taken, our family moved away to the US, but we didn't let the distance keep us apart. Whenever we made the annual, sometimes biennial, trek back to Denmark, we made a dutiful pilgrimage over to your station at Amalienborg Castle. Of course, you were probably a different man every time, but in my mind, you existed as one unchanging character. We'd grown up reading the classic Danish fairytale *The Steadfast Tin Soldier*, a Hans Christian Andersen story of a one-legged toy soldier that stands guard over a little boy's playroom. Your garb and stoic persona were straight out of that storybook. You were the definition of "steadfast."

Our yearly interactions with you followed a script. My sisters and I tried every trick we could think of to make you laugh, and every year we failed. Your poker face was as essential to your uniform as the hat atop your head. A smile was against your professional code.

In the summer of 2009, we visited for my Danish grandpa's birthday. I was sixteen, and doing a goofy dance for you: a disco that morphed into a sped-up "Cotton-Eyed Joe." My sisters, more witty than I, were probably firing jokes back and forth, scheming to get a smile from you. Our parents, never part of the show, looked on and served as our secondary audience.

Sometimes, when we entertained you, tourists would stop and watch, smile. Our tertiary audience. In this instance, though, it was just an old woman standing around with a camera. She watched us for a while, only half-interested, then took a step closer to you.

Ma'am, you said, *please step back.*

The woman didn't move. *I just need one photo . . .*

Ma'am, you said, shaking your head, *all visitors must keep a safe distance from the palace.*

The woman looked back at us and rolled her eyes, as if to say, *Can you believe this?* We could. We had your lines practically memorized—it was always fun to watch you navigate these small, civil acts of disobedience. You were instructed to protect the kingdom at *all costs*, which meant you bore that gun for a reason.

Ma'am—

Yes, she interrupted, *you're very good at that. Now let me take a picture, please.*

In the past, we'd seen tourists who didn't understand you at first, or who were slow to react, but this felt different. This woman understood you, yet still didn't *move*. Should we tell her? Intervene?

You were visibly uncomfortable. Finally, you hefted your rifle onto your shoulder in what was surely a calculated move. She tilted her head, watching. After a tense moment, she stepped back, and— sighing—turned to us.

That's my son, she said.

She gushed that it was your first day on the job. It wasn't easy to get selected for this post—did we know that? It was a big honor, one of the biggest honors in Denmark, to protect the Queen. *Go on, girls*, your mother said, *try to make him laugh again so I can get a picture in uniform for his mormor*.

Through most of your mother's speech, you stared on impassively—but were you blushing, now, under all that bearskin?

The Steadfast Tin Soldier is a story about a soldier's strength— his dedication and bravery in the line of duty—but it's also a love story. A paper ballerina lives near the tin soldier in a cardboard castle, and balances in arabesque—one leg arced behind her, obscured from the soldier's line of sight. He sees her one standing leg and immediately falls in love. After many adventures, the poor soldier eventually gets tossed into the playroom's roaring furnace. A breeze blows the paper dancer in, too, and the next morning the woman who cleans the fireplace finds a piece of glitter from the dancer's scarf resting next to the soldier, who has melted into a small tin heart.

What I love most about Andersen's tin soldier is that he sees only what he wants to see in his paper ballerina. There's a very real need, I believe, for this kind of self-serving deception in love. We misconstrue, and let ourselves get misconstrued, in service of giving others exactly what they need in a moment. As proud as your mother was, none of it was fully real to her, what you were doing. You were still a little boy playing soldier with a water gun in the backyard. That's how she had—wonderfully, completely, publicly—disarmed you.

Years later, I thought of you again when a coworker asked what my previous job was. *I was an active member of the Queen's Royal Guard*, I said, surprised by the lie even as the words took shape. *Black hat, rifle, everything.*

The man laughed, and I gave him my sternest look. *It's a big honor, actually, the highest honor in Denmark, getting chosen to protect the Queen.* So forceful was I in my defense that I became, suddenly, believable. The story spread and, weeks later, I was still left explaining this to everyone, how it was just a joke.

See? All these years later, and I'm still just trying to make you laugh.

≈ To the Young German Horsewoman, Chosen to Help with Réttir

ÓBYGGÐASETUR ÍSLANDS, ICELAND

by Pam Houston

To begin, I must admit I am no one you know, and ask you to excuse my forwardness.

I am a fifty-seven-year-old American woman who visited Iceland this September, and I happened to be at Óbyggðasetur when you and the men came riding down the dirt track in the North Valley, pushing ahead of you 1,500 sheep.

You had come all the way from Laugarfell hot springs, a distance of more than twenty kilometers, gathering sheep from the highlands along the east side of the Jökulsá river. I was high on the hillside when you arrived. I'd followed the men who, together with their sheepdogs, were pushing the straggling sheep down that final fence line, the one with the pens at the bottom, where they'd stay overnight, packed in like sardines and bleating like crazy, until tomorrow when you and the others would move them on down valley to the réttir.

There is no English equivalent for the word *réttir*, because it is both the name of the wheel, made from wood or stone, that holds hundreds of sheep in pie-slice compartments, *and* the name of the yearly event where farmers sort the sheep into that wheel, one pie slice per farmer. "*Réttir* means 'sheep party,'" one of the men I followed up the hillside had said.

As I watched you dismount, sling your saddle off your horse's back, and place it on the crossbar of a fence for airing, I decided it was your second summer in Iceland, and also that there is very likely a young man waiting for you back in Berlin who writes computer code and will one day have a very good job. Perhaps *last* summer you went home on the 15th of August so the two of you could have a beach holiday before you returned to university, and maybe when you told him, only a few weeks ago, that this year you planned to stay in Iceland until the end of September, till after the secondary réttir where you and the men will pick up all the strays, there was silence on the line for a good sixty seconds before he said he was late to have a beer with his mates.

Maybe if you were being honest with yourself, you would admit that you miss your Hanoverian gelding, Till, (a bright bay with high withers and a floaty, extended trot just made for the dressage ring) more than your code-writing boyfriend, but these Icelandic horses, with their stocky bodies, their get-up-and-go and their honest, ever-expanding hearts have gotten your attention, have made you forget (a little) even Till.

This summer when you arrived, the farmer took you up to the wild herd and let you choose a four-year-old gelding to train up by yourself, and you did: a flea-bitten gray with an unusually dark mane you named Naeturhiminn, (Naetur for short), Icelandic for "night sky." He was a good learner, a horse prone to making the right decision. The trust built between you all summer long, but never more than this day of the Gathering, tolting down the high sides of the valley shoulder to shoulder with a dozen men three times your age on horses they halter-broke before the turn of the century. Naetur followed those tried-and-true horses over ancient lava flows, leaping downhill over glacial erratics, dodging holes with a kind of intuition you'd never seen before, holes that would have snapped Till's long legs like matchsticks.

Together you were tireless, up and down the valley wall, finding the loners who hid in the crags and steeps or wandered into the highlands where they'd never survive the winter. Naetur never shied or stumbled—not when a particularly defiant ewe mocked charged him, not even when the caribou yearling, most likely abandoned by his mother and hanging with the ewes and lambs for the summer, came galumphing down the hill beside you, insisting that wherever those sheep were going, he was, too.

Don't think it hasn't occurred to you to put Naetur on a boat and take him back to Berlin and straight into endurance training, but then you think about the long, hot German summer, the stall he'd be forced to stand in every day, and how even if you could find a good turnout situation, he'd never graze again along a glacier-fed river or fill his lungs with this crystal air or doze under the northern lights, his legs tucked under him like a deer.

The farmer's wife brought out bread and apples, the mandatory shot of Brennivín. You kept your eyes on Naetur, checking for lameness, making sure he was cooled down. Then you were up and moving toward the sheep pen, the first one over the fence, *shuss-shuss-shuss*ing them toward the chute, moving half of them to the lower pen, so they would have a place to lie down tonight, enough room to turn around. Panicked lambs bleated for ewes and vice versa and you moved with the wave of them, advancing and receding, resisting and capitulating. You knew some half of these lambs would go to slaughter, but not tonight, not tomorrow.

This is how the world feeds the world, you thought, four solid months of bliss up in the highlands and then everything changes. You, too, were changing, the air in the pen prickled with the change. Even the men who'd been so cool all day, who wouldn't answer any of your questions except in Icelandic, who were simultaneously chafed and impressed that a girl could keep up, could hang in, could not lose her seat or her temper or her mind going up and down those steeps all day, just you and Naetur, one body, moving a lot of other bodies, food for the family, home and safe for the winter, more lambs the next spring. Even those men were tired and impatient, but not you.

No. You had burnished roses in your cheeks, the pure joy that came with twenty miles of hard riding in wild and clean terrain, with a job well done in a centuries-old tradition in which by some twist of fate you'd been allowed to fully participate, in this country that sits in the place where the North American and the European tectonic plates are pulling apart from each other at the rate of eighteen centimeters per year. There you were, saying *shuss-shuss-shuss* to those sheep in the pen, alive in every cell and as beautiful a human being as I have ever seen. You had a star inside your chest and it was glowing like a supernova. Your heart had expanded to the size of an Icelandic horse's, one named after the night sky, or a spring lamb's, set out to pasture with her twin sister and her mom, the whole summer ahead for grazing and play.

I am writing you now, because you may not have known how wondrous you were in that moment. My hope is that you will take that day into consideration as you make decisions about how to live your life.

≈ To the Lady of the Platform

NEW YORK, NEW YORK

by Jacquelyn Mitchard

I was queuing up to board the train when I saw you. I'd just made my way from the ticket counter in Grand Central Terminal, and so dazed was I by the sheer spin of that soaring chapel of transportation—the competition of commuter chatter and boom-box music and the smell of hotdogs grilling—that I almost ran right into you. I had to stagger so as not to trip over my own feet—a metaphor for our whole relationship. All forty minutes of it.

You wore flowy white trousers—the kind that would be called palazzo pants today—and a long, white, sleeveless vest with a hood. The vest was nearly floor-length, and swayed when you moved. It buttoned to the waist, showing just a peek of toned belly, and the hood hung back over your shoulders like a battlement of clouds. Your arms were proudly bare, firm and golden. You wore small gold hoops in your ears and, on your ring finger, a single gold band.

If I'd been wearing the same thing, I'd have been a nervous wreck, wishing I could have myself shrink-wrapped, terrified that a single grease mark would destroy my artful garb forever. After all, the platforms were grimy, the trains themselves skinned with dirt and rain. But you seemed to know that clothes were for wearing, and damn the consequences. I couldn't picture you in tears, pleading with the dry cleaner the way people plead in the ER, to try, just to please *try.*

I was dressed disposably, along the lines of how police reports describe the clothing of crime victims—as if they'd brought it on themselves by bad or boring attire: *She wore black cut-off jeans, a maroon shirt, and a blue-and-green striped sweater . . .* I was herding my kids to a friend's house in Southampton, a sort of storied mecca to Midwestern-me. The whole East Coast still seemed so big and bad and bold, it was as if I were in a movie about a flatlander with a nickel in her jeans and the dream of being a writer.

My children were still young then, the eldest barely past my shoulder. They carried an assortment of bags, both hard luggage and plastic sacks, all of which possessed animated lives of their own: dribbling food and bursting zippers, revealing tattered unmentionables. You were carrying a single square weekender of oxblood leather, and your children looked like you: blonde, faintly British in manner and affect, tossed together fashionably for sailing. When you spoke, they laughed appreciatively, as if what you said was large-minded and wise.

Behind you, my children were a rubble of rabbling boys. Accustomed to Wisconsin stillnesses, enchanted but also unnerved by competing levels of babble and bang, they kept turning up their own volume to compensate. You were too engaged to stare hungrily at another woman's attire. I overheard you speak to your kids of ice cream and sunset. I spoke to mine of staying the hell away from the edge of the platform.

I remember so little of that weekend in Southampton. What I remember instead is you. You, in your long, graceful, artful white vest, would always make the world come to you. I would always have to chase the world, thirsty, sweating, arms outstretched. Your children would inherit your insouciance and patience; mine would grow up perpetually squabbling and straining.

For years, I tried to be you. I tried to be reticent, beguilingly assembled, casually insightful. But as time went by, I realized that what you had was something that could never be purchased, something in your Yankee genes or your history that nothing could install in my own.

You were at home in your one world and probably understood that one was your limit, while I was like water filling the contours of every space I entered. I'm still this way. I still want everyone else's vegetable garden or fountain pen or relationship or angled bob or screen porch or turn of phrase. I still think that if I possessed those things, I would present that enviable, unruffled surface to the world. Strangers on the train platform would stare, transfixed, at me.

But here's what I know now, fifteen years after you and I intersected on that platform: the personality I was given is that of a frantic striver—one who always longs to be better and do better and make it better. There are gifts in that way of being, but mostly it's exhausting and sometimes no more efficacious than waiting coolly for the right moment. I won't ever strike people as a woman complete in her own skin. I can accept my nature all I want, but my nature is, immutably, that of a person who wants to change.

Once, I told a close friend about you. She listened carefully and asked questions, then laughed and said that you were probably a desperately status-conscious pill-popper who had to talk to her psychiatrist three times a day. And although it seemed disloyal to our relationship, I really wanted to believe my pal. In fact, I did believe her, for a day or two, and it was a crazy comfort to me: You were only human! You probably had recessed gums in a couple of places and maybe you liked to drink too much and were always thinking that your husband was going to leave you for the tennis pro. Maybe you shoplifted a couple of times. Perhaps you woke up crying and didn't know why.

But that didn't last. I soon went back to thinking of you in the way I always had, as my personal beacon, Our Lady of the Platform, the standard against which I could always reliably measure myself and be found wanting. It's not my friend's fault for trying to demythologize you. My friend doesn't know you the way I do. She couldn't possibly understand what I know to be true—that for any of this to work, for you or for me, you have to be . . . well, perfect.

≈ To the Italian Whose Name I Lost

FLORENCE, ITALY

by Julia Glass

I am dismayed to realize, just now, that I no longer remember your name—and that I have misplaced the small maroon book I carried everywhere that year, in which you wrote down, and then aggressively inked out, your address and phone number. This was way before email. This was in June of 1979. I was twenty-three years old, nine months into a yearlong fellowship to live and paint, no academic strings attached, in Paris—and to roam from city to city, looking at works of art that I had studied only in books.

Who, on such an odyssey, would miss Italy or Greece? But to travel alone through those countries as a woman was considered sheer, suicidal lunacy. So I had set out with another woman, one whom I thought of as a new friend. Quickly, however, we discovered that we were not compatible travelers—and I discovered that she was a bully. In the train from Venice to Florence, she delivered one of those eviscerating "Know what your problem is?" tirades. We parted ways on the platform.

The next morning, I faced the decision of whether to push on, traveling solo as a very young, very blonde, not-especially-intrepid American woman—or tuck tail and head back to Paris. First, however, I would enjoy one day in this extravagantly civilized city.

I had read that to steer clear of "man trouble," I should dress "nicely" and—swelter be damned—modestly: skirts below the knee, sleeves to the elbow, and never, ever shorts or T-shirts (hardly my style to begin with). My tiny suitcase was packed with discreet attire, including silky dresses from my grandmother, dresses you'd wear for dancing to Bunny Berigan on the Victrola.

That day I chose the prettiest, to raise my spirits. So there I was, wandering the paths of the Boboli Gardens in an antique party dress patterned with green foliage, stitched with opalescent sequins, when you approached me and said, grinning, "Hello, miss. Would you like a guide? I do not charge." I read your accent as British, an assumption reinforced by your pale, fiercely freckled skin and curly red hair. You wore a pair of thick-lensed glasses, giving you the look of a benignly mad professor. The gardens were safely crowded, and saying yes spared me from brooding about my inconvenient solitude.

You were indeed knowledgeable, expressively so, about the history of the garden, the palace, and the Medicis who'd lived there. From the lilt of your phrasing and the flaws in your grammar, I realized you were Italian, not English. How pleased you were by my confusion. You lived and worked in Lucca, but your favorite pastime on days off was to take a bus to Florence, where you honed your English by introducing yourself to anglophone tourists. So we had ourselves a bargain: I would converse; you would edify. You were well mannered, just a few years older than I, and passionately curious about my culture as well as my language.

Was the Pitti Palace closed that day? Perhaps. I don't know why we didn't go inside. You asked if I would like to see other gardens, villas, the homes of modern-day Medicis. Logically, I hesitated. But then I recalled how my friend had hectored me for being too timid. You waited, your eyes larger than life behind your glasses.

"Sure," I said. "Let's go."

In sandals, in my grandmother's frock, in the noonday heat of an Italian June, I followed you. Just like that, we were trekking through hedgerows and overgrown meadows, along cypress-cloistered lanes that led (as you promised) to views through iron gates of old, ornate houses, all seemingly deserted, their gardens luxuriant with oleander, poppies, and roses, teeming with bees. The sequins in my dress snagged on briars; my feet blistered; I felt my face and arms growing red (my complexion as pale as yours).

All the while we talked. You knew botany as well as art; you even knew the sky. When I marveled at the towering Tintoretto clouds—clouds I had never imagined as real—you told me their Latin name. You talked about your longing to visit America, about your only-child childhood. A good childhood: summers spent outdoors on the streets of Lucca and in the pine forests of Elba—an island I'd pictured as barren, Napoleon's final prison. I must let you show me Elba one day, as well as Lucca. Lucca, you bragged, produced the world's best olive oil. I must taste it!

When we reached a wide, sloping field near the summit of our hike, we paused to catch our breath. You looked around with an impish smile. You closed your eyes and spread your arms, scarecrow-style. What on earth were you doing? *Now*, I thought, *now he turns into a psycho*. Now I'm in trouble: man trouble.

But a few minutes later you opened your eyes and shrugged. When you were a child, you said, sometimes you would find a field like this, and you would hold your arms out straight, keeping perfectly still for a long while until butterflies alighted on your body.

No, I said. Not really.

But yes! Absolutely! This was no lie! As an adult, however, you seemed to have lost your uncanny magnetism. Still, now and again, you would try.

At last we reached a hilltop village. I asked if you would join me for dinner. Alas, you had to get back to Lucca. But I must visit you there, on my way to Greece! I handed you my notebook. Resting it on the hood of a car, you wrote studiously, legibly. I remember the quaint spiral of your 9s. "When willa you come?" you asked in your quirky Britalian accent. I told you I wasn't sure. I had to figure some things out first.

"But I must know you willa come." Your tone was urgent. I thanked you for the beautiful day. I told you that, honestly, I could not make a firm plan that very moment. I could call you in a day or two and—

You snatched back the book, took out your pen, and blacked out everything you'd written. "Wait!" I must have said. What you said next I remember perfectly: "I will not be able to support it. 'Willa she come? Willa she not come? Willa she come? Willa she not come?' No. I prefer to say goodbye." Tearfully, but also angrily, you walked away.

I stood there for a while. I told myself there was nothing tragic here, no regrets; your childlike obliteration of your name unsettled me. I didn't dare think about how lonely you were.

My grandmother's dress was ruined. I had the worst sunburn of my life. But after another two days in Florence, I traveled on, by myself: to Rome, Athens, Sounion, Delphi, Mykonos, followed by a grueling train trip back to Paris.

I haven't thought of you, not attentively, in years. Still, I'm dismayed to have forgotten your first name (Marco? Enzo? Gianni?). But as I began this letter, something hit me. I am in the middle of writing a novel, and wrapped up in its convoluted plot is a solitary boy named Ivo. He exists only in a children's picture book, but it's a very famous (fictitiously famous) picture book. He survives an earthquake and wrestles with an enchanted panther. At the climax of that book-within-a-book, Ivo stands in a forest clearing and holds out his arms. Small birds and butterflies land on his body. And that's when he saves the world.

≈ *To the Traveler Who Hid Cash in Her Underwear*

RWANDA–TANZANIA BORDER

by Ted Conover

Two nights earlier, as I signed into a Tanzanian guesthouse with Bradford the truck driver, I'd watched as he wrote "Kamba" under "tribe" in the register. When I asked him what I should put in that space on my form, thinking "American" or "WASP," he had to think about it for a moment. "Put 'Europe,'" he said.

I mention it because, as I saw you there in distress at the border post at Rusumo, I thought about our Euro-tribe, and what we are like, and the money that makes us different, and how much one traveler, like me, owes another, like you.

You were ahead of Bradford and me, having already gained entry to Rwanda, and as I saw you and your friend standing off to the side, in tank tops and handkerchiefs, ponytails askew and backpacks against the wall of the shed, I thought, *Who sticks around after clearing customs? What are you waiting for?* I would soon find out—because you approached me—that you had little choice, really, but to make a request unlike any that anyone—we hope—has ever had to make. An admission and a self-incrimination.

I nodded at you from my window of the truck cab, and you nodded back hesitantly, awkwardly, glancing around—something wrong. Meanwhile Bradford shouted out his truck window at the Rwandan border officer. It was a routine I'd seen before, when we entered Tanzania: he would argue then look away, as if by dismissing the demand for payment of duties he could make them go away. The Tanzanian official had compromised but this one looked as though he would not—he looked tough indeed, fierce and uncowed. Surely you were appraising him now.

Had you ever, in your earlier life, imagined yourself in such a place, in such a position? I don't think so. How could you have guessed that one humid morning, you would so fear a shakedown—or was it the rules about bringing in currency?—that you would attempt to rearrange your large stash of Deutsche Marks or kroner, deciding at the very last minute that a safer hiding place than your fanny pack was your underwear?

Never would you have pictured yourself stepping out of queue at the border hut and repairing to the fetid outhouse behind it, for the privacy that would allow you to secret those bills in warm places between skin and bra, skin and panties, where a guard was unlikely to reach.

The most unimaginable of all: what befell you in that Rwandan latrine. The moment's hesitation, the guilty bobbling in the penumbral cabin that somehow led to the epic slip and fall, your bills with the engraved drawings of pale-skinned ancestors in neither hand, nor wallet, nor money belt, nor held close by underthings; but rather fluttering darkly down toward that septic pool, to land with a splash, and force you now to turn to a fellow tribesman, the white guy in the truck, and ask for help.

Did I know enough French or Swahili or something to explain to the guard that you needed to hire somebody to help you? You dropped something valuable—okay, a lot of money—in that out-house. You—they—would need to take it apart and reach in there and get it out and then, maybe rinse it, or, God, probably boil it and then dry it and I guess come to some sort of arrangement so that you could wash your hands of this.

≈ To the Lady of the Blackberries

HAPPY CAMP, CALIFORNIA

by Kelly Ramsey

I remember the first time I saw you, on the weed-cracked sidewalk outside Double J Sports & Spirits, where the lost and itinerant of this town wait for a change of circumstance. But you weren't like the others. That day you were a barefoot outtake from Stephen King's *Carrie:* a woman covered in blood. Red wetting your hair, red-painted face, red covering every inch of skin on your skinny body. Red soaking through your baggy tank top and shorts, the outfit of a kid who borrowed clothes from someone else's mother.

You had covered yourself in blackberry juice. Blackberry, like any fruit, is a different color on the inside, one you might call fuchsia. I could see where the juice ran down your legs in rivulets and dried there. You grinned, teeth white in your hot pink face.

Who's *that*, I asked as we drove by in a government truck.

That's Crazy Stacy, Jeff said. Don't talk to her.

There you go on your bicycle. It is late at night, the town muffled by the blue cold of a place at the edge of the charted world. It is a town smaller than a postage stamp, as Charles Simic would have said, and near nothing. The end of dredge mining and the closure of the mill left people like shuttered storefronts: empty-handed, reflective, showing nothing but a mirror image of the steep green mountains and hard blue sky.

At this hour, the meth heads start to howl from their encampment under the Indian Creek bridge. At night, especially the first of the month when government checks arrive, they get higher than the Space Needle. It must feel amazing. How they holler, how they whoop and ballyhoo—at the moon, at fried chicken, at each other. I mistook you for one of them. You are not.

They say you come from a lot of money, actually. They say you don't do drugs at all, that you're just bipolar and refuse to take meds. They say your child, a towheaded boy of ten I like to call The Real Tom Sawyer, appears and vanishes, traveling the woods like a ghost. Once I saw him ten miles deep in the Marble Mountain Wilderness with nothing but a pair of Keds and a knapsack. He isn't with you now. They say he was taken away. After all, you live in a tent.

So many people here, though, have nowhere to go. They walk the highway all day, seldom with any apparent destination. They are rawboned, underdressed, hair in disarray, curses in their mouths. I call them Walkers. The older ones with grizzled beards I call Old Man Winter.

My father is homeless, too. I cannot look at you without thinking of him in faraway Wisconsin. I think he still has a truck to sleep in. Isn't a truck a home? I think my sister is helping him—food, clothes. The last time we saw him together, my sisters and I, he was near starvation after a decade's steady diet of Kessler, a brand of whiskey I saw on a dusty shelf in Double J the other day. My stomach lurched. He didn't believe us that the hospital was a good idea. *You women*, he hissed. *Always trying to tell me what to do*. Fine, I said. If he wants to die and he doesn't want our help, that's his choice. Go ahead and die then.

I must not have meant it, because I felt relieved when he survived. Still, I put off the next trip to Wisconsin for a year, a year that turned into five. I can't bear the thought of seeing him like that. So I barely think of him at all. The heart can only take so much, they say. I say it can take so much, then a bit more.

I sit on the porch of the government barracks where I'm stationed for the summer. I'm a visitor here, a temporary employee of the Forest Service. That word, "temporary," is how I've felt almost everywhere along my cross-country bushwhack through this life. I've taught English to immigrants in Texas, run an artist residency on an island in New England, started a magazine in Pittsburgh. I've become a backpacker, then a solo-er, climbed a volcano in Guatemala, thru-hiked the Grand Canyon, bagged a fourteener in Colorado. I've fallen from a climbing wall and heard my ankle pop like a hollow soda can. I have comforted other people's children. I have wondered whose child I am, supposedly grown now and far from home. I have wondered if home could be more than the musty cab of my small, high-mileage pickup truck, loaded again with a move's dented lampshades and loose cables.

But I'd like to stay here. Can I? Uncertain whether some higher authority has to grant me permission, I put down a deposit on a little cabin five miles up the Greyback Mountain Road. The owner, a stooped man named Ken with a straw cowboy hat and wily, watery blue eyes, immediately replaces the kitchen linoleum. He is excited for a tenant with a viable income. I'm excited about the sound of the creek rushing under the bedroom windows, and about all the firewood I'll feed into the cheerful maw of the wood stove. It will be a safe place for me, I can tell. A happy place.

You have no money nor place to live, yet a strange light illuminates your face. I guess a town is as much a home as a building. Especially one enclosed by mountains so thickly green they look covered in fur.

One of the Walkers, Eric, gets in a fight with a dumpster. That is to say, he points one swollen index finger at its unflinching face and yells. The dumpster doesn't defend itself, but Eric, a Karuk native with eel-black hair and heartbroken eyes, will not be mollified. *No*, he shouts. *Don't tell me that! This is your fault, yours. I will not be used like this!*

The dumpster stands directly across the highway from our Ranger Station. One of the foresters in the timber department takes a video of the fight. Everyone in the office shares it and laughs. *Have you seen this shit?* I laugh, too, then feel ashamed. It seems to me only a razor's edge of sanity, or money, keeps any of us from being out there ourselves, waging war against a steel box, weeping in broad daylight, calling out to God. We, too, would believe that it was not our fault.

Your bicycle wheels quietly by in the velvet night. I raise my hand in a silent wave, and you cheerfully wave back. We've never spoken, though once I stood behind you in line at the grocery store and watched you buy many loaves of bread. You were cordial to the checkout girl, a high schooler named Rebecca who got a new haircut this summer. Your voice was not a reedy hysterical whisper. It was mellow and calm. *Thank you*, you said. *Thank you so much.*

Somewhere in the Midwest, my father finds a place to sleep. Somewhere else, your son catches a fish with his bare hands. A storm rolls in over the mountain, over this remnant of a town where people squabble and have affairs and pick up their children from school. We watch the lightning with awe, bracing for the next wildfire. We talk about weather as if there were nothing else worth talking about, and really, is there?

It's a small place, but the store sells a brand of sourdough that isn't half bad. I am learning what I think you already know: the best places for blackberry picking aren't all in direct sun. Some ripen in the shade of trees drunk on the river, our river. That crush of current and rock that hushes us to sleep. Soon, the salmon will muscle upstream. We need very little to survive.

≈ REMORSE

≈ To the Logari Who Asked About the Sun

LOGAR PROVINCE, AFGHANISTAN

by Jamil Jan Kochai

I apologize if I seemed cold. It was just that I was afraid. You see, since the moment I arrived in Logar that summer of 2012, when I was nineteen, my uncles had been telling me to be wary of locals. No one could know I was back home, because word spread so quickly in our little village. In fact, my eldest uncle, Ahmadzia Maamaa—may Allah have mercy on his soul—very explicitly warned me not to tell anyone my father's name or that I had come from America. He escorted me about the countryside, wherever I went, to make sure I was safe. "I promised your father no harm would come to you here," he told me. "What harm?" I said, laughing, though I had an idea.

The tide was shifting then. Government forces were losing control. Militias set up checkpoints in the markets during the day, but the Taliban ran the roads at night. More than anything, though, my uncles were afraid of bandits. "A bandit," Ahmadzia Maamaa explained to me, "can be a Talib or a policeman or a militiaman or a shepherd or a shopkeeper or anybody at all."

This is all just to say that I had been explicitly ordered not to speak with someone like you—a stranger, a Logari, a "potential bandit"—on the day you approached me in the field behind my grandfather's compound. Ahmadzia Maamaa would have made me come inside with him, but the cows needed watching while they grazed, and Ahmadzia Maamaa had urgent business in Waghjān, which was why I was alone, tending to cows in an empty field, when you came strolling up to me.

I have to admit, Kaakaa: you looked so much like a Talib, with your big black beard and your woolen shawl and your black pakol. I half expected you to be hiding an AK beneath your pattu. Staring at the clay beneath my feet, I prayed you would pass by without a word, but you stopped and said salaam.

We exchanged greetings in Pashto, and I tried not to let my accent slip, not to reveal myself as a foreigner. I could tell you sensed something was wrong; what looked like suspicion—or curiosity—washed over your face. You asked me for my father's name. That was when a minor war played out inside of me. Not a war. A skirmish. A firefight. My first instinct was to lie. Just make up a name on the spot. A phantom father. Someone you couldn't recognize or condemn. Perhaps I could say that Ahmadzia Maamaa was my father. Claim I was my cousin. How would you know? But I've never been a good liar, or, honestly, a quick thinker. Besides, my father is my father. He destroyed his body to raise me up. How could I deny him then?

"I'm Dawa Jan's son," I said.

"Dawa Jan?" you said. "Hajji Alo's son?"

"That's the one," I said.

You smiled and told me that my father was once your classmate, that you had been friends decades ago, before the war(s). "Your father was a real palawan," you said. "Everyone was afraid of him."

"I'm still afraid of him," I said.

And you laughed, truly, from your belly, so that I was finally sure I was with a friend.

We talked for a bit about my family, your family, my life in America, your life in Logar. The sun was just beginning to set behind the black mountains in the distance, and before us all the rolling fields and the lonesome trees were taking on an incredible purplish hue, and it was as we were basking in the fading light of the countryside that you asked me if there was a sun in America.

"Pa Amerika ke mar sta?" you said.

I thought I misheard you. I apologized and asked you to repeat yourself.

"Pa Amerika ke mar sta?" you repeated.

You have to understand, Kaakaa, Pashto was the language I had grown up speaking, the language through which I had first learned to curse and joke and love. It was the language I had lost, bit by bit, in learning English, and it was precisely in these moments, when my understanding of my own language failed me, that I felt the falsest, and the least worthy of my father's name.

But you were so patient with me. You repeated yourself a third time, watched me shake my head, and went on to explain that your daughter had recently immigrated to London with her husband, and that she called you every night and complained that it was so foggy and dreary in London, it was as if the sun never rose. You said that she desperately missed the sunlight in Logar, and so you were wondering if it was the same in America, if the sun rose there.

I smiled, finally understanding, and explained that California was very sunny, very beautiful, but that nothing could compare to a Logari sunset, and you agreed, of course, and we stood there together in the evidence of Logar's splendor, just before darkness fell.

I returned to the States a few weeks later and wandered about California in a daze. I missed Logar so much. During my classes at Sac State, I would start daydreaming about the mountains and the trails and the mulberries and the wheat, and sometimes, when stuck in traffic on a hot day, a cold breeze would hit me square in the face with a scent of woodsmoke and barley that would transport me back to Logar. Even now, Kaakaa, I often think of our conversation in that field behind my grandfather's compound. I think about me and you and your daughter as well. I imagine her walking the foggy roads of London, through mist or rainfall, with only the memory of sunlight carrying her forward.

≈ To the Roomful of Travelers Watching Reality TV

LA PAZ, BOLIVIA

by Anna Vodicka

I have forgotten a great deal since 2006, but not the looks on your faces when I entered the hostel common room. In recent years, the memory has resurfaced with frequency. "Haunted" may be too strong a word—though I was fresh from the *mercado de las brujas*, the Witches' Market, that day, bag full of potions, mouth full of coca leaves for the altitude. My pulse throbbed from the steep climbs of La Paz and the heady scents and visions of the market: medicinal herbs, pots of feathers and glassy-eyed frogs, dried llama fetuses tied up with string, and vials of elixirs to ward off illness and debt, to bring love, prosperity, health, fortune.

You circled around the TV in beanbags and a sunken couch, deep in discussion until I walked in and silence fell like a spell cast on the room.

"What's wrong?" I asked.

You turned to me, all eight or ten of you: a local Bolivian desk clerk, a Romanian couple, a few Israelis post-mandatory service, faces from across the globe reflecting disbelief, grief, confusion, disgust, demand for an explanation.

A Polish girl, the other solo female traveler among us, broke the silence.

"Is it true? Is this what it's really like?"

It was Ivanka I saw first, or someone who looked like Ivanka, as rich girls on reality shows did in the early aughts—platinum blondes in designer bikinis with untraceable accents, who were enrolled in private boarding schools or universities but appeared already to be working professionals, employed as some hazy combination of model-actress-socialite, trailed always by cameras. In 2006, they were all Paris or Nicole or Ivanka to me, though I was an unreliable source on the subject, didn't own a TV, didn't pay attention. I felt a special disorientation before reality shows, a phenomenon critics promised wouldn't last.

In this episode, the rich girls in bikinis were washing cars. Or playacting washing cars. There were hoses and buckets of soapy water. There was a line of Hummers and Ferraris parked alongside a pool alongside a mansion alongside fountains and manicured hedges. But the girls concentrated primarily on the positions of their bodies before the camera. They sprayed each other, straddled the hoods of their boyfriends' sports cars, held hoses to the sky like so much shook champagne.

Occasionally, someone held a hose limply in the direction of a vehicle, laughed when they ruined the leather interior, but—perhaps the biggest spectacle, from the perspective of anyone in land-locked Bolivia—they mostly let the water run.

"This? No, no," I said. "I mean . . . yes. But . . . no."

Silence.

"Most Americans are not like this. No one has this much money. This isn't real!"

"It isn't real?" An Israeli guy pointed me again to the screen as if I had missed it. "It's happening."

You nodded in collective agreement. Who could refute the evidence, the scene before our eyes? This image we projected to the world, to Bolivia, land of the Water Wars, of the world's largest salt flat and the highest-from-sea-level city. Bolivia, where foreign gold mines sucked the land dry from below, and the sun baked it close from above, and the earth was cracked and fissured, exposed riverbeds rippling like all the water that wasn't there. It made me thirsty just to look at it.

My throat went dry. I flashed back to high school, Ivanka seductively pouting across the pages of *Seventeen*, she and Paris and Nicole as much a mystery to me and my rural Midwestern girlfriends as we would have been to them. None of us had ever seen New York.

And yet I simmered in guilt at the memory of long, hot showers, divine steam fogging over my reflection in the mirror.

I felt suddenly like a reluctant and ill-equipped ambassador, naïve and fumbling as a babe, though I was a freshly minted college grad, old enough to know . . . what? *The Real World?* Too-much-tuition's worth of Latin American literature? I barely felt qualified for my actual job, freelance copywriting for a healthcare marketing firm (a field that sounded suddenly ridiculous in Spanish, in countries where healthcare is a human right), let alone the role of national spokesperson. Alone, abroad, during the War on Terror, I was dodging questions about my president, working hard to mask my easy, credulous smile, my calcium-rich bones, straight from America's Dairyland.

I'd considered pinning a Canadian flag to my backpack—a tip from my fellow Americans. Before I left home, I'd made several trips to the salon to dye my naturally light blonde hair a less-conspicuous dark brown. The joke of the Fates or the brujas was on me: as soon as I hit the high-altitude Andes, the sun bleached every strand a raging bright orange. That's how I passed through South America: drafting convincing prose about advancements in robotic surgery, birthing centers, and microdermabrasion, with my head on fire.

Is this what it's really like?

A couple of Canadians looked guilty by association. Some of you grew so disgusted you turned to leave, and I couldn't blame you. I myself was searching frantically for a fire escape.

To my relief, one of you reached for the remote. With the click of the power button, the show was over.

I made a fast exit for my three-dollar bunk, though I can't say I slept that night, something gnawing at me beyond the usual discomforts of the shared dorm room. We parted ways the next day, all of us heading, eventually, toward some idea of home.

But I remembered you years later, when a real-life Ivanka breezed past me in an airport, full makeup, hair smoothed professionally in place, as if she'd just wrapped a photo shoot. She retreated to a private lounge, a boxy room of floor-to-ceiling glass. Bored, I settled in to watch with everyone else, suddenly more interested in the manicured life behind the glass than the messy world of connections and departures behind me.

I thought of you in 2010, when Bolivia signed into historic law the Rights of Mother Earth, "a living dynamic system made up of the undivided community of all living beings, who are all interconnected, interdependent and complementary, sharing a common destiny."

And again in 2016, when Bolivia suffered its worst drought in decades—residents allowed to fill only two jugs a day, every three to four days—and my country elected a reality TV star to its highest office, a man who boasts of plating his bathroom fixtures in gold.

Is this real? You ask, we ask.

They say that after a rain, a glassy surface of water settles over Bolivia's salt flats, converting the land into the world's largest mirror. I imagine the brujas, with their black braids and bowler hats, have something to do with this, holding a looking glass to the world. It takes a courage I didn't have to gaze into it, past the easy mirage of beauty or ugliness, a princess or a hag, to something real, something wounded, wrapped in great complexity and excruciating discomfort. I want to try again, with you. To practice looking in the mirror. To practice staying in the room.

≈ To Mario, 26-Year-Old Bestie to My 78-Year-Old Mom

SUNNYSIDE, WASHINGTON

by Faith Adiele

When Mom speaks of you, which is often, especially since the pandemic, she calls you Mario My Yard Man. And I have to remind her that one, as a white lady, she probably can't get away with saying that, and two, after nine years, I *know* who you are. Sure, I may need to be reminded that you were eight when you left Colima, on Mexico's Pacific Coast, for our dry, inland valley in Washington State. Ten when you left English Language Learner classes for the advanced track. Seventeen when you answered Mom's ad for a yard boy or girl. But in these nine years, whenever she comes to California or we travel, we're always shopping for "something science-y for Mario."

I know all about your love of science, your high school science-fair achievements. Though, after pushing Mom's ancient lawnmower around her scraggly backyard and raking piles of red leaves and helicopter pods beneath the maple and hacking back the orange trumpet vine stretching its tendrils toward the front door like an alien lifeform, you bonded through the screen door over politics. Two Democrats in a valley of Republican landowners.

I know all about the first time Mom wrote you a check. You stood silent, too polite to ask the chatty retired schoolteacher with the pink cheeks and mass of cowlicks why she'd handed you a paper strip printed with kittens. When you revealed that no one in your family had a bank account, instead standing in the line of farmworkers at the check-cashing and loan service on the highway, she shrieked.

"That's literal highway robbery! You're going to college, right? Okay, we're getting you a bank account!" When you were young, she'd advance you the occasional microloan, tiny amounts she wouldn't miss if you couldn't pay her back, but you always did. Now you rarely accept payment for yardwork or the pandemic provisions you deliver.

Like you, Mom was the first in a family of immigrants to go to college. She proofread your community college and scholarship applications carefully. You're a brilliant student, but we worry you're never going to graduate. Mom blames the grapes; I blame your boss. As a kid, you were working the fields with your parents. As a teen, you were overseeing adult crews. At twenty-six, you clock in six days a week, twelve to fourteen hours during harvest. Some quarters you can only take two classes; others, you can't enroll at all.

Mom says your plan was to become a biology teacher, but then you fell in love with vines. You still want your teaching credential, like her, but in the meantime, you've earned certificates in both vineyard and winery tech. Even though you were too young to drink at the time and had to spit out the wine you produced for your final, before driving straight to her house with a bottle.

You need that degree, Mom complains. You know how to grow the vines and make the wine. You've studied bookkeeping. You have years in the field. And yet, your boss hires managers with MBAs and makes you teach them to supervise you. The last idiot sprayed cheap pesticide on organic vines, despite your objections. His error cost tens of thousands of dollars. I wonder if you, with your brown skin and AA qualifications, could afford such a mistake.

"Poor Mario," Mom chirps into the phone. "And of course he's eating crap." She sounds half concerned, half disapproving, as if she herself weren't addicted to crap. I see you, tall and brown and plump, on the other side of the screen door. I know you call from work or school to organize your family to attend to "Mrs. Adiele," as you still call her: Your dad and brother insulating the cattery in winter and removing wasp nests in summer. Your mom, who doesn't speak much English, driving my mom, who doesn't drive or speak much Spanish, to the doctor or vet, your young sister translating from the backseat.

"Mario won't even let me pay them!" she marvels. That's where touring markets—Turkey for her seventieth birthday, Egypt for her seventy-fifth, Christmas in Mexico, not far from your home state—comes in. You may not accept payment for watering the lawn when she's away and scattering kibble for the yard cats, but you can't refuse a gift.

You reciprocate with books about political women—Michelle Obama's memoir, Elizabeth Warren's biography, Malala's story—that take their place in the study that used to be my bedroom. The last time I visited, I had to sleep on an airbed in the living room. The house cats sprawled atop me punctured the mattress, and I awoke facedown on the hardwood floor, choking on dust bunnies and fur.

"Never again!" I shouted.

And now, with the pandemic, it's come true. I couldn't visit if I wanted.

Since the pandemic, Mom says you bring groceries: One week, armfuls of pasta. Another week, eight rolls of toilet paper (the new currency), paper towels, bleach spray, coffee creamer (nonfat—you know what she likes), and sauce for last week's pasta. Once, four jars of her favorite peanut butter, special-ordered. Then you talk politics.

It's sweet. But I can't help wondering where you're standing during all this. Inside her tiny house? Wearing masks? Six feet apart?

It's sweet that you live with your parents and your two siblings and your brother's fiancée and child. Your love of family benefits mine. But I can't help being both concerned and saddened by the number of people leaving your house each day in search of work. By your long hours overseeing so-called essential workers who will likely catch the virus and crowd the free clinic for substandard care. It's happening up and down the valley.

"Mario and I are careful!" Mom snipes. Later, infection rates soar and the valley becomes the center of the epidemic in Washington. "I better not tell my daughter," she jokes to you, "or she'll yell at us."

"Please don't, Mrs. Adlele," you beg. "She'll come take you away from us!" She's surprised at the anxiety in your voice.

You probably know that we argued. I can't believe I have to debate science with her. Or with you, a former science-fair star. I can't believe the virus stretched its alien tendrils from western Washington, over the Cascade Mountains, to this backwater, carved from Native American lands and settled by European immigrant farmers like my grandparents.

But I suppose it makes sense. Poor rural towns filled with people like Mom and you—elderly white folks in and out of nursing homes and underpaid Latinx field hands—cluster along the reservation like grapes on the vine. The only one missing in this blend of the vulnerable is me.

I'm literally missing.

Even without the pandemic, you're there; I'm not. Even with your schedule, you call; I don't. I try. I teach Mom to install Netflix Teleparty and Hulu Watch Party, and we text jokes throughout the movies. Whenever I hear about a book that she'd like to read (or that I'd like her to read for me), I download it to her Kindle. I have meal kits and puzzles delivered. But for nine years you've shown up weekly for a woman you still address as Missus.

The pandemic reminds me that, though I know all about you, Mario, I don't know you. You and I have actually never met. When I think about it, I can't quite believe it. Though our lives are intertwined, an intricate calculus of companionship plus politics divided by science, I don't even know your phone number or your last name.

≈ To the Son of the Victim

SANTA ROSA, CALIFORNIA

by Sophie Haigney

I met you the day your father was shot and killed. I'd been in Oakland for a pink sunrise, watching police sweep a homeless encampment, gathering what we called "string" from residents who had nowhere—yet again—to go. I felt more outraged than usual and also maybe more useful. This was journalism, I suppose I was thinking, making sure the world knew what was happening right here. I wrote three hundred words for my newspaper's website in a café and was preparing to drive back across the Bay Bridge in brilliant golden morning light. Then I got a call.

An editor back at the office on Mission Street was listening to the police scanner and heard something unusual going on near Santa Rosa, about sixty miles northeast. Since I was already out, could I go? I could. I drove north, generalized dread already flushing cold through my veins, though I had no sense of what I was going toward. This is what the days were like, back then: waiting for something to happen, hoping it wouldn't, getting the call, driving, always driving, toward disaster.

There were black SWAT helicopters flying overhead and mixed reports from my editors: a robbery at two different addresses in Santa Rosa, three dead. Or maybe only one person was dead? Maybe they were related; maybe they weren't. Someone seemed to think that it had something to do with marijuana. I kept driving north into the brilliant sunlight, in a direction that—on other days or for other people—might have led to wine country or skiing in Tahoe.

Then the road turned into a vast sprawl of neon signs. I stopped at a gas station to buy a water bottle and a phone charger, a little shaky from hunger. I was listening to a song on repeat: *Heard you were rolling in the good times out West, went to the desert to find your destiny and place . . .*

I'd moved to San Francisco just a few months before to become a "breaking news reporter." The romance of breaking news was that you were just thrown out there, learning on your feet, somehow transforming into a real reporter in the process. I had wanted this badly, all of it: the crime scenes and fires, the early-morning wake-ups and late-night phone calls. But it turned out I hated showing up on people's doorsteps in the wake of disaster and death. One Friday, there had been reports of a hostage situation many miles north. While the details emerged online and over the radio, I did something unforgivable in the profession: I went to the bathroom, took deep breaths, and waited a few minutes until someone else was sent instead.

The first Santa Rosa address was a bust. Or rather it wasn't really an address at all—it described a long stretch of halfway-highway between two traffic lights. There were a few houses and I knocked on their doors but, to my relief, got no answer. I drove on, down a road that cut through farmland, where the distance between mailboxes grew longer. There were horses and shocks of green, as though drought had never struck here. This was the kind of place where neighbors could be relied upon to say, "I can't believe that something like this would happen here of all places." Then I saw the Sonoma County Sheriff's truck hulking beside one of the mail-boxes. This must be the place.

There were large cactuses and there was yellow tape. Even as I flashed my press pass, it was clear I wasn't going to get very close to the scene—to your house, a low white ranch house I could see from the driveway behind the kind of padlock gate that would keep horses in. A grizzled deputy with a red beard and sunglasses looked at me with disgust. "The family's not interested in talking, ma'am," he said.

"Can you tell me what's going on?" I asked. Reporting under conditions like this was always full of roadblocks, and the primary obstacle was usually someone in uniform.

"You've got to call the press line," he said. He was disgusted by me, and I by him. Sometimes the only thing that motivated me in my reporting was the stoic "no" of police officers and sheriff's deputies and flacks on the phone. I pulled up nearby to wait. I fiddled with my phone, checked for new statements from the different law enforcement agencies, texted friends in New York—a boy I loved was there—and then looked up to see you, leaning on a gate and looking straight at me through the windshield.

I grabbed my notebook and scrambled to get out of the car, up to the gate. We stood for a minute in the dusty early-afternoon heat and didn't say anything.

You were about my age, give or take. I was twenty-two. You had been crying, though you made a good attempt at hiding it, red rims around your eyes.

I can't remember what I started to say, maybe something like, *Hi, I'm a reporter, I know today must be a hard day, but I was wondering if you could tell me a little more about—*

"We're not talking to anybody right now," you said quietly, looking down. I looked down, too, and saw you were wearing dark leather cowboy boots.

"I'm really sorry to bother you, it's just that"—I was trying to figure out what to do with my hands, gesturing too much, probably—"we're hearing reports that someone was killed here last night and I wanted to know if you could tell me if that's true?"

To that, you said nothing; you looked at me and turned away, walking back toward the house. The cop was watching me from the car with the window rolled down. Maybe he shook his head, or maybe that's something I've imagined since then.

I drove away, back to the first set of addresses, and fielded calls from frustrated editors. Someone from the family—perhaps you?—had spoken earlier to the *Press Democrat* and confirmed that a man had been randomly tied up, tortured, and shot dead in the middle of the night. The suspects were a group of men who had mistaken the property for a cannabis farming operation—or perhaps it actually was one? Could I go back and find out? I could.

When I got there, I stayed in the car, engine on, watching the clock and hoping you wouldn't return. But you did, this time flanked by two men—boys?—who looked about your age. Maybe cousins or brothers or just friends. You recognized me and you looked my way almost imploring, as if to say, "I already *told* you: I need some time." The three of you walked toward a parked truck. I wish I'd given up then, but I instead followed numbly.

"You need to leave right now," said one of the other boys. I liked him for that.

"Can I just give you my phone number, in case you'd want to talk later?" I asked.

"Okay," you said, surprising me. But as I tried to write my number down, my pen ran dry. We stood awkwardly facing each other as I tried to sketch it, us just standing there in the brutal heat, your red-rimmed eyes behind sunglasses. Finally, I was ready to quit; I even shrugged. But then you pulled a pen out of your pocket, and you let me use it.

I have thought so often of this day—of my cruelty and your pain, of how powerful I was and how powerless I felt, of the pen you lent me, right in the moment of my defeat. What you must have felt that day remains impenetrable to me, even as I know more of the story, or at least as I know the bits of it that were reported in the following days, before everyone looked away. Your father was shot ten times while you and your mother were bound to chairs, with duct tape in your mouths. Four men and a woman were eventually arrested. More than a year later, a murder trial was ordered. It has yet to happen. That's one version of the story, but the ripple effects of that night are, I am sure, a much longer and more complicated story than could ever be written. No one has even tried, least of all me.

That day in Santa Rosa, I imagined that you hated me, but I now suspect you didn't think much of me at all. Probably I was part of the collateral of your grief, the random details—chipped nail polish, oddly-shaped clouds, the color of someone's hat—that one notices in the moments before or after catastrophe. If you remember me at all, I imagine it's like that: a girl standing improbably in the glare of sunlight and rising dust, borrowing your pen after hers runs dry, the sound of gunshot still fresh in your ears. Regardless, you were generous to me on a day when you had no reason to be. I wish I'd been kinder in return.

≈ To the Woman with the Restraining Order

HOODSPORT, WASHINGTON

by Meg Charlton

It was early spring in Washington State, when the flowers were blooming on the coast but the trails to the peaks were still impassable with snow. Cold enough that we barely saw anyone on our hike or on the logging roads that led to it. The few people we passed, we noticed.

First: a shiny orange VW van, old in the way that people call "lovingly restored," with two people lounging beside it in khaki canvas deck chairs, surveying the view below. Then, just a few minutes later: you. Your cars, old in the way that people just call "old," were parked at odd angles beside your circle of people and beers and pit bull mixes. From the safety of our rental car, we made some joke about #vanlife versus van life and laughed about those people in the VW playacting at what you were doing for real. But I think that, in that moment, we were all a little frightened of you, scared of dog bites and drunk people on remote roads. I think, if we'd had to choose right then, we would have thrown our lot in with those first people, with their twinkle lights and shiny bumpers and loving restorations.

My boyfriend drove as I stared out the window, our friend dozing in the backseat. I'd never had a boyfriend before, never had a valentine or a date to a wedding or a side of the bed. I was twenty-nine. I felt ashamed that it had taken me so long to reach such tiny milestones, and so I held my breath at each one, afraid I might spook him and fail to reach the next. He'd waffled about coming on this trip—to go visit a dear friend of mine—and when he finally booked his ticket, it was too late to get on the same flight as me. I remember being sad about that, because that was something else I'd never done, never gone to the airport with a man I loved or sat beside him as the earth slipped away beneath us.

But now, I was happy. We drove on, downhill, hugging the mountain in slaloming curves. The air was green and cool. We were sleepy and contented. I remember being so relaxed that I didn't realize we had gone off the road until we were dangling over the edge.

When I describe the accident, my limbs become props. My left arm is the road, my right hand, our car, and I glide the flat of my palm over the crook of my elbow to show how it happened, our car going straight, the road bending away. We stopped just in time, the passenger side midair, the driver's side skimming the gravel, the car balanced on its axle, hovering, as though it were levitating. *Oh shit*, he said. *Oh, shit.*

I looked down the sheer slope of the mountain, where the trees stuck up at us like bayonets. How abrupt, I thought, to die like this. I was sure that's what was coming—that if we moved, the car would fall and then it would be over, just like that. My boyfriend reached to open his door and I begged him not to, my voice rising. But he did. The car stayed balanced. I found the courage to climb out. While my friend and boyfriend stayed with the teetering sedan, I went to find help. To find you.

You said the dogs heard me first. I'd been sprinting uphill for about a mile, shouting as I went. I was out of breath. I said so little. *We've been in an accident, we need help.* And you acted instantly, so instantly it made me ashamed of my earlier jokes and judgments: your beers set down, dogs tied up, tasks delegated. You leapt into your old car and took me with you, speeding back down the mountain. You introduced the man with you as John, yourself as Mary. You dropped him off to wait with my boyfriend, while we went in search of a cell signal.

Once we reached the edge of the park, I was able to call 911. The troopers said they'd come, that we should stay where they could find us. So, parked beneath the tall pines, we waited.

You told me that you lived out here, in the parks. You gestured to the crystals cluttered on your dash. You mined them here, illegally, in the mountains, then sold them in the cities, on the streets, polished and blessed and imbued with your energy. But you didn't really care if anyone bought them. You went into town to find kids who were struggling, so you could bring them out to the woods to heal. They'd dry out, detox, get clean in this clean air. You'd show them God, you said, indicating the little Bible and the picture of an angel, also balanced by your windshield. That was what had saved you, after all. You could help them because you'd been there, too. You seemed so peaceful now, but it wasn't hard to imagine when you hadn't been.

I loved hearing you talk. It focused and soothed me. You had the radiant certainty common to people who've found God and found

God for real, people who don't even care if you believe, because they know they've got a direct line to the truth. I felt whatever those kids in Seattle or Olympia must have felt when you found them, like you'd suffered for us, in the Christian sense, so that you could be of service.

When we got back to our rental car, John seemed drunker, laughing and leaning on the wheels of our cliff-balanced sedan in a way that made my stomach lurch. I told him that the troopers were right behind us, on their way up the mountain, and, suddenly, he turned serious. *I gotta go*, he said, and gestured to you. *She's got a restraining order against me. We can't be within four hundred feet of each other.*

It was so casual, the way John said this. You nodded, sad and resolute, as though this were all an unfortunate accident as opposed to something you'd once demanded for your own protection. I followed your lead, said nothing. What business was it of mine? Hadn't he helped us? Weren't you with him? Maybe it was more complicated. Maybe it was another thing I had misjudged.

John vanished. You stayed. It was dark and cold and still you stayed, far from your campfire and all the food I'm sure you had up the hill. When the troopers finally arrived, I remember thinking John needn't have been so worried. They were harmless, joking and sympathetic. By the glare of their headlights, the tow truck hoisted the car back onto the road, righted it without a scratch. You left soon after. We drove back, shivering and silent, toward Seattle.

That spring, I often thought of you, Mary, of your crystals and your kindness and your rescues in the woods. Soon after that day on the mountain, my boyfriend and I broke up, another milestone, in its way. As it turned out, I'd misjudged him, too. After working so hard to make him stay, there was nothing I could do to make him leave me alone. I even looked into a restraining order of my own, just like yours, and was told it would be "ineffective." When I think of you now, this is what I remember: That honest stories all end strangely. That we will be mistaken and be humbled by it. That the world will surprise us, for better and also for worse. I wonder if you would agree, or whether you'd tell me it's more complicated.

≈ To the Woman We Met Before the Flood

PAI, THAILAND

by Maggie Shipstead

You had a way of speaking that was completely your own, vowels stretched out like chewing gum from a sassy kid's smile. "You want to watch a mooooovie?" you asked us. "You want a motocyyyycle? You want to go tuuuuubing?" When you listened, you tipped your head back and made a clipped, nasal sound of acknowledgment, something like *enh*. When emitted rapidly and repeatedly, it served as your verbal equivalent to nodding. Later, in the bungalow we rented from you, mimicry was irresistible. We asked each other over and over about tubing, about motorcycles, about movies. You were short, with a perm, in basketball shorts and rubber flip-flops, and we thought you said your name was Mrs. Prem, although we weren't sure. In any case, that's what we called you.

This was the summer after I graduated from college, and my then boyfriend had met some backpackers who'd recommended this little town, a hippie magnet northwest of Chiang Mai, near the border with Myanmar. We got off the bus after dark, crossed a bridge over a narrow, muddy river, rented one of your ramshackle bamboo huts. There, after our hilarity about you had subsided, after we'd gone out on the town and gotten into a drunken, excruciating conversation about how my boyfriend did not think he loved me, I lay crying for a long time on a thin mattress under a dingy mosquito net, until my sinuses were so full of snot and tears my whole face felt like it was made of hot lead. I was hurt and humiliated but also certain, Mrs. Prem, in the way only a twenty-two-year-old can be, that he *did* love me, that I should *not* break up with him but rather wait out this rough patch because definitely probably he would eventually have a miraculous epiphany about his as-yet-undetected but absolutely very real love for me.

In the morning, he and I began to rebuild, or at least to smooth over, set aside, quarantine. We checked into nicer lodgings across the river. Our new bungalow stood on square hardwood posts on the sloping, grassy river bank and had an actual bed with white sheets and a porch where we could sit and watch people drifting downstream in inner tubes. We ventured out into town and perused stalls selling sarongs and Buddhas; we slurped down tropical fruit smoothies and looked at posters advertising elephant rides and, I'm ashamed to say, planned to go on one the next day. (One more thing I know now but didn't then: don't ride elephants. It's inhumane.) We rented a scooter and rode out of town through hills and terraced paddies to visit some hot springs.

As we rode back through a forest, the afternoon turned dark as night, and big, fat raindrops started to fall, plunking down like pennies into a well. We stopped for a while, hoping it would pass, but eventually had to ride on through blowing sheets of water. I held on to my boyfriend as he leaned forward, straining to see, both of us shaking with cold. The headlight's beam flashed over an elephant standing in the trees just off the road, huge and shadowy, then gone.

Later, in a restaurant strung with bistro lights, rain loud on its corrugated roof, we ate a whole fish covered in peppers so hot we felt compelled to order pad thai afterward just to cool off our mouths. We were happy to be warm and dry, still jittery from the ride. We felt we'd had a close scrape. We joked about you, Mrs. Prem. You were one more piece of Scotch tape we stuck on our relationship. We made your listening noise. *Enh. Enh.* You were a character we could put on rather than be ourselves, rather than talk about anything that might upset our truce. Painfully full, mouths burning, we fell asleep in our bungalow to the sound of the rain, so much rain, rain that was running unseen down the surrounding hills in trickles and streams and torrents, swelling the river, which had been narrow enough that morning to throw a stone across, from a harmless channel into something else entirely. In the dark, the water rose, widened, swirled around the legs of our bungalow.

Dawn had not yet broken when the innkeeper pounded on our door to wake us. You need to go, he said, standing on our threshold, his clothes dripping wet. He aimed his flashlight behind him, illuminating a roiling plain of water just below his feet, as though our bungalow had been transformed into a boat while we slept. Blearily, hurriedly, we packed our things, heaved our duffels onto our shoulders and followed him down the bungalow's submerged steps. It was too dark to see the extent of the river, but I was chest-deep in it and conscious of its roaring, of the rain striking its surface hard enough to send up little explosions. Barefoot, balancing against the current, I picked my way squeamishly through sticky muck, stepping on sticks and leaves and whatever else was down there, thinking stupidly of snakes, less stupidly of tetanus.

We were lucky. We walked out of the river. We sheltered in the restaurant as the sky lightened, revealing a vast plain of churning brown water. Whole trees rushed by on the rapids, along with cars and sheets of metal and rafts of plastic and whole flotillas of half-submerged bamboo bungalows, their roofs sticking up like the prows of wrecked ships. The entire landscape was changed and obscured, unrecognizable, but when we looked for where your bungalows had been, Mrs. Prem, straining our eyes like mariners for a distant shore, we saw only water. Even our new bungalow, the sturdy one, had vanished—washed away—by the time the rain stopped and we went to fish our scooter out of the receding water, its basket full of leaves, its headlight full of dirty water. The streets were thick with mud and mosquitoes. Our clothes turned rigid with silt as they dried. We thought mostly of ourselves, not of you. Were you ever able to rebuild? We found a place to stay, figured out a bus for the next morning. All we wanted was to leave.

Eventually he said he loved me, Mrs. Prem, though I think it was more surrender than epiphany. Eventually we broke up. I want to construct some sort of parable from the pieces of this story, from the water rising in the night, the lost bungalow, the elephants in the laminated photos with tourists sitting on their necks, the apparitional elephant in the dark forest, and you on the edge of it all, a source of catchphrases and pathos. I want to pull some kind of metaphor about love from the mess. But I know enough now to know that love shape-shifts, might be the water or the wreckage, the captive animal or the wild one. I want to scold myself for how I thought my white-girl young-love tears—cried in your bamboo bungalow—were more important than the bungalow itself, soon to be broken apart and swept away. But my self-importance wasn't that important. It's not like I mattered in your story beyond being some anonymous girl who stayed one night and didn't want to go tubing. Getting on that bus was inevitable. The forward momentum of travel, like that of time itself, is a force of erasure. We move on. We leave behind. Our pasts fan out behind us like wakes on the surface of an impossibly immense flood, subsiding eventually into nothing.

≈ To the Servant Girl Who Shared My Toys

KARACHI, PAKISTAN

by Sheba Karim

I was nine years old, in the midst of a megacity, and completely alone. My mother spent her days running bureaucratic errands, my sister working through her trigonometry course book, determined to finish it before our return home. My grandfather was ill; my grandmother only spoke Urdu.

Inside the house was quiet, the dull hum of AC. Outside was life: drivers and guards, female servants walking to work, vendors announcing themselves in metallic singsong, donkeys, goats, mangy dogs and cats. But I was a girl from upstate New York, unfamiliar with the codes of Karachi's streets; people could tell I was foreign from the way I moved. Occasionally I'd observe from the roof, but in the day it was hot and at night there were mosquitos. So I mostly stayed in, reading a book, yearning for home.

Your main task was cleaning the floors. Twice a day, at least, you swept away the desert dust, wiped down the concrete with a wet rag; Cinderella in a low squat. I can't remember your face, but I remember thinking you looked dirty, and pretty. You were old enough to have breasts, old enough to be married, but you were just a kid. You were named Meraj, after the Prophet's night journey through the skies. You didn't laugh at my broken Urdu. No one minded our friendship, as long as it didn't interfere with your work.

I let you hold my toys, my books, my clothes. My mother started taking me to the neighborhood movie rental store. I'd sit on the bed and you'd sit on the floor, and we would watch pirated films on VHS: *Ferris Bueller's Day Off*, with every bad word censored; *A View to a Kill*, without the sex; *The Goonies*, which I'd already seen ten times. I remember the movies, but not your thoughts.

Some nights, the neighborhood would beat to the pulse of weddings. A house would turn disco dancer, draped with flashing bulbs and flower garlands, boxes of sweets paraded in and out of its gates. A colorful tent would be erected in the garden, or sometimes in the street itself, blocking traffic. We'd hear the feisty rhythm of the dholak drum. The air would smell of roasted meat. Neighbors would go to their roofs to watch the festivities.

You and I did, too, and one day we came up with a brilliant plan. We recorded ourselves singing and clapping wedding songs, played it from our roof full blast, and hid. A minute later, a curious few appeared on the nearby roofs, lured by the promise of a party, greeted instead by a tape recorder. We were delighted; we laughed with every limb. My memory of this evening is one of wonder: of being young, and un-alone, and clever, and free.

My last week in Karachi, I wanted to go to the ice cream parlor. My mother refused; she'd returned after a long day. We're going home soon, she said, you can have ice cream in America. But I'd been stuck inside since morning, thinking about ice cream. I was angry, and annoyed.

You were in my room, cleaning the floor, except you weren't. You were touching one of my things. I don't remember what, which shows how important it was to me.

I took it from you. I yelled at you for touching it, though I'd let you hold my things before. As I raised my arms, you cried, "No, no!" You assumed crash position: squatting down, head tucked against forearms as I pummeled my fists along the curve of your back. You did this instantly, instinctively—as if it were not the first time this had happened to you.

I didn't beat you for very long, or at least it didn't seem so to me. I stepped away, looking not at you but at my hands, which had never seemed so capable, or cruel. We kept it our secret, and we never spoke again.

You and I were once friends, but even my memory of you is all about me. I can't remember anything you said, except "No." Fault human nature, the Pakistani class hierarchy. Fault me being an ugly American, a daughter of immigrants who grew up in the land of kills. Distilled, it is this: I was a lonely child in a strange land, but I had power over you. I hit you because I could.

What happened to you, stranger? You may have risen with Asia; you may still be sweeping floors. The odds are stacked against a fairy tale, but Meraj is the Arabic word for "ascent," and your name evokes the most magical of flights. *If there is no justice in this world, try the next.* Maybe the burāq, that winged, mythical creature, strong horse body, beautiful female face, lifted you up as it did the Prophet, and flew you all the way to outer space.

≈ To the Keeper of the Fawn

CHISAGO CITY, MINNESOTA

by Sally Franson

We must have made quite a scene, the four of us, not slick, exactly, but certainly of the city, as skittish and wild-eyed on that rural highway as jackrabbits in a museum. Davinia, as I recall it, was screaming. Emma was on hold with the Department of Natural Resources. Gab was off looking for the other deer and I—well, you saw.

I was a mess. I'd never seen a deer, let alone a baby deer, get hit before. I'd never seen a car—the SUV in front of ours—drive off like it was nothing. Like hitting a fawn at sixty miles per hour was just something a person did on a summer Sunday during those golden hours between church and the ball game.

So my manners weren't their best when you drove up behind us in your Chrysler Town & Country, stepped out in your over-sized denim overalls. I must have at least asked your name though, because I remember the way you said it. *Larry.* A proud name, at least in your mouth, the kind of name you can trust, that gets up early to brew the coffee and stays up late fixing the toaster.

You walked over to that near-dead fawn and—bending down on arthritic knees—picked her up like a baby, then carried her to the tall grass on the road's edge. Just like that, like decency didn't cost you a whit. I'd wanted to do the same, but I worried about what city people worry about: ticks, parasites, injuries I didn't understand. Your movements said so much. They said: *The antidote to harm is so simple.* They said: *Love your neighbor. Try to help.*

The fawn thrashed. You stroked her flanks like a parent brushes a child's hair: slow, smooth strokes down her thin and dappled back. It mesmerized her. Mesmerized me, too. It seemed, for one viscous moment, like the story might have a happy ending. People coming together. Innocents saved. The afternoon sun turned the world wheat-colored, the wind blew off our distress.

Or it would have, had a truck not pulled up. I'm sure you remember the guy: sunburnt, shirtless, wraparound shades. Perhaps it was obvious to you, but it took me a minute to get that he was wasted. "That's so cool," was the first thing he said. "To see a little one that close." He knelt down on the ground right beside our fawn. I felt my lower abdomen clench. You kept your hands moving. "Take my picture, will you?" the man said to Gab, who stood nearby. "Text it to me." He grinned like a jack-o'-lantern. She only pretended to click and send.

"It's hurt," the man said, straightening. All authoritative, as if self-documentation brought out his inner clinician.

"The DNR is coming," I heard myself say in a voice so high and wan I'm surprised the wind didn't blow through me.

"DNR isn't gonna do nothing," he said, and picked the fawn up from right under your nose. Not the way you did, not like you cradle an infant. Like a butcher hauls meat.

"DON'T!" I shouted, kept shouting. "DON'T!" He appeared not to hear me. The fawn tucked her legs under her and let out a terrible cry. I'm highly strung by nature, but something else was now underway. Whatever thin line separates my selfhood from this animal's trembled at the sound like a plucked harp string. He paused. She stopped. He continued. She cried again. The sound waves shimmered and opened a hole that led to the bottom of the ocean. It was dark and strange and familiar. I stepped toward it. I fell in.

"It's not gonna make it," he said. "Broken ribs." When he put her down, you returned your hands to the fawn's fur. She stopped making that otherworldly cry, but that didn't restore me to the moment. I was, by then, long gone.

"Anyone have a knife?" I heard the man say from my vantage point on the ocean floor.

No one answered. In the silence, the guy went back to his truck. When he returned, he had a blue towel over his shoulder. I watched him tuck an X-Acto knife into the front pocket of his cargo pants, but when I tried to say something, to warn someone, my mouth filled with water.

That was around when Davinia got back into her car. She shut herself in her car and turned on the ignition. At her corporate job, she is asked often to serve on diversity panels. For these panels she is not paid an additional sum. She said later, "I'm so tired." She said, "I'm so tired of explaining people's ignorance to them." She gave up on the fawn. She didn't want to, as she said, *get into it*, having gotten into too much in her life already.

So we got into the car. Emma led me by the hand. Davinia was driving, she wanted to leave, we left. I wanted to stay, but as I said, I was gone already. People often mistake my cheerfulness for stronger stuff than it is. From the back window of the car, I watched you, your hands steadfastly on the fawn while you and the guy talked.

Negotiated, maybe. "Larry will protect her," Emma told me as she rubbed my goose-pimpled arm. "He won't let anything bad happen." My mind was soft and dissolute, my shirt soaking wet.

I was, I think it's fair to say, well out of my mind until well into the next day. That's when I discovered that there's a deer sanctuary in St. Croix Falls not fifteen miles away from where we'd met. When I remembered that I want to be a person about whom others say, *She won't let anything bad happen.* I didn't make that hole I fell in, but I did take a step toward it. It's my life's work to learn to walk in another direction.

Larry, I want to apologize for leaving the shoulder of the road. Next time I see another living creature in danger, I'll try walking in your shoes. The last image I have of you is from the Jeep's back window as we drove away. Crouched on the earth, protecting an innocent. How your knees must have ached. The Greek *hērōs* in origin means "to watch over, protect." You are the hero of this story, Larry. If the fawn is alive, it is because of your gentleness. I pray, though I believe in nothing but people, that the gentle inherit the earth.

≈ *To the Woman Harboring a Gringo*

SAN ISIDRO DEL GENERAL, COSTA RICA

by Jesse Donaldson

We met at an internet café in landlocked San Isidro—a hub for hikers en route to Mount Chirripó, and a retirement community for elderly Texans. The former never stayed long and the latter were always wishing they could afford a place by the sea. It was, I suppose, the Cleveland of Costa Rica. Pockets of side streets recalled its better days and the possibility, however faint, of better ones to come.

I was a college student teaching English an hour up the mountain, where I lived with eight adopted siblings, a coffee-farming father, and Doña Doris. Once a month I took an axle-shot bus into the city, bedded down at a cheap hostel, and bought fifteen-minute intervals of internet in a café where local boys played DOOM on chunky computers. I felt I was—if not an authentic traveler—at the very least somewhere between the *i* and the *n* of "inauthentic."

You asked me for help. I had just paid to look for a message from a girl I had a crush on back in Ohio and found none. I had hoped to impress her with my newfound knowledge of the world. She'd traveled to Kenya the year before and it had "changed everything." I wanted that same experience—mostly so we could sit on the quad come fall and commune over it together.

What you were asking, I couldn't fully parse. I had lied to the teaching program about my language "proficiency"—a broad and hazy term for those who don't aspire to fluency but also don't require a dictionary to order a meal. I told you I didn't understand. No comprende. You insisted. I asked you to repeat yourself—*Más despacio, por favor.*

Your story didn't make sense. There was an American at your house. A gringo. Some issue of money. Borracho. Borracho. He wouldn't leave. He had a daughter. You had a phone number. Would I call her? And could I translate? But no, I didn't understand. I shook my head. You pantomimed that I should come with you. Venga. Venga. See for myself.

The more you insisted I could help, the more I wanted to believe you were right. Venga. Venga. Vámonos. I followed through dusty streets to a part of town I'd never noticed. It wasn't far—maybe five to ten minutes—but it felt distant and, after a point, it occurred to me I could no longer retrace our steps.

Your house was one of hundreds like it in the suburbs of San Isidro. Colorful flaking paint. Sheet metal. A meager yard. The man's room—el Viejo—had its own entry. A garage or shed built over concrete slab. I saw mattress, blankets, bottles. Dark inside—the only light came from cracks in the siding—but once my eyes adjusted, he appeared. Shirtless. Wrapped in blankets. Rail thin. At the sight of you, angry. At the site of me, pleading. Drunk. Incoherent. Gray and sickly.

He ping-ponged between madnesses. He was a veteran. He was a captive. He was slurring. He was not drunk. He said you wanted to hurt him. *But then why would you bring me here?* He threatened to hurt you. You pleaded with me to help: *See what I deal with? See?*

I tried to talk. I mentioned the daughter. He called her a bitch. He called you a bitch. He called me a son of a bitch. You said he owed you rent money. There was no money. Empty bottles of the cheapest sugarcane booze were scattered everywhere, the sort of liquor that doesn't just dull the senses but eats holes in the brain.

The situation came into focus. A gringo viejo, an alcoholic who'd lost his savings to drink, and the woman who'd taken him in thinking she'd make a buck. He was a cautionary tale for the seventy thousand Americans living off Costa Rica's state-sponsored healthcare and testing how far their dollar could stretch. You were a cautionary tale for the Ticos who trusted foreigners, who conflated light skin with stable money. This particular gringo needed detox and medical care. You needed him out of your life. And so we came back to that daughter, that phone number you clutched in your hand, a lifeline.

As we walked back to the Internet café, I promised to call the daughter but tried to temper your expectations. I suggested you contact the police instead, but you said no. What I wanted most of all was for this to be over so I could return to the numb comfort of my inbox.

Together we dialed. No one was more surprised than me when she answered. This woman whose very existence I had doubted. I didn't know where to begin, but when I started to explain the situation she sighed a knowing sigh and cut me off—

"Don't get involved," she said. Short and direct. Not unkind but not welcoming either. While she appreciated my concern, this wasn't new terrain. Her father had been wandering drunk through Central America for years. She had received these calls before. She had contacted embassies. Traveled and found him. Been yelled at.

Been called ungrateful. She had given up. Gone home. Made her peace.

I pictured her back in the States. Late thirties? Early forties? At the kitchen phone, a pad of paper before her but no pen to take notes. The sort of woman who wears a zip-up fleece and pulls her hair back in a functional ponytail. She told us not to waste our long-distance money where it would do no good. To know that no help was coming and no good would come from this and no one would be saved.

I hung up. You looked at me expectedly. As if a solution had been found.

How could I explain in a language I didn't speak that while the man in your house might have a daughter, he was no longer a father? That sometimes we must cut loose the people we can no longer help? How could I comprehend at twenty-one—a decade before I would become a father myself—the ways in which we fail our children? I was still just a kid myself, a boy trying to impress a girl two thousand miles away, a wanderer hoping for a magic bean that would "change everything." You were a woman who needed more than I could offer.

I was left with only my elementary Spanish. Lo siento. Lo siento. Lo siento.

≈ FAREWELL

≈ To the Poet Who Disappeared

OKINAWA, JAPAN

by Akemi Johnson

You called the US military bases *sylvan* in your note to me,
and—I'll admit now—I had to look up the definition: "wooded."
Just like a poet, I thought, to use a word like that to describe a
military base.

You were farther north in Japan, traveling down the fire ring, on
a worldwide pilgrimage to climb and write about volcanoes. ("Had
to buy myself a gas mask in the end," you wrote me, "but I fumble
on.") You had found me on social media through mutual friends.
We made loose plans to meet once you arrived in Okinawa.

Okinawa is covered in US bases, and since the end of World
War II, a stream of Americans has made the islands their temporary
home. You called your visit a kind of homecoming, because you'd
lived on Kadena Air Base as a kid. You said you remembered "lots
of uncleared brush & forest & old fortress, lots of weird insects."

"At 6, 7, 8 years old it was a tropical paradise to me," you wrote.
"What's it like now?"

Not sylvan, I thought. Your description confused me, because
the bases I knew were manicured and sterile. After you wrote, I'd
sit in traffic on Route 58; look through the fences at the wide, neat

lawns; and wonder if forests were hidden in there. Maybe the bases had changed. Maybe your memory was faulty. Maybe a child could conjure woods from a line of scrawny, government-issued trees. I decided to ask you when we met.

I was in Okinawa because I, too, was researching a book. Half of my year on the island was over, and lately I had been feeling lonely and on edge. An American civilian, I felt just as foreign on the island's bases as off. I wondered why I had exiled myself to this remote area of the globe, severed from family and friends.

One night, I went to a party on Futenma, the Marine Corps base notorious for its place in the middle of Ginowan City. Surrounded by a squadron of pilots and their wives, I drank and drank and drank, even though I was taking medication that forbade me to drink. The next morning I woke with a ringing in my ears that—I never admit this to anyone, but I'm going to admit it to you—has never fully gone away.

Just before you were scheduled to arrive, I heard you read a poem on NPR. I was standing at the kitchen sink washing dishes and turned off the water to listen. I was delighted that you had a spot on *All Things Considered*, that the program had been relayed from Washington, DC, to the battery radio on my windowsill.

Then came horror. Your voice was an old recording. I learned that you had gone to hike a volcano on an island north of Okinawa three days earlier and never returned. Helicopters, dogs, and forty people were looking for you. The segment ended, "Craig Arnold, lost in Japan."

That morning, I had an appointment at the US consulate, where I asked about you. A Foreign Service officer assured me the situation was under control. They would find you.

They never did. The search teams scoured the small island, eventually surmising that a deer trail had led you off the edge of a cliff. They rappelled down that cliff and combed the area below, but you weren't there. Your loved ones were left with searing questions. In her beautiful book, an elegy to you, your partner, Rebecca Lindenberg, writes, "What makes a man impossible to find / on such a chip of land it's hardly there?"

We never met and never will, and I'm not here to tell your story. Others have done so in ways detailed and incandescent, and there is, of course, your writing, words that continue to speak.

I do want to tell you this:

Before I left Okinawa, I went to visit a small museum outside Futenma. At the end of a dead-end road, I parked along the rusted base fence. No one was around. Cicadas roared and a turtle-shaped tomb crouched nearby. Beyond the fence, on Futenma, there was some kind of monument: a white rock with a black plaque written in Japanese.

I peered at the rock, wondering what it meant, and then I noticed the dense, unruly foliage crowding around it. Branches heavy with leaves arched overhead. Of course. I'd seen only parts of the bases, the humorless buildings and hamburger joints. But the bases occupied so much space. Of course there were also areas like this—edges and corners left to the subtropics, wild and sylvan.

I stood there and thought of the word you had taught me. I thought about going home in a week. I thought about you on the base—six, seven, eight years old, amid the trees.

≈ To the Woman in the Earrings

PROVINCETOWN, MASSACHUSETTS

by T Kira Madden

The sky was blown out that afternoon, the waves a frothy green-gray. I'd been holed up in a small restaurant by the shore for hours, reading a Hawaiian dictionary, writing down different words for red: *'ula'ula, 'ehu, ua pūnoho.* I sat alone at a long communal table until you came in—you, your son, your daughter—and sat with me. You took one look at me and my dictionary and said, "Well that looks interesting!" and a warmth between us happened that simply.

"It is interesting," I said. "There are so many words for things."

You fidgeted with your crooked collar, swished your hands up and down your shirt as if to shoo something off. I watched as you eyed your daughter—maybe twenty, twenty-one—playing on her phone next to you. Your son, older, was texting with the cockeyed smile of someone in love, hiding the phone beneath the table as his thumbs twitched so quickly I felt it in our shared bench.

Your face was brightened by the window. You swiveled your head around, taking in the room. The fishing net hung in the corner. Tin cans sprouted with silverware. I wondered, then, how long you'd been waiting to come here to this town, this room. You turned back to me and said, "Excuse me, Dictionary," sweetly. Clever, perhaps you thought, calling me that. "Dictionary, you look like you belong here. What should we try?"

"The brussels sprouts," I said. I felt flattered by your assumption. That I could have the look of someone with inside knowledge of just the right thing.

"Then brussels sprouts it will be!"

On the picnic table between us, you laid out maps, pamphlets, plans for the day. I could tell you'd already studied them by the way you flipped right to a photo, as if surprised, to say, *Would you look at that* to your children. But your children didn't look. Your children kept on with their conversations, in their other places, their faces lit up by them. You pointed back down to a pamphlet and said, "Now *that's* a lighthouse!"

At this, your daughter tried to engage you in the business of her phone. She scrolled to something and said, "Look how stupid," chuckling with her hand over her mouth, hiding her teeth. You feigned interest, nodding, a guidebook still squeezed in your hand.

When the brussels sprouts arrived, you slapped both hands together. I watched you take the first bite and say, "That is so good," with your eyes closed. You pushed the red woven plate around to share, "I think this is the best of anything I've ever tasted," and your children shook their heads no thanks. You offered me a bite, too, your smile huge and open. I smiled back, "Already had some," but you were having a meal of it. A real occasion.

"What would *you* do with the day?" you wanted to know. "If you had just one day."

"The dunes," I said, "and take water. It's quite the hike."

"The dunes!" you repeated. "I thought so."

My father had been dead two years when I made this suggestion for the dunes. He'd slept for weeks in a fancy hospital with his brain intact and body spent, and he woke up to beg, "Please, one more day," then died. There was no joke to it; it was cliché and sentimental. There was no single plug to be pulled, but rather many machines—a tube of life straight to his throat—and we undid them. We did that.

Your children ate burgers. They indulged you some, nodding, *Sure, Mom*, and even, *Leave that girl alone she wants to read her book she doesn't fucking care.*

I project death onto everyone, everything. I have been this way always. In fact, I was trying to find the right phrase for death, for the many deaths of our lives, when I was writing down words for *red*. Brutal words. Bloody ones. The last day I spent with my father before his long sleep, we'd picked up dry cleaning. We'd nodded at the television—a special on Houdini. He'd asked me to stay over, then asked me again, and I left.

So when your kids who are grown people tap-tapped their phones as you smiled and ate, reaching for your jokes, awed at everything around you—the warm food, the lighthouse, the stranger with her strange dictionary—I thought, *they will regret this*. All the not-seeing.

One more day? What would it look like? My father and I never walked the dunes, though we did once live on them in another state. A different shore.

I wrote down more Hawaiian words. I wrote down facts about you, your family, the love in your body when you looked at them, because I didn't know what else to do with myself. I mouthed words for *red*. You tugged at your earring, excited. This was the best day ever, this weekend trip—maybe you felt that way, maybe you still do. I wonder. Your daughter spun a menu under her finger and your son said, "Can we go now?" You all stood up and we waved goodbye.

Your earrings—dangling things, made of sea glass and seashells. Expensive-looking, perfect for this beach town, precious and blue and all the way down to your shoulders. They didn't match you, I thought. Your flopping collar, your sweet maps; you didn't seem like a woman for earrings. I wish, now, that I'd asked where you'd found such a pair. You must have bought them just for this occasion.

≈ *To the Protagonist of a Too-Short Story*

US ROUTE 17, NEW YORK

by Carlynn Houghton

I lost you in a rest area on US Route 17 in upstate New York. The building's major architectural element was a windowed cupola in the ceiling. Under it, a large hexagonal atrium was lined with an Auntie Anne's Pretzels, a McDonald's, and a Sbarro. Families lined up to buy food and eat it at tables topped with red laminate. The white tiles on the floor were streaked with gray.

We called you the Sesame Seed, because that was how big you were. This was very early on, but already we had begun to make space for you in the future. Driving to Ithaca, I practiced singing along to Beatles songs on the radio. I imagined you singing with me. Then I imagined you embarrassed by my tunelessness. I enjoyed your embarrassment. It felt like an established trope. You were a very convenient baby, scheduled to arrive in March, when my twelve weeks of maternity leave would connect seamlessly with my ten weeks of summer holiday.

The blood was a thick schmear of crimson on a wad of toilet paper. I had been spotting for several days, but always brown, dried-up blood, which, according to the internet, was not a cause for concern. But this was fresh blood, blue with oxygen, roughly textured, like an illuminated letter. I knew what it meant. The stall doors and walls were painted black, little cubicles of polite inattention. Outside, automatic faucets turned on and off. Hand dryers drowned out speech. I felt protected by the setting, which seemed to place me firmly in the universe of an early Barbara Kingsolver short story. It seemed possible that grief could be held at bay by formal structures. Also, I was worried about your father. In the main hall, I took his arm and told him what had happened. At first he didn't understand. We had been in one story. Now we were in a different one.

The first story began on Atlantic Avenue. Waiting for the light to change, my eyes seemed to catch the particulates until I couldn't see. I crossed the street blindly, waving my arms at traffic. I bought a test at Duane Reade, and after five minutes, there was a blue cross instead of a horizontal line. I sent your father the photograph from my phone: a plus instead of a minus. I slept heavily in the afternoons. I felt my uterus shift and flex. My breasts no longer fit inside my bra. I told your father these things and he listened. As you and I fumbled empirically inside my body, he lived in a world defined by language. I was the intermediary, the witness, the one who turned lived experience into transmissible symbols. He took you at my word.

Now the story had turned into a dream story, the kind that ends when the protagonist wakes up. The kind, I tell my students, that makes me feel angry and betrayed as a reader, because I have invested my emotional energy in something that doesn't exist.

Your father looked over my head at a display case filled with scratch-off lottery tickets. "I really need you to drive," he said.

In the lot, he gave me the keys. I filled the car at the gas station and drove us home. The highway unrolled between the mountains.

The hoods of the cars ahead of us reflected the sun back against my eyes. We drove through the Delaware Water Gap, beside the river, below the trees. Blood dampened my blue linen pants. I let your father out at the house and found a parking spot on our street. The DVR had not recorded the World Cup final. We sat in front of the empty television in the living room. I drank a glass of white wine to give you something to live for, but you were already beyond temptation, beyond conflict, beyond change.

≈ *To the Follower of Cheikh Bamba*

DAKAR, SENEGAL

by Emmanuel Iduma

I met you when I arrived in Dakar from Lagos, and you invited me to your house. After our conversation, you handed me a postcard with a photograph of a man whose image I had seen on my drive into the city from the airport. The man's image was reproduced on drawings, lithographs, murals, glass paintings, almanacs, and postcards. It showed up on walls, windshields, doors, T-shirts, pendants: on any surface against which belief could be affirmed.

The photograph is of Cheikh Amadou Bamba, a Sufi mystic, and you consider yourself his follower. "I am a Muslim only because of him," you told me. I have set the postcard above my desk. I look at it intermittently as I write to you.

You insisted that I look at the postcard art until the Cheikh revealed himself to me. I write to you to tell you of how—once I returned home, and looked as you encouraged—F., who died recently, came into focus instead.

F. was a preacher in the Presbyterian Church of Nigeria, and before that an itinerant evangelist for the Scripture Union, a non-denominational Christian organization. I knew him all my life. The Cheikh, as you taught me, told the people of Senegal that as Black people they could be good Muslims. He produced a prodigious amount of tracts on the Quran, ritual, work, and the pacifist struggle against the French. He became so highly regarded that the colonial government sent him to exile.

Studying the gravitas of the Cheikh on the postcard you gave me, I was reminded of F., of one Sunday while we sang the closing hymn—decked in his cassocks, which had become extra white from the light that streamed into the chapel, as if to foreshadow a transfiguration. Both men, evoking saintliness, swirl together in my mind's eye. In writing of one, I slip into writing of the other.

How is it that in looking at the photograph of Cheikh Bamba, I became *aware* of F.—his death? From its Germanic and Old English roots, *awareness* infers watchfulness and vigilance. The state of being aware—like the potency of a presence in the dark. Once I looked at the image as you advised, I began to attend to the image on the postcard, to keep watch. I couldn't have kept watch *over* it—what audacity could I have mustered to cast a supervisory net over a culture I entered into as a stranger, one who has never been a Muslim, or Sufi? In taking note of the presence in the photograph, becoming curious about it, I offset an inner alarm, that of grief.

Later, when mindful of F. in his cassock, I considered the possibility of inhabiting the Cheikh's photograph myself. I returned to Dakar. I wore a similar dress as the Cheikh, posed in front of a similar shack. I mimicked his gravitas, and asked a photographer to record my pose.

I am attracted by the Cheikh's poise, a semblance of grace. I like his brilliant white. I like the shadow that falls aslant, and the little heap of fine sand near his feet. I like the 9-shape that his turban forms. I like what might seem like missing hands, and the hint of a leg. You had explained that the missing leg was symbolic of a man straddling two worlds. I like that many before me have looked so devotedly at this photograph that I seem to have learned to venerate secondhand, like a little boy who sees a painting and is convinced all bearded men carry invisible halos.

In order to return to Dakar, I convinced a cultural magazine to commission me to write about the Cheikh. We agreed I would be paid up front, to enable financial security while I conducted interviews with Islamic scholars and Mourides. The money never came, and I floundered. I did conduct interviews, relying on translators, on chance English words that fell through the cracks of French. But all the writing I did in those four weeks, about the Cheikh, was— believe me and excuse my duplicity—writing about wanting and failing to write about F. It was as if I intended to refract the light from his cassock through the saintliness of the Cheikh.

I remember that when you gave me the postcard, you encouraged me to write about the Cheikh, even though, you warned, "a lot has been written." I was reminded of Roland Barthes in the last week of his life. He had just completed his lectures, "La Préparation du roman," and he had announced that he wanted to write a novel—one he would never write—copying out a sketch for it day after day. The sketch comes to eight pages in his slender, sparse handwriting: he has given lectures for two years about the novel he wants to write and it comes to eight skeletal pages. When the subject is vast and vague, a writer traces the outline of the indiscernible.

In fact, the book by Barthes I should think about is his *Mourning Diary*, fragments written for over two years after his mother died. And Barthes, like me, is unable to talk about his bereavement without the anxiety of not knowing how to properly talk about it, as he writes in one of the entries: "I don't want to talk about it, for fear of making literature out of it—or without being sure of not doing so—although as a matter of fact literature originates within these truths."

Of all the miracles attributed to the Cheikh, none is more fabled than one performed aboard the ship deporting him from Senegal to Gabon in 1895, where he would begin his seven-year exile. Kept from praying, he broke free from his chains and cast a prayer mat on the surface of the sea. Then he climbed down the ship to affirm his submission. Once he was done he rolled up the mat and returned amidships. During the annual pilgrimage to Touba, the city he founded in Senegal, pilgrims honor this miracle one prayer out of a day's five, by turning their backs to Mecca, facing the sea. Cheikh Bamba had also authored an estimated twenty thousand mystical verses in Arabic. "My writings are my true miracles," he wrote.

Writing as a miracle.

In Dakar you told me I must make a pilgrimage to Touba to grasp the extent of his worldview, his spin on Islam, but also to ask God for anything. I was unable to go to Touba, even when I visited your country a second time. When you go on pilgrimage this year, would you pray for me? I am in need of a miracle, to write about F.

≈ To the Father of the Lost Chilean Son

CHILEAN BASE, ANTARCTICA

by Carin Clevidence

What I remember clearly even now is the phrase you used: *a stupid accident.*

I was working in Antarctica for the season on a Russian tourist ship, the *Alla Tarasova*. My friend Jasmine and I had been waiting on the pebble beach for the passengers to return from a tour of a nearby research station. You opened the door of the Chilean base and invited us in.

I don't remember your name, and over the years your face has faded to a vague impression of dark eyes and hair. Of the half dozen men there, you were the oldest and clearly the one in charge. You possessed a wistful gallantry to which I attributed to the fact that you were South American. *The flowers of Antarctica*, you called us, your English beautiful and assured.

Meeting anyone outside the world of our ship was a novelty: for most of the season we landed on desolate islands inhabited only by penguins. I'd traveled since childhood, but I'd never seen anything like Antarctica. It exploded every former sense of scale. We cruised past icebergs that stretched three miles long, and anchored in bays ringed by a dozen glaciers. I was in love with the austere purity and grandeur, the beauty of the constantly shifting sky. Now, as I sat in the workmanlike research lounge, I tried to imagine what it would be like to live here like you did; not to visit on a cruise ship with a hundred tourists, but to stay all winter through the long polar darkness, fully immersed in it.

We asked and answered the usual questions. Jasmine ran the onboard shop, I assisted the expedition leader. Neither of us had been here before. Already I knew I wanted to return.

You were from Santiago, where you had a wife and children. On the desk was a photograph of a young family. And beside it one of a boy, laughing with his head thrown back. "Your son?" I asked, though the resemblance was obvious. "How old is he?"

There was the faintest shift in the room.

"He was eight."

It took a moment for me to understand. I don't know what showed in my face.

"We lost him in a stupid accident."

You didn't elaborate. Graciously, you moved the conversation to something else. Tea was offered, and dry cookies of some kind. It was a short, friendly visit between people who found themselves for varied reasons at the bottom of the earth. My boss called us on the radio soon afterward, and Jasmine and I left to organize boat shuttles back to the ship.

I was, at the time, not yet thirty.

Later, after my children were born, I remembered our brief exchange. I was filled with the awful responsibility of motherhood, and still am. From the start my children have been wholly, irreplaceably themselves. Their vulnerability terrifies me.

When my daughter was ten, I took her to Antarctica. I was in my early forties, and the lens through which I saw the landscape had changed. I marveled again at the desolate islands hung with glaciers, the vistas of ice and snow, the albatross and whales, the enormous, variable sky. But this time, I found myself searching for traces of the people who had been there before us.

The try pots rusting in the tussock grass on a beach in South Georgia showed where sealers had camped a hundred or more years ago, to slaughter seals and render their blubber.

At Whalers Bay on Deception Island, I came across the remains of a cemetery all but destroyed in one of the island's volcanic eruptions. Two white crosses remained, makeshift and listing, bearing the years that encompassed a man's life. Again, I thought of you.

The last time I went to Antarctica was a month after my father died. The heart attack that killed him was wholly unexpected. We had planned to have Thanksgiving together the following week. I couldn't fully believe that he was gone. It felt as though the sun had vanished from the sky. I kept wanting to ask him a question, or tell him something, even as my sisters and I gathered at his house and wandered variously weeping through rooms filled with books and pillows and reading glasses he had only recently put down.

Going to Antarctica seemed like a dereliction of duty, or an attempt at escape. Nonetheless, the tickets had been bought months before. Staying would not bring him back.

And in some ways it was easier to be, temporarily, in a place with no connection to him. Or even to people. What I expected in the face of his unimaginable death was for the human world to grind to a halt. In Antarctica, it almost does.

Time operates differently there, as though measured with two separate clocks. One clock races madly and the other inches so slowly it seems to not move at all. As the ice recedes each spring, the brush-tailed penguins hurry to newly exposed hillsides to make their pebble nests. All austral summer the rookeries bustle with life. The penguins fight for space, steal each other's pebbles, mate, lay eggs, raise downy chicks, and try to protect them from the predatory skuas. In a few months the colonies empty again. The penguins scatter out to sea. The snow returns and the ice reforms, eventually doubling the size of the continent. And through the urgent cycle of the seasons, beneath the ice and snow and the rough pink feet of the penguins, the rock keeps its own geologic time, moving at a wholly different pace through the millennia.

Nothing in Antarctica is on a human scale—neither time nor space. On this trip, that vast indifference was a balm. Out my cabin window, at two or three or four in the morning, I watched a panorama of ice fields drenched in sulfurous yellow light, glaciers tinged with blues and violets, arched and crenellated icebergs like frozen castles. The sun didn't set. It feinted toward the horizon and then pulled back, as though having second thoughts. Everything felt upside down, and the external strangeness merged with my internal numb dislocation. There was a part of me that didn't want to go home.

My daughter is twenty now, living at college, applying to study-abroad programs an ocean away. Like the rest of the family, she loves to travel. My seventeen-year-old son leaves for college in the fall. In the meantime, he's working toward his private pilot's license. He has been learning to fly planes at the small local airport since he was twelve. I'm proud and afraid in equal measure. Twice in recent years I've attended the funerals of children their age, kids who died decades too soon, in stupid accidents. The awareness of their vulnerability never leaves me, even as I encourage them to spread their wings.

Their grandfather has been gone for two and a half years. On a recent visit to New York City, where he used to live, a fierce, illogical hope overcame me: I thought I might see him among the throngs of strangers in St. Mark's Place. I understand that he's dead, but even so, I kept searching the crowd for his long stride and dark hair, his observant, appreciative gaze, his sunny smile. It was useless, of course, no matter how hard I looked. There are over eight and a half million people in New York City. Not one of them is my dad.

I can't imagine the grief you carried when we met over two decades ago, that you carry still. Over the years I've wondered how you are. I picture you back in Santiago, your hair perhaps getting gray. You must be roughly my father's age, I realize. I think of how my children loved his stories about building a cabin on an island in Puget Sound or sailing in the Bahamas. I like to think you have grandchildren yourself.

Maybe they sometimes ask about the time you spent in Antarctica. Was it very cold? They want to know. Was it really night for the whole winter? And you tell them that it was cold but also beautiful, like nowhere else you've ever been. You tell them how the penguins sometimes looked, at a distance, like a line of children on their way to school. And how, after a winter of constant darkness, the sun crept back slowly, a little bit each day, though there were times you thought it never would.

≈ To the Man Who Had a Wife

COSHOCTON, OHIO

by Rachel Yoder

It was 1996, the summer before I left home for college, and everything was beautiful: that sun-drenched day in the teeming Appalachian foothills; that long-haired, easy-smiling girl of seventeen I used to be; even that dirty little town with its paper plant and steel plant and industrial pipe plant puffing the sky to haze and the air to a sweetly chemical stench. Three rivers converged at its center and ran high and muddy always, always.

I first saw you in the little tourist trap on the east side of town—a restored canal-era town of which I'd almost been queen—as I had lunch with my piano teacher, a woman from church. You sat at a picnic table next to us, up the hill a bit, a man who looked like any other in that place, skinny and ratty, in jeans and a T-shirt and ball cap. You face has faded over all these years, the details. I could no longer describe you to a law enforcement official, but your essence remains: cocky, clever, smirking.

Were you also eating? Who knows? You were just there, until I noticed what you wanted me to: a hole in the crotch of your jeans with no underwear underneath. Were I the me of now, I would have cackled with laughter, pointed and called you out, but I was a girl from the Mennonite commune twenty minutes away. I was smart and nice and obeyed my father.

I looked away, told my piano teacher you were "weird." I didn't know what else to say. I can't remember where I went next, but it must have been somewhere on Main Street in that tiny town, to the one clothing boutique where I liked to try on Guess? jeans and study the Fossil watches. To the gas station. The bank. At first, I wrote you off as a simple coincidence of a small town. *Overreacting*, I said to myself. But after I saw you once, twice, and then again, I knew you were following me. I could no longer minimize your hunched form, the pickup in which I spotted you; your low, ugly gaze.

I wonder how it made you feel to stalk me. Did you feel like an animal, heart racing, a high-pitched alertness electrifying every last cell? Because that's how I felt.

I sped to the public library, because my mother worked there and I thought I'd be safe. I told her what was happening, that a man was following me. Did I mention that you had exposed yourself? I imagine I did, though I'd also believe if I hadn't, for my mother and I had never talked about sex, desire, men and women and all that could mean.

I wandered through the stacks to comfort myself, picking random books that looked interesting, as was my habit, my favorite indulgence. But then, as if I were in a bad thriller, I pulled a book from the shelf and, through the space it opened, saw your face staring back at me.

I ran to my mother at the reference desk. We called the police. I hid up in the employee break room—shady and cool and dead quiet—until they came and took a limp statement from me. Nothing they could really do, they said. Just keep a look-out. Call them if I see him again. For the next hour, I swelled with anger, then shrunk down inside my helplessness, back and forth, unable to reconcile the two. Finally, I wound back up. I ventured back downstairs and out into the day.

Why did I need to go to the grocery store? What could a girl of seventeen possibly need to get? Why didn't I just get in my old Volkswagen and speed away on the roller-coaster roads, up and over and through hills and gullies, slamming from third gear into fourth, taking each turn entirely too fast? I remember now: I did not want my day to be overtaken by fear. I went to the store and wandered the aisles to prove you had no control over me. But inexplicably—even after I'd waited hours at the library and taken care that no one was trailing me—you were there, turning quickly to examine a row of crackers, as if that's what you were looking for.

I'm sure I swore under my breath as I stormed to the front of the store to dial the police department on a pay phone. Once connected, the operator put me on hold. As I waited, you sauntered toward me, picked up the pay phone right beside mine, dialed and then muttered in low tones, though you'd never dropped a quarter in the slot. I could have reached out and touched you. I could have slapped you. I could have screamed. Instead I waited, silent and seething.

Still on hold, I watched as you hung up and walked away. How dare you keep following me. How dare you come so close. I was about to explode. And then I did.

I ran after you, through the automatic sliding doors, past grandmothers and toddlers examining flowers, out into the afternoon heat, and yelled: "Hey! HEY! Stop following me! You've been following me all day and you need to stop."

You paused, along with everyone else out there. All eyes turned to me, the hysterical girl, yelling. What was my problem? Why was I making a scene? I didn't care. All I wanted was for everyone in earshot, out of earshot, in the entire town, or world, to know what you had done.

You turned to me, spread your arms wide, palms up. "Darlin'," you said. "I have a wife." As if a wife would keep you from doing such a thing. As if you were worthy of calling me "darling."

Now, more than twenty years later, the person I'd like to speak to is that girl of the summer of 1996, now a stranger to me as well. I'd tell her what a good job—what a wonderful and brave job—she did, yelling at you. Tell her that she is strong and beyond capable, that she should keep yelling, whenever she wants, that it will serve her well in the years to come. I want to tell her that the shame she feels isn't hers. It belongs to you, and her work over time will be to find ways to give it back. That she is not small and powerless despite what you did, despite the fact that you got away with it.

Though I'd like to claim I have nothing, nothing, nothing more to say to you, stranger, in my mind I am yelling, still yelling, will always be yelling: *Stop. Stop.*

Stop following me.

≈ To the One Who Was Supposed to Get Away

KO PHA NGAN, THAILAND

by Lavinia Spalding

What I remember, fifteen years on, is not your face or hair or hands, nor the beach or the full moon above us that night. I remember the safety cone. It was bright orange, brand new, and perfectly incongruous—so we stared at it for seven straight hours.

My friend swung by twice to check on me, maybe three times.

"I'm good," I said dreamily, as you studied the plastic cone or the silver sea of tinsel before us or the spectacle to our right—hundreds of barefoot bodies gyrating to a techno laser lightshow. Perhaps you looked behind us to the dreadlocked girl with the vacant eyes performing fire poi, twirling and swaying inside her trance of flaming hoops.

I wanted to stand up when the giant paper lanterns drifted like white sparks into the sky, burning ash flakes from a campfire. I should have scrawled my wish on paper and flown it into that blackness, or joined the mob of dancers and truly belonged, then, to the tens of thousands on our tourist-trap party island in Thailand. I contemplated finding my sandals. Instead I stayed captive, promised to one small square of sand and one plastic cone and you.

We admired its pointy shape, its cheerful hue, its phantom-tollbooth quality, while we talked. Of Amsterdam, America. Of love and sex and opium, travel, philosophy, altered states, higher powers, politics, prostitution. We talked of meditation and monogamy, and we talked of us, but also of him, my devoted Army sergeant waiting in Florida. And so, while bodies in the water coupled, not twenty feet away, you and I would not touch. Still, of all the drugs that night—and there were many—longing was the strongest.

At dawn, the light revealed our crescent beach, gift-wrapped in broken Singha bottles and cigarette butts, plastic cups and abandoned footwear. We said goodbye, eyes closed, clutching. You smelled of salt and smoke, and I took one long drag off your shirt before we separated.

Nearby, a college kid wearing only shorts and a white shell necklace lay passed out on the sand. Remember? His camera balanced on his sunburned stomach. A passerby stopped, plucked it up, and I was about to yell, protest, but the thief stepped back, took one photo of the kid, returned the camera, and walked on. We laughed, one last laugh along with one final glance at our orange traffic cone, our own undeveloped snapshot to tell the story. *Danger*, it warned. *Proceed with caution. Keep your distance.*

We did. Morning ended our affair of words and headlines and secrets laid out like a newspaper on a breakfast table, now folded and tucked away. We would never have this again. We would never have another night so exquisitely our own.

Until, of course, you ruined it. Not once or twice, but three whole fucking times.

First: after the water taxi ferried us back to the big island and everyone slept away the day in dark huts and shady hammocks.

That evening, you sauntered past my bar table. Mundane greeting, blithe conversation, and a cocky justification of why you kept company with the teenage Thai girl: saving her from pervy old white guys, you said, as I looked on in disbelief—because wouldn't she rather be with you: young and virile?

Second: the next night, same thing, only this time you left with a local sex worker your own age and a bit taller than you. I shouldn't have been shocked—you were off the map, and so Dutch, my friends said by way of explanation, and whatever, you couldn't care less. But where did that leave me? Us? Our sweet stretch of numinous night? Nowhere. Seven hours of life, swept away. Now, thinking of us, I saw not only pristine white sand and lapping waves, but also garbage clinging to the shore.

Still, when I left the island later that week—though I didn't seek you out to say goodbye—I somehow knew your memory would get off easy. My mind was already rinsing it clean, sanitizing it for a wistful someday. Those hours would remain sacrosanct, unsullied by follow-up, or any expectation of it. I would carry only an image of two strangers, one lost night, and a perfect never-again.

I still remember what you said fifteen years ago, as the sun stirred over the sea and the chemicals drained from our bodies. You were happy, you whispered, that I was faithful to my sergeant—it meant we wouldn't ruin this. Nothing would ruin it.

But you found me, last week, sent a message through Facebook. Proving, at last, that never-agains are the new happily-ever-afters. Elusive, illusory, now a relic of a lost era of travel. We weren't lovers and we won't be friends, and now you've made it so we can't even be strangers. We were never more than two paper lanterns drifting separately into blackness, wishes unfulfilled, bracing for the fall.

≈ To the Stranger My Doctor Heard All About

PORTLAND, OREGON

by Robin Romm

Today I sat in the pediatrician's office with my four-month-old daughter. She lay on a blue vinyl table, the sound of a sudden summer rain percussive against the shaded window.

"How are you doing?" the doctor asked me.

I want to be doing better than I am. The baby has been very, very ill, and now here she is, spryly kicking her little perfect legs. Yesterday, I told the doctor, she pulled out the nasal gastric tube, the tube through which we force-feed her the calories she needs to grow, and I got to take her out of the house without it. Oh, how good it felt to be a mother who dissolved into the day. I went to a café. Oh, a baby, people said with their distracted smiles before they went back to looking at their phones. But then she wouldn't take enough calories, and we had to place it again, the baby screaming as we snaked the thing down her throat. I'm so sick of her tube, I said to the doctor. I hate it, hate it, hate it.

What is it about the tube, she wanted to know, that has become such a flash point? After all, look at that growing girl!

That's when I mentioned you. There are a lot of you, but I will start with just you, at the fancy grocery store near my house. You, with your brown hair that you have been neglecting to cut, your ethically made T-shirt and your second-hand jeans. You started toward us to say hello to her, my Annie, my dear, sweet new baby, and then you saw the tube, and you backed away.

Oh, your face said, the way the eyebrows raise up and the skin becomes stretched somewhat. Oh, oh. What could be worse than a sick baby? You didn't want to bother me. You didn't want to be bothered. You were protecting something, yourself probably, but maybe me. You were just buying shrimp to make dinner. The world was falling apart. The whole world—the news on a constant loop of dread and doom—and you thought you saw a fresh and tiny baby, a tired mother, those precious and real good things, simple things, and you remembered your little baby, a little boy, the way his smell made you feel like you finally belonged to the human race. You remembered his tiny fat forearms. And you were going to fawn and delight in us, but what confronted you was actually just another horror. A sick baby.

I tried to tell the pediatrician about how sad it made me, for myself and for Annie, to watch people do this, over and over and over and over and over. How it makes me feel like staying in the house, but how staying in the house makes me nuts.

I am rusty, writing this letter to you. I have not written anything since this baby was born. I have not written about her, the way her tiny hands ball around mine. The way her blue eyes, darker around the rim, sizzle like sparklers when she sees me. Oh, she seems to say with her baby eyes, her mouth open in so much joy. *This is awesome! That is my MAMA!*

Her spirit, I felt it before I was even pregnant with her. Pregnant, instead, with a baby I would miscarry, I sat in the car and I felt this insistent fluttering, like a being trying to tell me something, and I knew we would have a second baby, though we had been told we almost certainly would never conceive. But then she managed to get to us, this steadfast spirit. Two lost pregnancies and then one that stuck. She wanted to be here with us in our funky old house on the corner. She chose us, and here she finally is, having caught a working boat to us at last.

Having a sick baby, it turns out, is all-consuming. You cannot even write an email. You cannot even remember where your phone is, ever. Every night, you go wandering around the house, looking for your phone, and so does your husband, and you just wonder all the time—*Where is the thing I thought I had? Why can't I find it?*

You backed away and it took you a split second to do it. If I'm honest, I don't even really remember your hair or what you wore. I dismissed you, too.

My mother had tubes hanging from her nose. She lumbered along, hauling oxygen, her diaphragm damaged from radiation. And maybe Annie's tube reminds me of this, and you backing away from us brings back a bodily memory of what it felt like, a lifetime ago, when my young mother became ill, then disfigured, then erased—even before she died.

The other weekend, we went to the beach, and I wandered the booths of the farmer's market with Annie in a carrier, and a woman approached me. She was probably in her fifties, with blondish gray hair that fell around her face, her glowing skin. She wore no makeup. And she peered at Annie, and she said, "Awww, look at that beautiful girl," and she asked me what the tube was for, and I told her. And she nodded and she fawned.

"Look at my wife," the woman's husband said. "Her own kids won't give her any babies! Just dogs!" And she looked surprised and I smiled at her and she smiled at me and we went back to feeling the peaches, to feeling the sea wind on our faces. And I thought about her the whole rest of the day, the way she didn't project pity or fear, the way she just looked at Annie as she was.

That's the rarest kind of stranger, isn't it? The kind that makes you feel known.

≈ *To the Deliveryman Who Gave Me a Lift*

CARACAS, VENEZUELA

by Lucas Mann

On the back of your motorcycle, I clung to you, ducking in the hopes that the police wouldn't see my exposed hair. You wore a fake red leather jacket that felt sticky on my hands, and a black helmet—your only helmet, you said, because you never had passengers. The sky was ash, the air hot and thick even as it rushed into my face. The city—a city I would never see again—crept up the hillsides around us.

We met in a DHL in northern Caracas. The sun was setting, which I had been told by everyone should be my cue to get off the streets, but I'd just spent the last of my bolivars on a Kit Kat bar. My remaining cash—the exact amount I'd been told would cover a cab to the airport the next morning—was locked in a hotel safe eight miles away. I'd been in Venezuela for a month on a small grant to write about baseball players, the application for which gently exaggerated my Spanish-speaking abilities. You had no reason to know any of this, of course.

You had no reason to know, either, that I'm not an adventurous traveler by nature. That I am afraid of heights and speed and change of most kinds. That I'd been having a rougher-than-usual year. That the night before I left for Venezuela, I had driven around by myself in a panic, finally stopping at a mall to watch *The Hangover Part II* in an empty theater, weeping and hyperventilating, wondering if there was any way to refund nonrefundable tickets.

There wasn't, and so I went, and instead of danger I found the type of kindness cities seem to reserve for visitors. In an alley at midnight, a cab driver exchanged my American dollars at the fair black-market rate, shook my hand, and wished me well. In a little city called Tinaquillo, a family took me in for weeks. The mother made me arepas every morning; her daughter dropped me wherever I needed to be dropped on her way to work. At a baseball academy in the jungle, women who labored in the kitchens snuck me water bottles to take back to the bare room where I was crashing, so I wouldn't dehydrate in the June heat. And finally, back in Caracas, a bevy of strangers guided me through your city; telling me where not to go, showing me when it was time to turn around.

I'm ashamed to say that I had begun to do that thing that travelers do. I'd started a narrative in my mind, every life that had contacted mine becoming an extra detail in a story about how I had been transformed in the unlikeliest of places. In a far-off land full of violence and poverty—Chávez weak and cancerous in Cuba, churning unease on every news channel and in every coffee-shop argument, machine-gunned military boys at seemingly arbitrary checkpoints on the highway—kind faces lined up to remind me about the good in the world.

You became the last kind face. You had a usual end-of-the-day delivery route, taking packages from satellite shops to a shipping center south of the city. I was beginning to unravel at the DHL service desk as the clerk told me, again, that this branch was closing for the weekend, that she had to go home to make dinner, that it wasn't her problem what happened to me when she left. I said I'd walk home if she gave me a map, and then she giggled, ran a long, painted fingernail along her neck and said, "No walking." There was a tiny space on the seat of your bike, between you and the swollen parcel bag bungeed to your back fender. It was big enough for a person.

We were together an hour. You had deadlines, so you drove quickly—to another small DHL shop, to the shipping center on the outskirts of the city, back to my hotel. I wish I remembered more about the ride: it should be the climax, the most exciting part of this story. But really, a city at night is a city at night. And wind in your hair is wind in your hair. We knifed between honking, bumper-to-bumper cars. Lights flickered on the mountainsides like blinking eyes.

You dropped me off at the side of the highway near the center of the city. You gestured that my hotel was just above the embankment, and you were late, so you'd take me no farther. You handed me a business card, like I might ever have a use for it again.

The drive was nothing. It was how we got from one place to another. You wouldn't bother to talk about it, I'm sure. I do talk about it, though, this moment when I was just a stowaway. I talk about it like it was something miraculous, but it never sounds as miraculous as it felt. And always sooner than I expected, I'm at the end of the story.

≈ To the Girl I Didn't Love on the Last Bus Home

GUANACASTE, COSTA RICA

by Jeremy B. Jones

If it hadn't been for you, I would have stared at those fences for hours as the bus rumbled through grazing land from the coast. *Cercas vivas*, everyone called them: "living fences." In truth, they were merely branches chopped from trees, stuck in the ground and strung with barbed wire. And yet those limbs sprouted buds, tiny branches reaching out and up. I loved the audacity of those living fences, so when I took the only open seat on the bus, beside you, I fixed my eyes on the window. I'd brought a novel by Fernando Contreras Castro and you noticed: *Única Mirando al Mar*, a book you loved.

You were studying to be a teacher, on your way back to your village. I was on my way back to the exhaust-filled capital city after a weekend at the beach. My Spanish must have been middling, the pages of my novel lined with translation like bad midrash. But I bumbled along as we talked about literature and the strangeness of language. You schooled me on all the ways I could use *echar*—to throw, to grab, to chase, to pour, to to to. I told you about the endless flexibility of *get*—get on, get out, get going, get lost.

We were young—early twenties—and soon talking about the

beautiful complexity of your country. A place with giant oropendola birds weaving baskets in trees and chopped branches growing from the soil and whole communities living in trash dumps. A country without an army, fighting no one's wars. I envied that you knew where you were going: back to a small town where you were born and would one day be a teacher.

I was running away from my own small town in the North Carolina mountains, where everyone told me I would be a teacher— like my dad before me, like my grandmothers before him. I may have told you about my people. About how they'd been holed up in those mountains for 250 years. About how I'd grown up on one hundred acres of land passed down for generations. Or maybe I simply told you I was a university student, studying sustainable development and seeing the world.

I didn't have the language to explain that I felt squeezed by the generational weight of my family's land—the predestination of staying put, of abiding. I wish I could have told you about my great-great-grandparents' house, about how if you stand on the hill beside it, you can see clear across the creek to the cemetery where we all end up. Everyone is in that ground—Ray and Betty and Albert and Azalee and William and Clara— sinking back generations. The smallness of living a whole life on one piece of land and then being buried in it terrified me. So I left. I caught that bus running through Costa Rica to get lost.

The sun was setting. Do you remember? The whole world seemed awash in sepia, the wide-reaching trees and the humped Brahman cows all yellow. I don't know how it happened, but you fell asleep, leaning your whole body into me. Your head on my shoulder. Your leg pressed perfectly into mine.

I liked it. I shifted my body to make it softer, fashioned it to hold you better. You were pretty, but it wasn't just that. We hadn't flirted—I couldn't flirt; it required a fluency I hadn't acquired. Did I even know your name? What I liked was settling into my seat with you. I imagined we were on our way back to your town together, where your mother would teach me to make tortillas and tease me about rolling my *r*s and you would read to wide-eyed students beneath a mango tree. You and I would sit on a porch—in just this position—after a not-so-long day, talking about nothing, while that very same sun dropped behind those cows and displaced branches. We'd go inside to our small bed in our small house in our small town and fall asleep until birds called us up. Then we'd start all over.

I shouldn't have wanted that. I was young and free and on my way back to a city of museums and clubs and sparkling twenty-something girls, but as we bumped along, suddenly all I wanted in the world was to climb off that bus when we reached the dirt road to your town. To carry your bag for you and never look back.

You know the moral, I'm sure. I didn't love you. You didn't love me. You woke up and we made small talk and you carried your own bag down that road to your house. But in the hour that you let your body rest on mine, I could see the future: I would go back to that land along Clear Creek, the land from which I'd been grown. Not then and not for some years, but I would return. I would graft my branch back onto the trunk instead of enjoying the small buds on the road alone. *Echar de menos*, isn't it? To pine for? I pined for a porch and a falling sun.

I hope that you have that now. I hope your students write you notes, that your kids gather at your feet, that your mother teaches some other man to make tortillas. Here in the Blue Ridge Mountains, my boys are blowing bubbles in the yard. Lightning bugs are easing out. My wife has settled into a chair beside me, and the headstone of my great-great-great-great-great-great-grandfather up the road calls out to me like an old song I'll never tire of hearing. I lean back, get comfortable. I let my body rest, just the way you showed me to.

ACKNOWLEDGMENTS

Years ago, when I was in the throes of launching a literary magazine, I read John Steinbeck's *East of Eden*, and came upon this claim: "There are no good collaborations, whether in music, in art, in poetry . . . the group never invents anything." I underlined it, not in recognition, but in rejection. *Not so*, everything in me said. Collaborating was at the heart of my creative life, and the power of it awed me daily.

This book is the fruit of collaborations upon collaborations. I have so many people to thank.

I must begin with Ed Cohen, the founding donor of *Off Assignment*, who removed the most daunting barrier between an idea and its fruition. Ed, this book was born of your conviction and kindness. I am beyond grateful for what you set in motion. Vince Errico, bottomless thanks for joining forces with me as a cofounder and for meeting my zeal with equanimity and wisdom. You always saw something exceptional in "Letter to a Stranger" and toiled to give it a nonprofit platform. Anne Fadiman, thank you for getting a copy of this manuscript into the right hands; that act of generosity and good faith made all the difference. Thank you to the rest of *OA*'s Board members—Robert Wertheimer, Kathryn Besemer, and Rick Passov—for the mentorship and ongoing support. I'm deeply fortunate for the ways you bolster and guide me.

So many generous souls supported *OA* early on and helped usher "Letter to a Stranger" into existence: Lavinia Spalding, Marcia DeSanctis, Ted Conover, Pico Iyer, Rolf Potts, Mary Morris, Andrew Rowat, Andy Isaacson, David Farley, Tony Perrottet, Elisabeth

Eaves, Julia Cooke—all of you nourished this project with your enthusiasm, as well as your words. So many others propelled "Letter to a Stranger" forward—an inevitably partial list: Jamie Andersson, Ali Francis, Jina Moore, Kristina Ensminger, Alfred Megally, Jaime Green, Andy Omel, Kate Essig, Meron Hadero, Katie Aldrich, Olaniyi Omiwale, Don George, Maggie Yellen, Sarah Jampel, Sam Benson Smith, Jackson Barnett, Willa Young, Louise Langheier, Fred Strebeigh, Anne Keene, Elaina Plott, Graham Duncan, Alex Sheshunoff, Mary Holderness, Colleen Cotter, Richard Deming, Mark Oppenheimer, Steven Brill, Glory Edim, Deborah Burke and Peter McCann, Susan Orlean, Michael Segal, Paul Haigney, Roger Austin, Conor Flynn, Jotham Burrello, Alexander Lumans, Michael Cunningham, Gideon Lewis-Kraus, Aaron Lammer, Briallen Hopper, Gay Talese, Anna McDonald, V. Stephanie Carendi, John D'Agata, Jenna Wortham, Anna Ziegler, Ajay Kulkarni, David Gimbel, Leslie Kwok Potter, Bianca Wendt, Harriet Clark, Melissa Febos, Erik Rydholm, Rob Giampietro, Amy Hungerford, Hyman Milstein, Wesley and Evan LePatner, Sarah Smith, Marc Fitten, Gregory Walsh, Erik DeLuca, Kathryn and Bob Gronke, Charlotte Foote, Sheryl Dluginski, Robert Nankin, Willa Brown, Robert Boynton, Kathleen Masterson, Mara Manus, Tomek Roszkowski, Mary Vascellaro, Tom Davis, Adam Sexton, Arianne Cohen, Chris Rubin, Gregory Marshall, Aidan Walsh, Brad Wolfe, Brian O'Connor, Michelle Rushefsky, Jason Toups, and John and Rita Murray. Thank you for deploying your talent, resources and platforms to lend *OA* and "Letter to a Stranger" momentum. Grants from both the New York State Council on the Arts and the Reader's Digest Foundation funded the original publication of so many essays in this collection. For this backing, I am so grateful.

I have so many *OA* editors—past and present—thank for their skillful curation of the "Letter to a Stranger" column. Katy Osborn and Sophie Haigney loved "Letter to a Stranger" into existence—with style, conviction, and a great deal of hustle. Joshua Tranen and Sarah Holder shaped so many early stories, and Sarah and Sophie helped mold the original book proposal, laying such helpful groundwork. Candace Rose Rardon brought vision and passion to our first print volume; I'd have been lost without you, Candace. Julia Calagiovanni, Sam DiSalvo, Nicole Clark, Lenora Todaro, Rachel Veroff, Tekendra Parmar, Jordan Cutler-Tietjen, and Maggie Milstein curated dozens of "Letters" and made *Off Assignment* a sturdy home for extraordinary stories. Finally, Anya Tchoupakov, Aube Rey Lescure, Claudia Crook, and Stephan Sveshnikov injected new life into the "Letter to a Stranger" vision and brought spectacular writers into the fold. Anya and Aube, this book is notably better thanks to your miraculous entrance in 2020. Emphatic thanks to you all.

Many wise readers lent me feedback on parts (or the entirety) of this manuscript—Lavinia Spalding, Anna Vodicka, Dustin Dunaway, Anya Tchoupakov, Aube Rey Lescure, and Vivian Lee— whose eagle-eyed line edits were critical. Leslie Jamison, thank you for being my sounding board, my enthusiast, my first contributor, my recruiter of more contributors, my wise reader, and the friend who keeps my head above water, year after year. Your impact on this book is almost too immense to track.

Chris Clemans, you were the dream agent for this essay collection—so alert to its promise, resolute in finding the right publisher, and hands-on in curating the ultimate manuscript. It's hard to do justice to my gratitude, Chris. Thanks also to Roma Panganiban at

Janklow & Nesbit for the care you put into the manuscript, and to Lynn Nesbit, who made sure it reached Chris and Roma in the first place.

Amy Gash: Chris assured me you were the ideal editor for this book, and what a matchmaker he is. Your love for this book has buoyed me, and your decisive guidance made its pieces coalesce at last into a beautiful anthology. Thank you—and the entire Algonquin team, including Brunson Hoole, Cathy Schott, Stephanie Mendoza, Kelly Doyle, and Lauren Moseley—for championing this collection. Dominic Trevett: much gratitude for the cartographic table of contents. Jaya Miceli: what a blessing to have your art on this book's cover. Thank you for your imagination and skill.

Everything I create—and complete—is the result of my partner's daily support and love. Owen Murray, I am so fortunate for all the ways you back me up and make sure I get to the desk, day after day. To the Kinder women—my mom, Mary Therese, and sisters, Katie and Molly—your support is such an infinite force; I feel it always. We lost my father right as I was tying up edits on this collection, a loss that illuminates anew what this book taught me: there are beautiful ways to be haunted. My world-wandering father, you're in these pages.

Finally, to the authors in this book: Thank you for saying yes to the invitation to write a letter to a stranger. You knew what I meant; you glimpsed the story's edges; you traced it all out—with such beauty, humanity, and care—onto the page. Collaborating with each of you was an honor and a joy.

ABOUT THE CONTRIBUTORS

JENESSA ABRAMS is a Norman Mailer Fiction Fellow and has been awarded fellowships and grants from the MacDowell Colony, Ucross Foundation, the Vermont Studio Center, and Columbia University, where she earned her MFA in fiction and literary translation. Her writing has been nominated for a Pushcart Prize and published in *Tin House*, *Guernica*, *The Rumpus*, *BOMB Magazine* and elsewhere. Currently, she teaches writing at Rutgers University.

AMBER MEADOW ADAMS is Lower Mohawk of the Six Nations at Grand River. She holds a PhD in Indigenous Studies from the University at Buffalo and a BA in Literature and Writing from Columbia University. Her short fiction and scholarship have been published in the UK, US, and Canada. She is currently reworking her doctoral research on the Haudenosaunee story of Creation into a novel.

FAITH ADIELE is the author of two memoirs—*Meeting Faith*, a Buddhist travelogue that won the PEN Open Book Award, and *The Nigerian-Nordic Girl's Guide to Lady Problems*, subject of the PBS documentary *My Journey Home*, and coeditor of *Coming of Age Around the World: A Multicultural Anthology*. She founded VONA Travel, the nation's first writing workshop for travelers of color, and writes travel stories for the Calm app.

MICHAEL AGRESTA has published nonfiction and fiction in *The Atlantic*, *Slate*, *The Wall Street Journal*, *Wired*, *The Southern Review*, *Boston Review*, *Conjunctions*, and others. He writes regularly on art and culture for *Texas Monthly* and *The Texas Observer*. He has received residencies from the MacDowell Colony, Blue Mountain Center, and VCCA. His MFA is from the Michener Center for Writers in Austin, Texas, where he lives.

HOWARD AXELROD is the author of *The Stars in Our Pockets* and *The Point of Vanishing*, the latter of which was named one of the best books of 2015 by Slate and the Chicago Tribune. His essays have appeared in *The New York Times*, *The Paris Review* online, *O Magazine*, *Politico*, *Salon*, and *VQR*. He is the director of the Creative Writing Program at Loyola University in Chicago.

ERICA CAVANAGH grew up in Rochester, NY, a place whose abolition and suffrage history deeply influence her interests and writing. During her Peace Corps service in Benin, she worked with women and children on access to education, health, and economic resources. Her nonfiction has appeared in *The Missouri Review*, *North American Review*, *Bellevue Literary Review*, *The Journal*, and elsewhere. She teaches creative nonfiction and food studies at James Madison University.

MEG CHARLTON is a writer and producer based in New York City. Her journalism has appeared in *VICE*, *Slate*, *Atlas Obscura*, *The Today Show*, and others. Her fiction has been featured in *Blunderbuss Magazine* and performed by Liars' League London. She is currently at work on a novel.

CARIN CLEVIDENCE is the author of a novel, *The House on Salt Hay Road*, as well as travel essays and short stories appearing in *O Magazine*, *OZY*, *Panorama*, *The Michigan Quarterly Review*, and elsewhere. She has worked as a deckhand in Baja, Mexico, and an assistant expedition leader in Antarctica. She has received a Rona Jaffe Foundation Writers' Award; fellowships from the Fine Arts Work Center, the Elizabeth Kostova Foundation, and Sustainable Arts; and residencies at Yaddo, MacDowell, and Marble House. She is currently at work on a novel set onboard a ship in Antarctica.

TED CONOVER is the author of six books, including *Newjack*, *The Routes of Man*, *Rolling Nowhere*, *Immersion*, *Coyotes*, and *Whiteout*. He has written articles for *The New York Times Magazine*, *The New*

Yorker, *The Atlantic*, *Vanity Fair*, *National Geographic Magazine*, and *Smithsonian Magazine*. He directs the Arthur L. Carter Journalism Institute at New York University.

JESSE DONALDSON was born in Kentucky, educated in Texas, and now lives in Oregon. He is the author of *The More They Disappear* and *On Homesickness*. His work has recently appeared in *Gulf Coast* and *The Oxford American*.

SALLY FRANSON is the author of the novel *A Lady's Guide to Selling Out*. Her writing has appeared in *The Guardian*, *San Francisco Chronicle*, and *Best American Travel Writing*, among other places. She lives in Minneapolis.

JULIA GLASS is the author of a story collection and five novels, including *A House Among the Trees* and the National Book Award–winning *Three Junes*. She has also won fellowships from the NEA, the New York Foundation for the Arts, and the Radcliffe Institute for Advanced Study. A Massachusetts resident, Glass is a Distinguished Writer-in-Residence at Emerson College and a cofounder of Twenty Summers, a nonprofit arts and culture festival in Provincetown.

NAOMI GORDON-LOEBL is a writer, educator, and fellow at Type Media Center. Her work has been published in *The New York Times*, *Harper's*, *The Nation*, *Complex*, *Hazlitt*, and elsewhere. She is the recipient of residencies and fellowships from Lambda Literary, Monson Arts, and the Vermont Studio Center. She was born, raised, and still lives in Brooklyn.

LAUREN GROFF is the author of two short-story collections, *Florida* and *Delicate Edible Birds*, and the novels *The Monsters of Templeton*, *Arcadia*, and *Fates and Furies*, the latter of which was a finalist for the National Book Award and National Book Critics Circle Award. She was a 2018 Guggenheim Fellow and lives with her husband and two sons in Gainesville, Florida.

MERON HADERO is an Ethiopian-American whose short stories have been shortlisted for the Caine Prize for African Writing and appear in *Best American Short Stories, Ploughshares, McSweeney's Quarterly Concern, Zyzzyva, The New England Review, The Iowa Review, The Missouri Review*, among others. She's also published in *The New York Times Book Review* and *The Displaced: Refugee Writers on Refugee Lives*. Meron has been a fellow at San Jose State University's Steinbeck Center, Yaddo, Ragdale, and MacDowell.

SOPHIE HAIGNEY has written for *The New York Times, The New Yorker, New York Magazine, The Economist, The Atlantic, Slate, The Nation*, and *The Boston Globe*. She was *Off Assignment's* first managing editor and helped get the "Letter to a Stranger" column off the ground.

CARLYNN HOUGHTON earned her MFA from the University of Iowa Writers' Workshop. She is a recipient of the Michener-Copernicus Fellowship and teaches at the Chapin School in Manhattan.

PAM HOUSTON is the author of the memoir *Deep Creek: Finding Hope in the High Country*, as well as five other books, including the novel *Contents May Have Shifted* and the short-story collection *Cowboys Are My Weakness*.

VANESSA HUA is a bestselling novelist and a columnist for the *San Francisco Chronicle*. Her novel, *A River of Stars*, was named to *The Washington Post's* and NPR's Best Books of 2018 lists. Her short-story collection, *Deceit and Other Possibilities*, received an Asian/Pacific American Award in Literature and was a finalist for a California Book Award.

EMMANUEL IDUMA is the author of *A Stranger's Pose*, a book of travel stories, which was longlisted for the 2019 Royal Society of Literature's Ondaatje Prize. His stories and essays have been published widely, including in *Best American Travel Writing 2020, Aperture, LitHub*,

The Millions, Art in America, and *The New York Review of Books Daily.*
He divides his time between Lagos and New York.

PICO IYER is the author of fifteen books, translated into twenty-three
languages, including, in 2019, two twinned books on his adopted
home, *Autumn Light* and *A Beginner's Guide to Japan.* For more than
a quarter-century, he's been a constant contributor to *Time.* He has
also written for *The New York Times, The New York Review of Books,
Harper's, Granta,* and more than 250 other periodicals worldwide.

LESLIE JAMISON penned the first-ever "Letter to a Stranger" for *Off
Assignment,* revisiting memories of Nicaragua, where she worked as
a Spanish teacher. She is the author of *The Recovering; The Empathy
Exams; Make It Scream, Make it Burn;* and the novel *The Gin Closet.*

AKEMI JOHNSON is the author of *Night in the American Village:
Women in the Shadow of the U.S. Military Bases in Okinawa,* which
was shortlisted for the William Saroyan International Prize for
Writing. A former Fulbright scholar to Japan, Akemi has contributed
to *The Nation,* NPR's *All Things Considered,* and *Code Switch, Travel
+ Leisure,* Anthony Bourdain's *Explore Parts Unknown,* and other
publications. She lives in Northern California.

JEREMY B. JONES is the author of *Bearwallow: A Personal History of a
Mountain Homeland,* which won the 2014 Appalachian Book of the
Year in nonfiction and was awarded gold in the 2015 Independent
Publisher Book Awards in memoir. His essays have been named nota-
ble in *Best American Essays* and published in *Oxford American, The
Iowa Review,* and *Brevity.*

SHEBA KARIM is the author of four novels: *Skunk Girl, That Thing We
Call a Heart, Mariam Sharma Hits the Road,* and *The Marvelous Mirza
Girls.* She is the editor of the anthology *Alchemy: The Tranquebar Book
of Erotic Short Stories 2.* She is a writer-in-residence at Vanderbilt
University and received her MFA from the Iowa Writers' Workshop.

COLLEEN KINDER has written essays and articles for *The New York Times Magazine*, *The New Republic*, *Virginia Quarterly Review*, *The Wall Street Journal*, *A Public Space*, *Atlantic.com*, *Creative Nonfiction*, *AFAR*, and *Best American Travel Writing 2013*. A graduate of the Iowa Nonfiction Writing Program, she has received fellowships from Yaddo, MacDowell, Ucross, and the Fulbright. She is the cofounder of *Off Assignment* and teaches for Yale Summer Session in France.

JAMIL JAN KOCHAI is the author of *99 Nights in Logar*, a finalist for the PEN/Hemingway Award for Debut Novel and the DSC Prize for South Asian Literature. He was born in an Afghan refugee camp in Peshawar, Pakistan, but he originally hails from Logar, Afghanistan. His short stories and essays have appeared in *The New Yorker*, *The New York Times*, *Los Angeles Times*, *Ploughshares*, and *The O. Henry Prize Stories 2018*. Currently, he is a Stegner Fellow at Stanford University.

ELIZABETH KOLBERT is the author of *Field Notes from a Catastrophe* and the Pulitzer Prize–winning book *The Sixth Extinction: An Unnatural History*. She is a staff writer at *The New Yorker*.

AVIYA KUSHNER grew up in a Hebrew-speaking home in New York. She is the author of *The Grammar of God*, a National Jewish Book Award Finalist, Sami Rohr Prize Finalist, and one of *Publishers Weekly's* Top 10 Religion Stories of the Year; *Eve and All the Wrong Men*; and *Wolf Lamb Bomb*.

MADELAINE LUCAS is an Australian writer and musician currently based in Brooklyn, New York. Her short story "Ruins" was awarded the Elizabeth Jolley Prize in 2018, and her nonfiction writing has appeared in *Paris Review Daily*, *The Believer*, *Literary Hub*, *Catapult*, and *The Lifted Brow*. She is a senior editor of the literary annual *NOON* and a graduate of the MFA program at Columbia University.

ALEXANDER LUMANS was awarded a 2018 NEA Creative Writing Grant in Fiction. He also received a fellowship to the 2015 Arctic Circle Residency, and he was the Spring 2014 Philip Roth Resident at Bucknell University. While currently at work on a novel set in the Arctic, he teaches at University of Colorado Denver and Lighthouse Writers Workshop.

JULIE LUNDE currently lives in Tucson, where she is a nonfiction MFA candidate at the University of Arizona. Her previous work may be found at *Queen Mob's Teahouse*, *Pigeon Pages*, and *Underwater New York*.

LUCAS MANN is the author of *Class A: Baseball in the Middle of Everywhere*, *Lord Fear: A Memoir*, and *Captive Audience: On Love and Reality Television*. His essays have appeared in *The Washington Post*, *Guernica*, *BuzzFeed*, and *The Los Angeles Review of Books*, among others. A recipient of fellowships from the National Endowment for the Arts and United States Artists, he teaches writing at the University of Massachusetts Dartmouth.

T KIRA MADDEN is a lesbian hapa writer, photographer, and amateur magician. She serves as the founding editor-in-chief of *No Tokens*, and is the author of *Long Live the Tribe of Fatherless Girls*.

EMILY MATCHAR is a journalist based mostly in Hong Kong, but sometimes in Pittsboro, North Carolina.

SARAH MENKEDICK is the author of *Ordinary Insanity: Fear and the Silent Crisis of Motherhood in America* and *Homing Instincts: Early Motherhood on a Midwestern Farm*. Her work has been featured in *Harper's*, *The New York Times*, *The Washington Post*, *The Los Angeles Times*, *The Guardian*, *The Kenyon Review*, *Guernica*, *Oxford American*, and elsewhere. She lives with her family in Pittsburgh.

JACQUELYN MITCHARD is a *New York Times* bestselling author of twelve novels for adults, including *The Deep End of the Ocean*, which was the inaugural selection of the Oprah Winfrey Book Club and also made into a major feature film. She is a professor of creative writing at Vermont College of Fine Arts and lives on Cape Cod with her family.

CRAIG MOD is a Japan-based author and photographer. His books include *Kissa by Kissa*, *Koya Bound*, and *Art Space Tokyo*. He is a MacDowell, VCCA, and Ragdale fellow. His writing and photography has appeared in *Eater*, *The Atlantic*, *California Sunday Magazine*, *The New Yorker*, and other publications.

MATTHEW OLZMANN is the author of three collections of poems including *Mezzanines*, which was selected for the 2011 Kundiman Prize; *Contradictions in the Design*; and the forthcoming *Constellation Route*. He teaches at Dartmouth College and in the MFA Program for Writers at Warren Wilson College.

PETER ORNER is the author of two novels, *The Second Coming of Mavala Shikongo* and *Love and Shame and Love* and two story collections, *Esther Stories* and *Last Car Over the Sagamore Bridge*. His essay collection *Am I Alone Here?* was a finalist for the National Book Critics Circle Award. Peter has been awarded the Rome Prize, a Guggenheim Fellowship, and a Lannan Foundation Literary Fellowship.

KEIJA PARSSINEN is the author of *The Ruins of Us*, which won a Michener-Copernicus Award, and *The Unraveling of Mercy Louis*. A graduate of Princeton University and the Iowa Writers' Workshop, she is an assistant professor of creative writing at the University of Tulsa. Her work has appeared or is forthcoming in *Salon*, *Slice*, *The Brooklyn Quarterly*, *New Delta Review*, *This Land*, *Five Chapters*, *Marie Claire*, and elsewhere.

GREGORY PARDLO is the author of two poetry collections, including *Digest*, which won the 2015 Pulitzer Prize for Poetry, and the memoir in essays, *Air Traffic*. He is poetry editor of *Virginia Quarterly Review*, and teaches in the graduate creative writing program at Rutgers University–Camden.

DAVID PARKER JR. is a fiction and freelance writer in the mountains of Western North Carolina. He lived in New Orleans for fifteen years and five hurricanes and graduated from the University of New

Orleans MFA program somewhere along the way. He has published in *The Nation*, *Maclean's*, *New Orleans Magazine*, *Offbeat Magazine*, *Blue Ridge Outdoors*, and many more. His fiction, creative nonfiction, and poetry have been anthologized in *Louisiana in Words*, *Soul is Bulletproof*, and *Fuck Poems*. He adventures often with his wife, two children, and a crooked canoe.

SARAH PERRY is the author of the memoir *After the Eclipse*, which was named a *New York Times Book Review* Editors' Choice, a Poets & Writers Notable Nonfiction Debut, and a Barnes and Noble Discover Great New Writers pick. Sarah lives in Brooklyn, New York.

KIKI PETROSINO is the author of four books of poetry, most recently *White Blood: A Lyric of Virginia*. She is a professor of poetry at the University of Virginia, where she teaches in the creative writing program. Her awards include a Pushcart Prize and a Fellowship in Literature from the National Endowment for the Arts.

LIA PURPURA is the author of the essay collections *All the Fierce Tethers*, *On Looking*, *Increase*, and *Rough Likeness*, and the poetry collections *It Shouldn't Have Been Beautiful*, *King Baby*, *Stone Sky Lifting*, and *The Brighter the Veil*. She has published poems and essays in *Agni Magazine*, *Orion*, *The New Republic*, *The New Yorker*, *The Paris Review*, and *Ploughshares*. A finalist for the National Book Critics Circle Award, she has been awarded fellowships from the NEA, the Fulbright, and the Guggenheim Foundation.

KELLY RAMSEY writes fiction, memoir, and adventure narrative. Her work has appeared online and in print, and she has received two fellowships from the MacDowell Colony. She was cofounder of the artists' residency program the Lighthouse Works. She is a wildland firefighter in Northern California.

YING REINHARDT is a Malaysian writer based in Germany. Her writing has appeared in *Roads & Kingdoms*, *BootsnAll*, *Traveloka*, and *Marie Claire*. She is currently working on a memoir of her time on board Costa cruise ships.

IRINA REYN is the author of three novels, *What Happened to Anna K.*, *The Imperial Wife*, and *Mother Country*. She teaches fiction writing at the University of Pittsburgh.

ROBIN ROMM is the author of the story collection *The Mother Garden*, which was a finalist for the PEN USA prize, and the memoir *The Mercy Papers*, which was named a Best Book of the Year by *The New York Times*, *The San Francisco Chronicle*, and *Entertainment Weekly*. She is the editor of the anthology *Double Bind: Women on Ambition* and currently teaches in the low-residency MFA program in writing at Warren Wilson College.

ANJALI SACHDEVA's work has been published in *Creative Nonfiction* and *The Best American Nonrequired Reading*, among others. She teaches for the University of Pittsburgh and the low-residency MFA program at Randolph College and is the recipient of a 2020 NEA Literature Fellowship. Her story collection, *All the Names They Used for God*, was the winner of the 2019 Chautauqua Prize and an NPR Best Book of 2018.

ANNIE SCHWEIKERT is an archivist and occasionally a writer in the San Francisco Bay Area.

MAGGIE SHIPSTEAD is the author of *Astonish Me* and *Seating Arrangements*, which won the Dylan Thomas Prize and the *L.A. Times* Book Prize for First Fiction. She is a graduate of the Iowa Writers' Workshop and a former Wallace Stegner Fellow at Stanford. Her work has appeared in *The New York Times*, *The Washington Post*, *The Guardian*, *The Wall Street Journal*, *Travel + Leisure*, *Departures*, *Condé Nast Traveler*, *Outside*, *The Best American Short Stories*, and *The Best American Sports Writing*.

ARIA BETH SLOSS is the author of *Autobiography of Us*, a novel. Her short stories have appeared in several publications, including *Glimmer Train*, *Ploughshares*, *One Story*, and *Best American Short Stories 2015*. She lives in New York City.

LAVINIA SPALDING is series editor of *The Best Women's Travel Writing*, author of *Writing Away*, and coauthor of *With a Measure of Grace*. She introduced the e-book edition of Edith Wharton's classic travelogue *A Motor-Flight Through France*, and her work appears in numerous print and online publications, including *Tin House*, *Post Road*, *Inkwell*, *World Hum*, *Yoga Journal*, and *Sunset*.

MARGO STEINES is a native New Yorker and journeyman ironworker. Her work has been published in *Essay Daily*, *december*, *Tits and Sass*, *The New York Times*, and *Brevity*.

MEERA SUBRAMANIAN is an award-winning independent journalist and author of *A River Runs Again: India's Natural World in Crisis*, finalist for the 2016 Orion Book Award. She occasionally loiters around academia, including most recently as Princeton University's Barron Visiting Professor in the Environment and the Humanities. Based in Cape Cod, she's a perpetual wanderer who can't stop planting perennials.

RACHEL SWEARINGEN is the author of the prize-winning story collection *How to Walk on Water*. Her work has appeared in *VICE*, *The Missouri Review*, *Kenyon Review*, *American Short Fiction*, and elsewhere. She is the recipient of several awards, including a Rona Jaffe Foundation Writers' Award. She lives in Chicago and teaches at the School of the Art Institute.

MICHELLE TEA's collection of essays, *Against Memoir*, is the recipient of the 2019 PEN/Diamonstein-Spielvogel Award for the Art of the Essay. She is the author of over a dozen books in various genres, including *Valencia*, which won a Lambda Literary Award for Best Lesbian Fiction, and most recently, the *Astro Baby* children's astrology series. Her writing has appeared in *Harper's*, *Cosmopolitan*, *The Believer*, *Marie Clare*, *n+1*, *BuzzFeed*, and many other print and web publications.

MONET PATRICE THOMAS is a Black American writer and poet living abroad. She holds an MFA in creative writing from the Inland Northwest Center for Writers in Spokane, Washington. Currently, she's the Interviews Editor at *The Rumpus*.

PETER TURCHI is the author of *Maps of the Imagination: The Writer as Cartographer*, among five other books. He coedited three anthologies: *A Kite in the Wind: Fiction Writers on their Craft*, *The Story Behind the Story*, and *Bringing the Devil to His Knees*. His writing has appeared in *Tin House*, *The Huffington Post*, *Ploughshares*, *Story*, and *The Colorado Review*. He has received fellowships from the National Endowment for the Arts and the John Simon Guggenheim Memorial Foundation.

RAKSHA VASUDEVAN is an Indian-Canadian economist and writer. Her work has appeared or is forthcoming in the *Threepenny Review*, *LitHub*, *Guernica* and more.

ANNA VODICKA's essays and travel writing have appeared in *AFAR*, *Brevity*, *Guernica*, *Harvard Review*, *McSweeney's Internet Tendency*, *Longreads*, *Paste*, Lonely Planet's *An Innocent Abroad*, and *Best Women's Travel Writing 2017*, and earned fellowships to Vermont Studio Center and Hedgebrook. She teaches creative writing at Seattle's Hugo House and to women incarcerated at the King County Jail.

CUTTER WOOD is the author of *Love and Death in the Sunshine State*. His work has appeared in *Harper's*, *Virginia Quarterly Review*, and other publications, and he has been awarded fellowships by the National Endowment for the Arts, the Bread Loaf Writers' Conference, and the University of Iowa. He lives in Brooklyn.

RACHEL YODER is the author of the novel *Nightbitch* and a founding editor of *draft: the journal of process*. She lives in Iowa City with her husband and son.